Automating Government

Automating Government: How AI Will Revolutionise Public Services is a timely and authoritative guide for political leaders, senior managers, and public officials confronting the challenges and opportunities of artificial intelligence. Through dozens of global case studies and clear analysis, it explores how AI can transform public services, such as predictive healthcare, automated social services, and real-time transport systems, leading to improved outcomes and lower costs.

While the potential is considerable, the implications are far from straightforward. The book addresses the following critical questions: What will happen to jobs? Can we trust machines to make decisions about people's lives? Will AI reduce inequality or entrench it further?

Rich in practical insight and grounded in real-world examples, *Automating Government* sets out a roadmap for responsible, effective AI adoption in the public sector. It challenges readers to see AI not simply as a tool for efficiency but as a means to build a more capable, inclusive and accountable state fit for the demands of the twenty-first century.

Jeremy N. White has over 40 years of experience in technology and venture capital financing in Europe and the United States and has been involved in over 50 acquisitions while raising more than £100 million in development capital for his companies. He is currently an Honorary Visiting Professor at Bayes Business School in London, where he teaches behavioural corporate strategy to postgraduate students as well as serving on the global advisory board.

Massimiliano Filippi is a governance and management professional with over a decade of experience in the insurance and financial services sectors across Italy, Europe, and the United States. He is currently leading innovation and regulatory-driven projects at Italy's top insurance group. He earned an Executive MBA from Bayes Business School in London.

Automating Government

How AI Will Revolutionise Public Services

Jeremy N. White
Massimiliano Filippi

Routledge
Taylor & Francis Group
LONDON AND NEW YORK

Designed cover image: Getty Images - WANAN YOSSINGKUM
Cover design Helena Spicer

First published 2026
by Routledge
4 Park Square, Milton Park, Abingdon, Oxon OX14 4RN

and by Routledge
605 Third Avenue, New York, NY 10158

Routledge is an imprint of the Taylor & Francis Group, an informa business

British Library Cataloguing-in-Publication Data
A catalogue record for this book is available from the British Library

ISBN: 978-1-041-14312-3 (hbk)
ISBN: 978-1-041-12284-5 (pbk)
ISBN: 978-1-003-67389-7 (ebk)

DOI: 10.4324/9781003673897

Typeset in Adobe Garamond Pro
by Apex CoVantage, LLC

Contents

Figures and Tables

Figures

Tables

Boxes

About the Authors

Professor Jeremy N. White has over 40 years of experience in technology and venture capital financing in Europe and the United States and has been involved in over 50 acquisitions while raising more than £100 million in development capital for his companies. He founded one of the first e-commerce companies in the United Kingdom. He took the company public on the London Stock Exchange in 2000 with a market capitalisation of £250 million. Professor White has served on the boards of a number of quoted and private companies in addition to numerous government committees. He was Deputy Chairman of the HRH Prince's Business Trust, and he is a member of the board of the Pepperdine University in California. White has an MBA from Bayes Business School and an MA in Psychology from Pepperdine University. He is currently an Honorary Visiting Professor at Bayes Business School in London, where he teaches behavioural corporate strategy to postgraduate students as well as serving on the global advisory board. He is the author of *Making Better Strategic Decisions: How to Develop Robust Decision-Making to Avoid Organisational Disasters* (Routledge, 2024).

Massimiliano Filippi is a governance and management professional with over a decade of experience in the insurance and financial services sectors across Italy, Europe, and the United States. Throughout his career, he has held senior positions at prestigious consultancy firms, specialising in process optimisation, regulatory compliance, and internal control. He is currently part of Italy's leading insurance group, managing cross-functional innovation initiatives and regulatory-driven projects to enhance governance and drive business development. Mr Filippi earned an Executive MBA from Bayes Business School in London, a Master's degree in Economics and Law and an undergraduate degree in Economics and Corporate Management from the European University of Rome. He is a Chartered Public Accountant and legal auditor in Italy.

Preface

I have spent my career in technology, from security automation in the 1980s to business software and the internet in the late 1990s, and now into the emerging, transformational domain of AI.

Over the decades, a consistent theme has tied these disparate technologies together: the drive to make processes more efficient, both in terms of service delivery and cost-effectiveness. In many ways, AI feels like a logical progression. The internet and email dramatically improved communication and access to knowledge, but they can be seen as evolutions of the telegraph, telex, and fax. I recall, in the mid-1980s, sitting in an office in New York trying to close an acquisition and faxing documents back and forth to our bankers in London. We were thrilled by the miraculous new fax technology that enabled us to complete a complex transaction without being in the same room. How far we have come.

Today, ChatGPT ranks among the most visited websites in the world, and the contrast between human and machine capabilities is starker than ever.

In the 1870s, London was home to over a million domestic servants, an indispensable workforce that sustained middle- and upper-class households. That profession has virtually disappeared. The shift was not mourned as a social tragedy. It was driven by rising educational opportunities, broader career choices, and a quiet technological revolution: vacuum cleaners, washing machines, dishwashers, and central heating, which replaced much of the manual labour. Society adapted. People found new employment, often more rewarding and less physically demanding.

A similar transition is now under way in the realm of low-level administrative work. In a BBC interview in May 2025, Neil Lawrence of DeepMind highlighted the vast gap between human and computer processing speeds, noting that while the average human processes information at around 2,000 bits per minute (bpm), modern computers can reach up to 600 billion bpm, some 300 million times faster. As AI systems take over routine clerical tasks, we may come to view this displacement not with nostalgia but with relief. Just as few now lament the passing of the servant class, the obsolescence of routine administrative roles may ultimately be welcomed as progress.

The demand for government services is self-evident. Perhaps because of our experience with commercial platforms like Amazon, we now expect fast, high-quality, and efficient service from government agencies. Yet those agencies face relentless challenges: funding constraints, outdated technology, convoluted regulations, and the unforgiving glare of social media.

There is no shortage of demand for better service, whether it is booking a GP appointment or a driving test, applying for planning permission, or navigating one of the hundreds of daily interactions that citizens have with public bodies. At last, AI offers a glimmer of hope that a better way exists. It holds the potential to deliver a win–win outcome. Public servants, who face daily challenges of overwhelming demand, frustrated users, and scarce resources, may enjoy greater job satisfaction when they can offer more effective support. Citizens will receive faster, less frustrating service.

My academic work on decision-making, outlined in my previous book, *Make Better Strategic Decisions* (Routledge, 2024), highlights the many traps and pitfalls that await those who seek change. As Niccolò Machiavelli astutely observed in *The Prince*, written over 500 years ago:

> It ought to be borne in mind that there is nothing more difficult to handle, more doubtful of success, nor more dangerous to manage, than to take the lead in the introduction of a new order of things. For the innovator has for enemies all those who have done well under the old conditions, and lukewarm defenders in those who may do well under the new.

AI offers enormous potential for improving efficiency, and this, rather than simplistic cost-cutting, should be its principal aim in government. Yet the challenge of harnessing its power will require a depth of strategic focus, institutional reform, and political courage that is conspicuously lacking in today's public institutions.

Massimiliano and I hope this book offers useful insight into both the opportunities and the challenges ahead. Above all, we hope it inspires those responsible for delivering public services to engage actively with the possibilities that AI brings.

I wish to express my thanks to my editor, Rebecca Marsh at Routledge, for her encouragement and steadfast support throughout this project, and to Grace Collier for her work on the book's production. To Helena Spicer for the cover design. My thanks also go to my co-author, Massimiliano, whose insight, dedication, and good humour made the process of creating this book both productive and enjoyable. As always, I owe a special debt to my family, whose patience and understanding sustain me as I continue the search for answers to today's most pressing strategic challenges.

Jeremy N. White

I would like to express my deepest gratitude to Professor White for the opportunity to co-author this book. His insight, guidance, and support have been instrumental throughout this endeavour, and I will carry his counsel and vision with me in both my personal and professional life.

I am also profoundly grateful to my family and friends for their unwavering support during this demanding yet enriching experience. Their belief in me has been a constant source of strength.

Massimiliano Filippi

Glossary

Aadhaar System India's nationwide biometric identification platform. It integrates AI to streamline welfare distribution, verify identities, and reduce fraud by ensuring benefits reach the intended recipients efficiently.

Accountability (AI Context) A core ethical principle requiring that AI systems and their outcomes are traceable to responsible human actors, ensuring transparency, oversight, and recourse in case of errors or harm.

Agentic AI An emerging class of AI systems designed to operate independently in pursuit of defined objectives, with capabilities to sense their environment, make decisions, and learn over time.

AI Act (EU Artificial Intelligence Act) A regulation by the European Union (Regulation (EU) 2024/1689) establishing harmonised rules for the development, deployment, and use of AI systems within the EU, based on risk categorisation and ethical principles, with extra-territorial effects for global providers.

AI Agents Autonomous digital entities designed to perceive their environment, interpret information, and take action towards defined objectives. Commonly integrated within multi-agent systems and built to collaborate with humans or other agents to optimise workflows and automate decision-making processes.

AI Code of Ethics A structured framework of moral principles guiding the ethical development and deployment of AI systems. It promotes fairness, transparency, inclusivity, and data privacy to ensure that AI technologies are used responsibly and for the benefit of society.

AI-Enabled Predictive Analytics The use of AI to analyse historical and real-time data, identifying patterns and predicting outcomes to inform proactive governance and decision-making in areas such as healthcare, policing, and social services.

AI Governance Structured sets of principles, policies, and procedures guiding the responsible development, deployment, and oversight of AI systems, emphasising transparency, fairness, accountability, and human rights.

AI System (EU AI Act Definition) A machine-based system designed to operate with varying levels of autonomy, capable of inferring how to generate outputs (predictions, recommendations, decisions) from input data, thereby influencing physical or virtual environments.

Algorithm A structured sequence of rules or instructions – typically encoded in software – that drives problem-solving and task execution in AI systems, forming the foundation for functions like classification, prediction, and optimisation.

Algorithmic Decision-Making The process by which AI systems make or assist in making decisions, often automating tasks previously performed by humans. It requires transparency and explainability to ensure fairness and accountability.

Annexes (EU AI Act) Supplementary documents within the EU AI Act detailing specific requirements for technical documentation, registration, and compliance.

Application Programming Interface (API) A standardised interface comprising protocols and tools that enable seamless communication and data exchange between software systems. It is crucial for integrating AI capabilities into existing government platforms and ensuring interoperability across services.

Artificial General Intelligence (AGI) A hypothetical form of AI characterised by human-level intelligence and the ability to generalise across diverse tasks and contexts. Distinguished from narrow AI by its versatility and still regarded as a long-term research objective rather than a present-day capability.

Artificial Intelligence (AI) A broad field of computer science focused on creating systems capable of performing tasks that typically require human intelligence, such as perception, reasoning, learning, and decision-making.

Automated Decision Systems (ADS) Government or organisational systems that use AI algorithms to make or support decisions affecting individuals or groups, such as eligibility for services, resource allocation, or law enforcement actions.

Bidirectional Encoder Representations from Transformers (BERT) A machine learning framework designed to support natural language processing tasks, enabling AI systems to understand and interpret dialogue in applications such as telephone support systems and to generate human language with greater accuracy and efficiency.

Biometric Systems AI-driven systems that use unique biological characteristics (e.g. fingerprints, facial recognition) for identification, authentication, or categorisation. Subject to strict regulation due to privacy and discrimination risks.

Blockchain A decentralised, tamper-proof digital ledger technology used to enhance transparency, security, and trust in AI-driven public services, such as land registries and transaction records.

Citizen Co-Creation/Participatory Governance Models where citizens actively collaborate with government in the design, development, and oversight of AI systems, fostering trust, transparency, and alignment with community needs.

Common Service Centres (CSCs) India's network of rural digital hubs that provide access to AI-driven e-governance services, digital literacy, and social benefits, helping to bridge the digital divide.

Data Governance The management of the availability, usability, integrity, and security of data within an organisation or system, which is crucial for high-quality AI outcomes and compliance with privacy regulations.

Data Infrastructure The foundational digital systems, technologies, and processes enabling the collection, storage, processing, and sharing of data for AI applications in the public sector.

Data Lake A centralised infrastructure for storing vast amounts of raw diverse data, designed to support AI-driven analysis and insight generation.

Data Protection Impact Assessment (DPIA) The systematic identification, assessment, and reduction of privacy and data protection risks typically carried out when processing personal data is likely to present a high risk to individuals' rights and freedoms.

Data Tampering The unauthorised modification, deletion, or manipulation of data, often by cybercriminals for malicious purposes like financial gain, espionage, or sabotage.

Deepfake AI-generated synthetic media (images, audio, video) that convincingly mimics real people or events.

Deployers (EU AI Act) Entities (natural or legal persons, public authorities, agencies) that use AI systems under their authority, excluding personal, non-professional activities.

Digital Divide The gap between individuals or communities with and without access to digital technologies and the internet, affecting equitable participation in AI-enhanced public services.

Ethical AI The development and deployment of AI systems in accordance with principles such as fairness, transparency, privacy, non-discrimination, safety, and respect for human rights.

Explainability/Explainable AI The ability of AI systems to provide understandable and interpretable reasons for their outputs or decisions, critical for accountability and trust.

Exposure Management The comprehensive set of information collected, consolidated, and analysed to support an organisation's cybersecurity exposure management efforts, providing a clear view of potential vulnerabilities and risks across its digital environment.

Foundation Model A large-scale AI model, trained on extensive datasets, designed for adaptability across diverse tasks, including generative AI applications.

General-Purpose AI (GPAI) Models Large-scale AI systems designed for a wide range of applications, not limited to a specific task.

High-Risk AI Systems (EU AI Act) AI applications that could significantly impact public health, safety, fundamental rights, or the environment (e.g. biometric identification, law enforcement, critical infrastructure), subject to the most stringent regulatory requirements.

Human Oversight The principle that humans must supervise, intervene in, or override AI system decisions, especially in high-risk or sensitive applications, to ensure ethical and lawful outcomes.

Hybrid Workflows Work processes that combine human expertise and AI capabilities, often leading to more efficient, accurate, and responsive public services.

Immutability (Blockchain Context) The characteristic of blockchain records that prevents alteration or tampering, ensuring data integrity and trustworthiness in public registries and transactions.

Inclusivity Ensuring that AI systems and digital services are accessible and beneficial to all segments of society, including marginalised or vulnerable populations.

Interoperability The ability of different systems, devices, or organisations to work together and exchange data seamlessly, which is essential for integrated AI solutions in government.

IoT (Internet of Things) A network of interconnected devices and sensors that collect and transmit data, often analysed by AI to optimise public services such as energy management, transportation, and waste collection.

Limited-Risk AI Systems (EU AI Act) AI systems that may pose risks of manipulation or deception (e.g. chatbots), requiring transparency measures such as user notification when interacting with AI.

Large Language Model (LLM) An AI model trained on vast text datasets to comprehend, generate, and process human language; it enables advanced chatbots, document analysis, and other language-driven applications within government services.

Machine Learning A subset of AI involving algorithms that learn from data to improve their performance over time, widely used in predictive analytics, pattern recognition, and automation.

Membership Inference A privacy attack targeting machine learning models, where an adversary seeks to identify whether a particular data point was part of the model's training dataset.

Minimal-Risk AI Systems (EU AI Act) AI systems posing negligible risk (e.g. spam filters), not subject to mandatory requirements but encouraged to adhere to general ethical principles.

Model Inversion A security and privacy risk in machine learning in which an attacker uses the outputs of a trained model to deduce details about its training data, model parameters, or sensitive attributes of individuals represented in the dataset.

Model Manipulation A manipulation that involves deliberately altering a machine learning model's internal parameters, activations, or structure to change its behaviour, outputs, or capabilities.

M-Pesa A mobile banking service in Kenya and other countries that leverages AI for fraud detection, personalised financial services, and customer support, significantly advancing financial inclusion.

OECD AI Principles Internationally recognised guidelines for trustworthy, human-centric AI, focusing on values such as inclusiveness, fairness, transparency, accountability, and respect for human rights.

Personalisation The use of AI to tailor public services and interactions with individual needs and circumstances, enhancing efficiency and user experience.

Predictive Policing The application of AI and machine learning to analyse data and predict potential criminal activity, raising both effectiveness and ethical concerns regarding bias and privacy.

Proactive Governance A governance model where governments anticipate and address citizen needs through AI-driven predictions and interventions, rather than reacting to issues after they arise.

Public Trust (AI Context) The confidence citizens have in government use of AI, built through transparency, accountability, ethical practices, and effective communication about risks and benefits.

Risk Categorisation (EU AI Act) The classification of AI systems into unacceptable, high, limited, or minimal risk, which determines the level of regulatory scrutiny and requirements.

Supervised Learning A machine learning technique where algorithms are trained on labelled data, allowing them to learn patterns and make predictions or classifications.

Tax Assessment AI (e.g. Ve.Ra.) AI tools used by tax authorities to analyse financial data, identify tax evasion risks, and support compliance while balancing transparency, privacy, and fairness.

Transparency (AI Context) The obligation to make the functioning, logic, and decision-making processes of AI systems understandable and accessible to users and regulators.

Unacceptable Risk AI Systems (EU AI Act) AI systems prohibited under the EU AI Act due to their incompatibility with fundamental rights and EU values (e.g. social scoring, real-time biometric surveillance).

Ve.Ra. (Verification of Financial Relationships) An AI-based tool used by the Italian Revenue Agency for risk analysis in tax compliance, which employs supervised learning to identify high-risk profiles and support tax audits.

List of Acronyms and Abbreviations

AI – Artificial Intelligence

ADS – Automated Decision Systems

CSCs – Common Service Centres

DHS – Department of Homeland Security

EDIHs – European Digital Innovation Hubs
EU – European Union
FCA – Financial Conduct Authority
FDA – United States Food and Drug Administration
GDP – Gross Domestic Product
GPAI – General-Purpose AI
ICE – Immigration and Customs Enforcement
IoT – Internet of Things
LLMs – Large Language Models
MGX – Specific company in Stargate Project context
NHS – National Health Service
NYCEDC – New York City Economic Development Corporation
OECD – Organisation for Economic Co-operation and Development
SMEs – Small and Medium-sized Enterprises
TBI – Tony Blair Institute
UAE – United Arab Emirates
UN – United Nations
UNESCO – United Nations Educational, Scientific and Cultural Organisation
USCIS – United States Citizenship and Immigration Services
VLEs – Village Level Entrepreneurs
Ve.Ra. – Verification of Financial Relationships

List of Specialised Initiatives, Programmes, and Projects

AI Act Service Desk – EU support resource for AI regulation compliance
AI Continent Action Plan – European Commission's roadmap for AI
AI Factories – European Commission's AI infrastructure initiative
AI Gigafactories – Large-scale AI chip facilities in the EU
AI Skills Academy – EU talent initiative
Apply AI Strategy – EU plan for sector-specific AI adoption
Asylum Text Analytics – USCIS AI tool for asylum applications
CityOS – Barcelona's urban data and AI platform
Data Union Strategy – EU cross-border data sharing initiative

Digital Inclusion Action Plan – UK government digital access strategy

Digital Street – UK Land Registry blockchain project

Domain Awareness System – New York City's surveillance and analytics platform

Flood Hub – Google's AI-powered disaster prediction system

HIGP – Hiroshima Process International Guiding Principles

M-Pesa – Mobile money service in Kenya and other countries

M-Shwari – M-Pesa-linked savings and loan product

NYC AI Action Plan – New York City's AI governance strategy

Predicted to Naturalize – USCIS AI tool for citizenship eligibility

PredPol – Predictive policing tool (Los Angeles)

Stargate Project – US AI infrastructure initiative

Strategic Subject List – Chicago Police Department predictive analytics tool

Talent Pool – EU AI talent initiative

vTaiwan – Taiwan's digital participatory governance platform

Zuri – Safaricom's AI-powered chatbot

List of Regulatory and Governance Frameworks

AI Act – Artificial Intelligence Act (EU regulation)

AI Bill of Rights – US White House Blueprint for AI

GDPR – General Data Protection Regulation

Hiroshima AI Process – G7 international AI governance initiative

Hiroshima Process International Code of Conduct for Organisations Developing Advanced AI Systems

United Nations Governing AI for Humanity framework

United Nations System White Paper on AI Governance

Government Agencies and Authorities

Agenzia delle Entrate – Italian Revenue Agency

HM Land Registry – His Majesty's Land Registry (UK)

Ministry for Children – New Zealand government department

Ministry of State for Local Issues and Anti-Corruption – Albania

National Agency of Public Registry – Georgia

Republic of Estonia Ministry of Justice and Digital Affairs – Estonia

List of Technical and Analytical Terms

Annex I, III, IV, VIII, IX, XI, XII, XIII – Specific sections of the EU AI Act

Blockchain – Distributed ledger technology

Neural Networks – Type of AI model

Random Forests – Type of AI model

Supervised Learning – Machine learning approach

Introduction

In 1900, an estimated 40 per cent of the United States workforce was engaged in agricultural production. Today, because of the impact of automation, less than 2 per cent remain in the sector. In the United Kingdom, where industrialisation began earlier, 10 per cent of the workforce was employed in agriculture; now, it is less than 1 per cent. Job losses in one sector have been absorbed by others. Few would wish us to return to manual farming, with its higher food costs, physical hardship, and diversion of workers from more economically productive activities. We have welcomed automation and the benefits it brings to society. Artificial intelligence (AI) offers similar advantages. The key difference is the compression of time. The automation of agriculture was relatively slow, allowing for steady adaptation. The impact of AI will be far faster, perhaps within five years, bringing enormous benefits but also significant disruption to those displaced.

In a world increasingly shaped by digital transformation, we are witnessing remarkable improvements in service. Consider the smooth experience of shopping on Amazon, with its rapid search functions, competitive pricing, frictionless payment options, and astonishingly fast delivery, all supported by real-time updates. With Uber, users receive instant pricing, live tracking of their driver, and seamless payment, powered by the computing strength of a smartphone. These everyday experiences have shaped the expectations of modern consumers. By contrast, public service interactions are often disappointing, frustrating, and inefficient. It does not have to be this way.

The integration of AI into public service marks one of the most significant, and potentially unprecedented, shifts in modern governance. What makes this change so consequential is that it transfers decision-making power from people to machines. Algorithms, rather than human judgement, will increasingly determine outcomes that affect citizens' lives. This shift has the potential to dramatically improve service quality while reducing costs.

DOI: 10.4324/9781003673897-1

AI has become a major political issue and is often promoted as a near-magical solution to the economic stagnation facing many Western countries. In October 2023, President Biden stated: 'Artificial Intelligence is driving change at an unprecedented pace. It has the potential to solve some of our toughest challenges, from curing diseases to tackling climate change.'[1] The President of the European Commission, Ursula von der Leyen, said: 'AI can open new horizons for medical research, energy efficiency, and education. But we must guide it with strong human-centred values.'[2] British Prime Minister Sir Keir Starmer, in January 2025, declared: 'Artificial Intelligence will drive incredible change in our country. From teachers personalising lessons, to supporting small businesses with their record-keeping, to speeding up planning applications, it has the potential to transform the lives of working people.'[3] President Donald Trump promoted his vision of AI through the Stargate Project, claiming: 'This is the largest AI infrastructure project in history . . . ushering in a new golden age for America.'[4]

Governments around the world are at the start of an AI revolution, one that promises not just to redefine how services are delivered but to reshape the nature of governance itself. AI is altering not only administrative efficiency but also the way decisions are made. It is influencing how governments formulate policy and make choices that affect every citizen. This transformation presents profound opportunities but also complex challenges, particularly around accountability, transparency, and the continuing role of human oversight.

The promise of AI in public service is clear. It can streamline bureaucratic processes by automating repetitive tasks, personalise service delivery, forecast societal needs with extraordinary accuracy, and achieve all this while reducing costs and improving service quality. Yet, these advantages are set against real obstacles: budget constraints, legacy IT systems, excessive regulation, and a cultural resistance to change, often driven by fear of the unknown and the inertia typical of large bureaucracies.

Imagine public transport systems that adjust in real time to traffic patterns, healthcare systems that predict disease outbreaks before they escalate, or social services that proactively identify and support at-risk populations. These are not distant dreams but emerging realities powered by AI, offering governments the ability to do more with fewer resources while enhancing the quality and accessibility of public services.

Still, this potential must be balanced against serious concerns. As AI replaces tasks traditionally performed by humans, especially in administrative roles, millions of jobs are at risk. Ethical issues are widespread, from algorithmic bias to the erosion of privacy in data-rich systems. The digital divide also threatens to widen inequality, leaving already marginalised communities further behind. Whether AI becomes a tool for social progress or a source of new division will depend on how governments confront these tensions.

The digital divide is significant in Africa. According to a recent survey from *TechRepublic*, 'a single institute at Harvard has more computing power than all African-owned AI data centers in the continent combined'.[5]

In 2025, Amazon, Meta, Microsoft, Google, and Open AI invested more than $300 billion in AI, much of this on infrastructure – an expenditure almost as large as Canada's national budget.

AI is not a panacea for government reform. It is a powerful tool operating within a complex ecosystem of legacy data, policy complexity, fiscal constraints, and rapidly developing technology. This book, *Automating Government: How AI Will Revolutionise Public Services*, is not simply a technical guide to AI applications. It is a roadmap to understanding and navigating the far-reaching societal shifts that AI will bring. Through case studies, analysis, and practical guidance, it offers public servants, policymakers, and leaders the insight they need to lead with confidence.

You will find stories of success, failure, and lessons learned. From Estonia's pioneering digital governance model to the ethical missteps of predictive policing in the United States, these examples reflect the complexity and nuance of real-world AI adoption. The book explores the promise of transformation, the cost of disruption, and the strategies required to ensure AI is deployed responsibly.

At its heart, this book is a call to action. It asks public leaders to view AI not merely as a tool for efficiency but an opportunity to create a more inclusive, transparent, and responsive state. It calls for ethical frameworks that promote equity and accountability, participatory governance that involves citizens in shaping solutions, and sustained investment in workforce development. Together, these elements can transform how essential public services are delivered. As explored in this book, unlocking AI's potential will require significant investment. A recent report suggests that the UK will need to allocate at least £4 billion annually in additional public technology spending over the next five years. While a £20 billion commitment is substantial, it represents less than one-fifth of the cost of the UK's largely abandoned HS2 high-speed rail project, which has yielded little national benefit. By contrast, as we aim to show, AI has the potential to benefit millions across multiple sectors.

The integration of AI into government is not an end state. It is part of a continuous journey to improve public services and meet citizens' evolving expectations. That journey demands vision, courage and an unshakeable commitment to the public good. This book is intended as a guide for that journey, offering tools and insights to navigate the complexities that lie ahead.

As we explore these themes together, let us remember that the aim of government is not simply to administer but to serve. In the age of AI, this mission remains the same, but the methods, technologies, and mindset must adapt. By aligning technological progress with human values, we can create a future in which AI supports a more just, capable, and inclusive society.

Notes

1 The White House (2023), Remarks by President Biden and Vice President Harris on the administration's commitment to advancing the safe, secure, and trustworthy development and use of artificial intelligence, https://bidenwhitehouse.archives.gov/briefing-room/speeches-remarks/2023/10/30/remarks-by-president-biden-and-vice-president-harris-on-the-administrations-commitment-to-advancing-the-safe-secure-and-trustworthy-development-and-use-of-artificial-intelligence/ (accessed on 28 March 2025).

2 Reuters (2025), Quotes from EU chief von der Leyen's AI speech at Paris summit, www.reuters.com/technology/artificial-intelligence/quotes-eu-chief-von-der-leyens-ai-speech-paris-summit-2025-02-11/? (accessed on 28 March 2025).
3 Government of the UK (2025), Prime Minister sets out blueprint to turbocharge AI, www.gov.uk/government/news/prime-minister-sets-out-blueprint-to-turbocharge-ai? (accessed on 28 March 2025).
4 The American Presidency Project (2025), Remarks on artificial intelligence infrastructure development and an exchange with reporters, www.presidency.ucsb.edu/documents/remarks-artificial-intelligence-infrastructure-development-and-exchange-with-reporters? (accessed on 28 March 2025).
5 TechRepublic (2025), Global divide: Only 32 countries host AI data centers, www.techrepublic.com/article/news-only-32-countries-host-data-centers-2025/ (accessed on 28 March 2025).

Part I

Understanding the AI Revolution and Its Implications for Government

Chapter 1

The Dawn of AI in Public Service

On a quiet morning in 2025, a citizen logs into their municipal portal to apply for a building permit. Instead of enduring months of waiting, filing paper documents, and making repeated visits to city offices, they receive a response within minutes. An artificial intelligence (AI) system has reviewed their application, cross-checked it against zoning regulations, and issued a preliminary approval almost instantaneously. Elsewhere in the city, a social services caseworker consults an AI assistant to analyse the complexities of a family's situation, gaining insights that support more effective coordination of services. Meanwhile at city hall, predictive algorithms reshape the rhythms of urban life, optimising transportation routes in real time to reduce costs and shorten commute times for thousands of residents.

These are not scenes from speculative fiction. They are happening now, and they illustrate the profound changes that AI is bringing to government operations. AI has moved from being a futuristic concept to becoming a driving force behind a quiet transformation in public service delivery. Its integration is not only improving efficiency but also fundamentally reshaping how governments interact with citizens, manage resources, and make decisions.

Unlike previous waves of technological change, such as the introduction of computers or the rise of the internet, the potential of AI reaches far beyond the enhancement of existing systems. It offers the possibility of redesigning them entirely.

There is widespread public debate about AI. Is it a force for good or ill? How can we protect ourselves from harm caused by AI? Will we lose control over our lives, with important personal decisions being made by impersonal, and at times flawed, software programs?

DOI: 10.4324/9781003673897-3

These are important and legitimate questions that are causing deep concern among both politicians and the public.

At this early stage in the book, we feel it is important to offer some clarification. Our aim is to unpack the rather nebulous concept of artificial intelligence and explain how its application to public service should be understood.

We can begin by considering two broad categories of AI application: routine task automation, and complex problem-solving and decision support. These two modes are often conflated in public debates, yet they have distinct implications for governance, ethics, risk, and workforce impact.

Let us start with the first category, routine task automation. AI can greatly improve efficiency in managing predictable, rule-based administrative tasks. Examples include supporting patients through hospital systems, processing standardised applications such as planning permissions, answering frequently asked questions, and handling tax refunds. These tasks are generally transactional in nature and follow established procedures.

In such cases, AI can reduce waiting times, lower operating costs, minimise errors or inconsistencies, and improve user satisfaction. This form of automation is typically less contentious, as it replicates services already in place. AI excels at sifting through large datasets, making clear-cut classifications, and flagging more nuanced cases for human review.

The second category, complex problem-solving and decision support, involves AI systems that are used for analytical reasoning, pattern recognition, or predictive modelling. Examples include identifying children at risk within social care, optimising the allocation of emergency response resources, detecting fraud in tax returns, or supporting policy decisions through simulation and scenario analysis.

In this area, the stakes are higher and the consequences more serious. These applications require human judgement and discretion. They often involve ethical trade-offs and demand a greater degree of accountability and transparency in decision-making.

There may be some overlap between the two categories, but we believe they offer a useful way to frame how AI can be applied. Other perspectives can also provide insight into the broader implications of AI for public service, as shown in Table 1.1. For example:

- Efficiency versus legitimacy: AI offers the promise of faster, cheaper, and more scalable public service delivery. At the same time, it risks undermining public trust when decisions appear impersonal, opaque, or unfair.
- Centralisation versus local empowerment: Since the Second World War, the United Kingdom has seen a strong shift towards centralisation, often at the expense of local autonomy. This issue is highlighted in Sam Freedman's recent book, *Failed State*. AI has the potential to support local decision-making by providing more tailored insights.
- Standardisation versus personalisation: AI is effective at applying rules consistently and at scale, but many decisions benefit from individualised, person-centred responses.

- Displacement versus augmentation of human roles: A key question is whether AI should be used to support and enhance human judgement, or whether it will ultimately replace human roles entirely.
- Short-term deployment versus long-term transformation: There is a tension between using AI to automate existing processes and using it to rethink how public services are designed and delivered.
- Innovation versus compliance: Strict adherence to rules can improve consistency and accountability but may also limit creativity and discourage innovation.

Whichever way you consider these dimensions, opportunities, and risks of AI, one thing is certain: AI is reshaping the very foundations of public administration.

Participatory Governance and AI: Engaging Citizens

The transformative potential of AI in public service is best realised when citizens are actively involved in shaping how it is implemented. Participatory governance models, in which citizens work alongside governments to design, develop, and oversee AI systems, help ensure that technology reflects the values and needs of the communities it is intended to serve. This approach not only builds trust and transparency but also supports the creation of solutions that are both equitable and responsive.

A leading example of participatory governance is Barcelona's Decidim platform, an open-source tool enabling citizens to propose, debate, and vote on municipal policies. Decidim uses AI to process large volumes of citizen input, identifying recurring themes and shared priorities. This ensures that policymaking is responsive to public sentiment, not just bureaucratic or political agendas. By directly involving citizens in AI-supported projects, such as urban planning algorithms or traffic optimisation systems, governments can develop solutions that genuinely reflect community needs.

Table 1.1 Ways of thinking about AI

Dimension	*Opportunity*	*Threat*
Efficiency vs. Legitimacy	Faster, cheaper services	Loss of trust, perceived unfairness
Centralisation vs. Local	Scalable coordination	Disempowerment of local actors
Standardisation vs. Personalisation	Consistent rules	Risk of bias or perceived inequity
Displacement vs. Augmentation	Productivity gains	Job loss, skills obsolescence
Short-term vs. Long-term	Quick wins	Failure to transform broken systems

Source: Authors' elaboration

Taiwan's vTaiwan initiative provides another compelling example. This digital platform collects public opinion on proposed legislation and uses AI to synthesise thousands of comments into actionable insights for policymakers.

During debates on ride-sharing regulations, vTaiwan successfully facilitated dialogue among stakeholders, balancing the interests of the public, regulators, and private companies. The AI-supported synthesis of diverse viewpoints enabled more informed and inclusive policy outcomes.

Even in emerging economies, participatory governance is proving effective. In Brazil, a participatory budgeting project in Belo Horizonte utilises AI to analyse citizen proposals for municipal investments. This system ensures that the voices of underserved populations are heard, guiding decisions on public infrastructure and services.

Governments can further develop participatory governance by establishing citizen assemblies on AI. These assemblies, made up of diverse representatives, would deliberate on the ethical, social, and technical implications of AI in governance. For example, before deploying AI in predictive policing, an assembly could weigh the benefits of crime prevention against the risks of bias or privacy infringement, helping to shape the system's design accordingly. This participatory model not only builds trust but also enables citizens to play an active role in shaping the technologies that affect their lives.

Bridging the Digital Divide in Early AI Initiatives

While AI offers enormous potential to transform public services, its benefits may be unevenly distributed because of the digital divide. Access to the internet, levels of digital literacy, and trust in technology vary significantly across socio-economic groups and age cohorts. These disparities create barriers that must be addressed if access to AI-enabled services is to be fair and inclusive.

India's Common Service Centres (CSCs) provide a compelling example of how governments can bridge the digital divide. Located in rural and underserved areas, these centres give citizens access to AI-enabled e-governance services.

A villager without internet access, for example, can visit a CSC to apply for government benefits or register a complaint, with the assistance of a local entrepreneur who helps navigate the system. AI operates behind the scenes to streamline processes, verify identities, and detect fraudulent applications, improving efficiency while promoting inclusion.

In Kenya, the AI-powered chatbot Eva demonstrates another innovative approach. Designed to assist citizens in accessing government services, Eva works via SMS, eliminating the need for smartphones or high-speed internet. Citizens can inquire about their tax status, register for social programmes, or file complaints through simple text messages. This initiative highlights how AI can be adapted to the technological realities of underserved populations.

Similarly, Estonia has placed inclusivity at the centre of its widely respected digital governance model. Its e-Residency programme uses AI to streamline administrative processes for both residents and international users. At the same time, the government has invested in digital literacy initiatives to ensure that all citizens, including older adults and those in rural areas, are able to access AI-enhanced services. This dual focus on technological innovation and public education provides a valuable model for overcoming barriers to adoption.

Access to digital services is a critical issue shaping the UK's social and professional landscape. A growing proportion of government services now require internet access, often through a computer or smartphone. Internet penetration is high, with 97.8 per cent of the population online as of early 2025. However, approximately 2.2 per cent, or around 1.28 million people, remain offline.

This digital exclusion is especially pronounced among vulnerable groups, including older adults and low-income households, who face significant barriers in accessing essential online services. Government initiatives such as the Digital Inclusion Action Plan aim to bridge this gap by providing devices and digital skills training, although substantial challenges remain.[1]

However, bridging the digital divide is not solely a technological challenge. It also requires addressing social and psychological factors, including public trust in government systems. Some communities are hesitant to engage with AI due to concerns about surveillance, misuse of personal data, or fears linked to immigration status. In such cases, technical solutions must be combined with clear communication strategies to explain the benefits of AI while acknowledging and addressing the associated risks.

France offers a useful example. Public awareness campaigns around its national health data platform emphasised both the safeguards in place and the potential health benefits of AI-generated insights. This approach helped to build public trust by being transparent and relatable.

A more contentious example is found in the United States, where AI is increasingly being used in immigration enforcement. Many undocumented immigrants fear that engaging with government services could lead to their data being used to facilitate arrest or deportation. The US Department of Homeland Security (DHS), along with its agencies such as US Citizenship and Immigration Services (USCIS) and Immigration and Customs Enforcement (ICE), has integrated AI into several key decision-making processes.[2]

USCIS, for instance uses AI tools like Predicted to Naturalise to assess eligibility for citizenship and Asylum Text Analytics to screen asylum applications for potential fraud. At the US border, AI enhances surveillance technologies at the border, such as drones and sensor towers equipped with machine learning to detect illegal crossings.[3] These AI systems are capable of distinguishing between people, animals, and vehicles, which helps reduce false alarms and improve accuracy.

AI also plays a role in deportation decisions. Tools such as the Hurricane Score used by ICE help determine the terms of electronic surveillance for individuals awaiting immigration hearings. Predictive algorithms are being used to identify people for deportation more quickly, thereby accelerating enforcement processes.[4]

However, these developments raise serious concerns. Critics point to the potential for bias, data misuse, and the lack of transparency in how such tools are developed and applied. They argue that AI-driven systems may result in inaccurate or discriminatory outcomes, further undermining civil rights protections for already vulnerable populations.

The need for transparency, independent oversight, and ethical review is therefore critical. Governments must ensure that AI systems do not disproportionately or unfairly affect immigrant communities and that accountability mechanisms are in place to protect individual rights.

Conclusion

The rise of AI represents not just a technological shift but a fundamental opportunity to reshape how governments serve their citizens, engage with them, and are held accountable. AI should not be viewed merely as a tool for improving efficiency but as a transformative force capable of redefining the principles and practices of governance itself.

The integration of AI into public services is more than a technical upgrade. It represents a profound reimagining of the relationship between citizens and the institutions that serve them. From Barcelona's participatory platforms to India's rural service centres, we are seeing a global shift in which technology acts as a bridge rather than a barrier.

The true potential of AI in public service does not lie in the sophistication of its algorithms but in its ability to help create systems that are more responsive, inclusive, and transparent. As governments and citizens work together to apply these emerging technologies, we are beginning a new chapter in public administration, one that brings innovation, ethics, and human-centred design into closer alignment to support a more equitable and intelligent future.

Notes

1 Think Digital Partners (2025), UK Government to tackle digital exclusion, www.thinkdigitalpartners.com/news/2025/02/26/uk-government-to-tackle-digital-exclusion/ (accessed on 24 March 2025).
2 U.S. Department of Homeland Security (No date), United States Citizenship and Immigration Services – AI use cases, www.dhs.gov/ai/use-case-inventory/uscis (accessed on 24 March 2025).
3 CNBC (2025), How Trump's mass deportation plan can use AI to extend immigration crackdown, www.cnbc.com/2024/12/01/trump-mass-deportation-plan-ai-immigration-border.html (accessed on 24 March 2025).
4 U.S. Department of Homeland Security (No date), United States Citizenship and Immigration Services – AI use cases, www.dhs.gov/ai/use-case-inventory/uscis (accessed on 24 March 2025).

Chapter 2

AI's Potential

Transforming Public Service Delivery

The integration of artificial intelligence (AI) into public service delivery is not simply a technological upgrade; it represents a seismic shift in how governments carry out their responsibilities. From improving the efficiency of routine tasks to personalising citizen interactions and anticipating broader societal challenges, AI has the potential to transform the traditional bureaucratic systems into agile, data-driven engines of public service delivery. The opportunities are vast, but realising them will require detailed planning, significant upfront investment to update existing IT infrastructure, and a commitment to fairness and transparency.

According to a 2024 report by the Tony Blair Institute (TBI) in the UK, approximately 40 per cent of public-sector tasks could be partially automated by using advanced tools such as machine learning, large language models (LLMs), and AI-enabled robotics. The report estimates that these innovations could save around one-fifth of the total time currently spent by the six million-strong public-sector workforce.

To put that in perspective, saving 20 per cent of workforce time equates to roughly 245 million employee days per year. Even if this estimate is overstated by a factor of ten, the potential efficiency gains are enormous. The report suggests that administrative and back-office functions stand to benefit the most, with potential time savings of up to 27 per cent. In contrast, frontline roles such as healthcare professionals and teachers would see smaller efficiencies of around 11 per cent, reflecting the unique complexities and interpersonal demands of their work.

AI-driven efficiencies, the TBI claims, could save the UK public sector up to £41 billion annually, equivalent to 1.5 per cent of GDP, assuming optimal utilisation. Notably, these savings would stem largely from reducing overtime and improving

DOI: 10.4324/9781003673897-4

resource allocation, rather than large-scale job cuts. Realising such significant savings, of course, demands upfront investment. Investing an estimated £4 billion per year would result in a benefit-cost ratio of 9:1 when fully operational.[1]

In a recent article, UK Prime Minister Keir Starmer said: 'The government can be more efficient by using AI and technology,' adding, 'We're essentially asking businesses across the country to be more efficient, to look at AI and tech in the way that they do their business [and] I want the same challenge in government.'[2]

While the spotlight on AI reflects its contemporary relevance, the way it is often presented by politicians as a miracle solution bringing low-cost efficiency to a wide range of services is overly simplistic and geared towards sound bites. Presenting AI as a low-cost, high-efficiency solution risks obscuring the broader and more complex challenges involved in its integration into the provision of public service delivery. A more grounded conversation is needed, one that acknowledges not only the promise of innovation but also the real costs, logistical hurdles, and the need for thoughtful regulation and ethical oversight. Only through such a balanced approach can we begin to harness the potential of AI in a manner that is equitable, responsible, and sustainable.

A New Paradigm for Public Service

The traditional image of public service delivery often evokes frustration: long queues, challenging paperwork, unanswered helplines and emails, inconsistent advice, and time-consuming delays. Bureaucratic inefficiency has long been a global challenge, slowing progress and undermining public trust in government institutions.

AI is beginning to change this narrative. By automating repetitive tasks, incorporating predictive decision-making, and enabling more personalised services, it is gradually but fundamentally altering the relationship between governments and citizens.

In India, for example, the government's Aadhaar system, a nationwide biometric database, uses AI to streamline welfare distribution. It verifies identities in seconds, reducing fraud and ensuring that subsidies and benefits reach the intended recipients. [3]

Similarly, in Denmark and Italy, AI tools in tax administration identify patterns of evasion and improve the efficiency of the tax collection processes, resulting in the recovery of millions in lost revenue.

These examples highlight how AI is not only improving efficiency but also strengthening accountability and fairness in public service delivery. However, the transformative potential of AI extends far beyond these applications.

AI in Action: Revolutionising Service Delivery

AI is proving invaluable across various domains of public service. Its applications are as diverse as the numerous challenges governments face. As the following examples illustrate, there are significant advancements in areas such as urban planning, health, infrastructure management, and tax audits.

Urban Planning and Transportation

Urban areas, with their dense populations and complex systems, present some of government's most pressing management challenges. AI is helping city planners tackle these issues with unprecedented precision. For example, Singapore's Urban Redevelopment Authority employs AI to analyse traffic patterns, population density, and land use data to optimise urban planning decisions. The result is a city that is not only more efficient but also more liveable.

Similarly, AI is revolutionising public transportation systems. In Helsinki, Finland, AI-powered predictive algorithms adjust bus and train schedules in real time based on passenger flow data. This minimises wait times, reduces overcrowding, and ensures efficient use of resources. By making public transport more reliable and user-friendly, these systems encourage sustainable commuting habits, contributing to environmental goals.

Public Health and Crisis Management

The role of AI in public health has gained prominence in recent years, particularly during the COVID-19 pandemic. AI models were instrumental in tracking the spread of the virus, predicting infection hotspots, and optimising the distribution of medical supplies. In South Korea, AI-enabled contact tracing systems helped contain outbreaks by identifying potential transmission chains quickly and accurately.

Beyond pandemic response, AI is transforming everyday healthcare administration. In Rwanda, AI-powered diagnostic tools address healthcare inequities by providing accurate, early detection of conditions like malaria and tuberculosis in underserved regions. These AI tools, combined with mobile health units, have significantly improved health outcomes in remote areas.

In the United Kingdom, NHS England has an AI team working on a range of projects. AI is being trialled to predict patient demand, helping to ensure hospitals are adequately staffed and resources are allocated efficiently. These predictive systems also support preventive care by identifying individuals at high risk of chronic disease and recommending early interventions.

In the report *AI in London Healthcare: The Reality Behind the Hype* (March 2025), the authors highlight several fundamental challenges: navigating governance and regulation, securing sustainable funding, building digital infrastructure, and ensuring that staff have the knowledge and capacity to engage with new technologies. A key insight from the report is the need for a more strategic and collaborative approach to AI adoption, as well as the importance of sharing best practices and avoiding duplication.[4]

Infrastructure and Environmental Management

AI is enhancing the management and maintenance of public infrastructure. Predictive maintenance systems, powered by machine learning, analyse sensor data to identify potential infrastructure failures before they occur. Japan's railway operators, for example, use AI to monitor track conditions, preventing costly and dangerous disruptions.

In environmental management, AI enables governments to monitor and protect natural resources more effectively. Norway's forestry authorities use AI to analyse satellite imagery, detecting illegal logging activities in real time and aiding enforcement efforts. Similarly, cities such as Los Angeles use AI systems to monitor air quality and predict pollution levels, enabling targeted interventions to improve public health.

Expanding Citizen Responsiveness

AI's ability to respond and adapt to citizens' needs lies at the heart of its transformative potential. By providing personalised services and real-time feedback, AI helps ensure that public provision evolves in step with citizens' changing needs.

Real-Time Feedback Systems

AI offers governments the ability to create real-time citizen feedback systems, providing a continuous loop of communication and adaptation. Barcelona's CityOS integrates AI with Internet of Things (IoT) sensors to monitor public services, including waste management, traffic flow, and energy consumption. Citizens can report issues via a mobile app, and the system immediately identifies, prioritises, and dispatches resources to address them.

Tools like AI-driven sentiment analysis, used during public consultations, help governments gauge public opinion and refine policies in real time. Imagine a public transportation system that adapts schedules and routes based on commuter feedback or a city council that dynamically tailors public services based on real-time citizen input.

Citizen-Centric Public Service

AI enables unprecedented personalisation of public services. Estonia's digital governance platform provides an excellent example of personalisation at scale. By analysing life events, such as the birth of a child or the retirement of a citizen, AI systems proactively offer relevant services, from tax credits to healthcare registration. This proactive approach reduces the administrative burden on citizens, transforming interactions with government from transactional to relational.

Predictive Analytics and Proactive Governance

Predictive analytics, a subset of AI, is enabling governments to shift from reactive to proactive service delivery. By analysing historical and real-time data, AI systems can identify patterns, predict outcomes, and inform decision-making.

Predictive analytics has been implemented in several cities, demonstrating both its potential benefits and associated challenges. In a project that sounds like something out of the Spielberg movie *Minority Report*, the Chicago Police Department introduced the Strategic Subject List, a machine-learning-based system designed to identify individuals at high risk of being involved in violent crime. A University of Chicago study reported that the model could predict crimes with 90 per cent accuracy, though concerns were raised about potential biases in the response of law enforcement. New York City employs the Domain Awareness System, which integrates data from surveillance cameras, licence plate readers, and social media to detect crime patterns. This system enhances situational awareness; however, it has faced criticism regarding privacy concerns and a lack of transparency. Similarly, the Los Angeles Police Department used PredPol, a tool that analysed past crime data to predict high-risk areas for criminal activity; there were concerns about over-policing in some communities, leading to the programme's discontinuation.[5] These cases highlight the growing role of predictive analytics in law enforcement, offering potential crime prevention benefits while also raising concerns about bias, privacy, and the ethical implications of data-driven analytics.

Proactive governance enhances public services by anticipating needs and implementing solutions before issues arise. One example of proactive public services is *application-free* child benefits, where eligible families automatically receive benefits upon a child's birth without the need for paperwork. This streamlines service delivery and reduces bureaucratic hurdles; however, concerns about errors, fraud, and waste will no doubt be prominent in public and political debate. Early intervention by social services is another area where predictive analytics identifies at-risk populations, for example, families vulnerable to homelessness. By acting early, governments can address long-term challenges and reduce the costs associated with chronic homelessness. Economic planning and fiscal responsibility also benefit from proactive governance.

At a time when most municipalities face severe financial pressure, advanced analytics help forecast revenue trends, monitor expenditure patterns, and identify fiscal risks, ensuring economic stability and transparency. This data-driven approach reduces financial uncertainties and enhances government accountability.

Proactive governance is being adopted in several countries to improve the accessibility, efficiency, and transparency of public services. In Pakistan, a notable example predating AI, although the principles would be the same, was introduced in Punjab in 2011. Under this model, government officials actively solicit citizen feedback on service quality: citizens receive SMS requests for input, while service providers document service delivery using smartphones. The initiative has generated over four million feedback requests and has led to measurable improvements in service delivery and staff behaviour. An AI-driven model would rapidly analyse the data and draw out salient points using advanced statistical techniques without the user needing any programming skills. AI could also link into existing databases to identify trends and even apply mapping technologies. Albania has adopted a similar approach through an SMS campaign launched by the Ministry of State for Local Issues and Anti-Corruption; the campaign aims to combat corruption by encouraging proactive citizen engagement to break the cycle of unethical practices.[6] Estonia has also made significant strides in proactive public services, designing systems that require minimal user interaction while ensuring accessibility, particularly for socially disadvantaged groups. New Zealand has adopted a similar approach, focusing on making government services more user-friendly and efficient with minimal citizen effort. Austria has embraced proactive public services by redesigning government interactions to be more accessible and effective, increasing policy impact.[7] Additionally, Estonia and other Baltic countries have pioneered event services, where multiple authorities collaborate to provide services automatically in response to significant life events, such as having a child or starting a business, without requiring citizens to make formal requests.[8]

These initiatives highlight how proactive governance can improve service delivery, reduce bureaucratic hurdles, and foster greater transparency and citizen engagement.

Disaster Management

In disaster management, predictive models are proving to be lifesaving. The Indian state of Odisha, prone to cyclones, uses AI to predict storm paths and coordinate evacuation efforts, which has significantly reduced casualties in recent years. Similarly, in California, AI systems analyse weather patterns, vegetation data, and historical wildfire information to predict high-risk areas, enabling pre-emptive measures.

Social Services and Vulnerable Populations

Predictive analytics is transforming social services by helping agencies identify at-risk populations and allocate resources more effectively. In New Zealand, the Ministry for Children uses AI to analyse data from sources, such as health and education records, to identify children in vulnerable situations. This enables social workers to intervene earlier, prevent potential crises, and improve outcomes for families. Of course, it is important to stress that in most cases AI is not deciding what action to take; it is providing valuable guidance to help professionals make better decisions.

Enhancing AI with Emerging Technologies

The integration of AI with other emerging technologies, such as the Internet of Things (IoT) and blockchain, further amplifies its potential in public service delivery. IoT devices are capable of generating vast amounts of real-time data, which AI systems can analyse to optimise resource allocation. For example, smart grid systems use IoT sensors and AI to monitor energy consumption, predict demand, and reduce wastage.

Blockchain, on the other hand, enhances transparency and trust in AI-driven systems. The UK's HM Land Registry is actively exploring the use of blockchain-secured databases to ensure tamper-proof records. Linking AI and blockchain technology can streamline the process of verifying and updating these records.

The Digital Street project by His Majesty's Land Registry aims to modernise land registration and property transactions in the UK using blockchain technology.[9] Launched in 2017, it explores distributed ledgers for secure, transparent property records, smart contracts for automated transactions, and real estate tokenisation for broader investment access. Prototypes using Corda have been developed for digital identity verification and contract signing, with blockchain integration promising real-time land register updates. While the project roadmap has been updated in October 2024, no official launch date has been set, as research and testing continue to ensure a smooth implementation.[10]

This combination has been particularly effective in Georgia, the first country to integrate blockchain technology into its land registration system, which has enhanced security, transparency, and efficiency. Launched in 2016 through a collaboration between Bitfury and the National Agency of Public Registry, the system operates as a backend layer within the existing digital registry.[11] By using Exonum's platform blockchain timestamping, and anchoring records to the Bitcoin blockchain, it ensures immutability and prevents fraud.[12] Citizens can easily verify property ownership online, while automated verification streamlines transactions. Recognised globally for its efficiency and anti-corruption impact, Georgia's success was driven by legal reforms, digital mapping, and strong political support, serving as a model for other nations.

Overcoming Challenges to AI Integration

While the benefits of AI in public service delivery are undeniable, its implementation is not without challenges. Governments face significant obstacles related to data management, infrastructure, ethics, and public trust.

Bridging the Digital Divide

India's Common Service Centres and Kenya's M-Pesa demonstrate how mobile technology and community hubs can bring AI-enhanced services to underserved populations. Expanding digital literacy and facilitating affordable internet access are essential components of these efforts.

India's Common Service Centres (CSCs) play a crucial role in bridging the digital divide by providing essential digital services to rural and remote areas. These centres serve as last-mile delivery points, offering services such as Aadhaar registration (India's national digital identity system) banking,[13] financial planning, telemedicine, education, and e-commerce support, ensuring broader access to government initiatives. By promoting digital literacy, CSCs empower rural communities to navigate and utilise online services effectively. Equipped with high-speed broadband and modern infrastructure, they facilitate e-governance, financial inclusion, and other critical services while also creating economic opportunities by supporting Village Level Entrepreneurs (VLEs) who manage these centres.[14] Innovative models, such as GPS-enabled mobile vans, further extend these services to the most remote areas. The integration of AI into CSCs has the potential to enhance service delivery by automating routine tasks, improving data-driven decision-making, and personalising user experiences. For instance, AI-powered education and skill development programmes can adapt content to local needs, improving digital literacy and employability; in e-commerce and AgriTech, AI can optimise supply chains, predict market trends, and better connect rural producers with national markets. Despite its potential, AI integration faces significant challenges including infrastructure limitations, data privacy concerns, and the need for equitable access to technology-driven services. However, overcoming these obstacles presents an opportunity for CSCs to become more efficient, user-centric, and innovative, further advancing digital inclusion and socio-economic development in rural India.

M-Pesa, launched in Kenya in 2007 by Safaricom, was a groundbreaking mobile banking service designed to provide financial services to the unbanked and underbanked population, and it is now integrating AI into its operating systems. Its name, meaning 'mobile money' in Swahili, reflects its core function of enabling seamless financial transactions. The service allows users to send and receive money both domestically and internationally, deposit and withdraw cash at agent locations, make retail purchases, and pay bills, including utilities, school fees, and taxes. Additionally, M-Pesa offers financial services such as loans and savings through platforms like M-Shwari and KCB M-Pesa. Since its introduction, M-Pesa has revolutionised Kenya's financial sector by significantly increasing financial inclusion, which rose from 23 per cent in 2007 to over 84 per cent by 2021.[15] It has contributed to poverty reduction, lifting around 2 per cent of households out of extreme poverty, and has boosted household income and spending.[16] The platform has also improved the velocity of money, accelerating the circulation of cash within the economy. Initially launched in Kenya, M-Pesa has expanded to several countries, including Tanzania, Mozambique, the Democratic Republic of Congo, Egypt, India, and Afghanistan. Merchants can integrate M-Pesa into their payment systems by registering with Safaricom, enabling them to serve a wider customer base while ensuring secure and efficient transactions.

M-Pesa is incorporating AI to improve security, customer service, and financial inclusion. AI-driven fraud detection systems analyse transaction patterns to identify and prevent fraudulent activities such as identity theft and social engineering scams. Personalised financial services, including savings and loan products through M-Shwari and KCB-M-Pesa, are tailored based on users' transaction history. Safaricom's AI-powered chatbot Zuri enhances customer service by efficiently handling queries, while predictive analytics help forecast M-Pesa adoption and usage, aiding in strategic planning. Looking ahead, M-Pesa plans to leverage AI for even greater personalisation of financial products, enhanced real-time fraud prevention, and improved credit scoring to expand loan access. AI-driven budgeting tools could offer personalised financial advice, while predictive cash flow management could assist businesses in optimising transactions and loan applications. The potential introduction of voice-activated transactions would improve accessibility for users with limited literacy or visual impairments.[17] However, challenges such as data privacy concerns and digital literacy gaps must be addressed to ensure equitable access and ethical AI implementation.

The two cases offer compelling examples of how technology can bridge the digital divide in developing regions, demonstrating that successful digital inclusion depends on a combination of appropriate infrastructure, locally relevant services, and a clear understanding of user needs. As these programmes increasingly incorporate AI technologies, from personalised financial services to adaptive educational content, they illustrate how digital solutions can be both innovative and accessible, creating economic opportunities while addressing the specific challenges faced by underserved communities. The success of these models provides valuable lessons for expanding digital access globally while helping to mitigate the risk of deepening inequalities across the digital divide.

Building Public Trust

New York City has taken significant steps towards AI governance. Various initiatives contribute to responsible AI implementation and building public trust in these technologies, and we examine these in detail later in the book. The Automated Decision Systems (ADS) Task Force, created under Local Law 49 of 2018, evaluates the use of algorithms to promote fairness and equity, addressing concerns about bias and discrimination. In October 2023, the city launched the Artificial Intelligence Action Plan, outlining strategies for assessing AI tools, managing risks, and integrating AI responsibly within government agencies.[18] Additionally, the NYC Economic Development Corporation (NYCEDC) is forming an AI Advisory Council to promote AI-driven economic growth and innovation while ensuring ethical considerations remain a priority.[19] Transparency, public engagement, and clear governance structures are key components of these initiatives, helping to build public confidence in AI-driven decision-making. However, while these efforts promote accountability and the responsible use of AI, New York does not yet have a dedicated organisation focused on AI oversight in public services. Strengthening public trust will require continued transparency, community involvement, and safeguards against AI-related risks.

The Role of AI in Achieving Environmental Benefits

AI is increasingly recognised as a powerful tool for tackling global environmental challenges, providing advanced solutions across a range of domains. However, its deployment also raises important concerns about responsible implementation, as training and operating AI models demand significant energy and other resources throughout their lifecycle.

AI enables unprecedented advances in climate science and response strategies through sophisticated modelling and prediction capabilities. The technology analyses vast datasets to forecast weather patterns, track greenhouse gas emissions, and project climate change impacts with increasing precision. This enhanced understanding empowers policymakers to develop targeted mitigation strategies. In practical applications, AI has demonstrated remarkable success in reducing energy consumption, as evidenced by Google DeepMind's optimisation of data centre cooling systems. The technology also strengthens disaster preparedness through early warning systems for floods, hurricanes, and wildfires, with innovations like Google's Flood Hub providing crucial advance notice of potential disasters.

In the renewable energy sector, AI is driving significant improvements in efficiency and reliability. The technology enables precise prediction of energy output from wind and solar sources, facilitating smoother integration of renewable power into existing grids. Smart grid systems powered by AI can dynamically balance energy supply and demand, supporting the transition to sustainable energy sources. Predictive maintenance capabilities help identify potential equipment issues before they cause disruptions, maximising the performance and longevity of renewable infrastructure.

Conservation efforts have been revolutionised by AI-powered monitoring systems. Advanced image recognition algorithms, coupled with motion-sensing cameras and drones, provide real-time tracking of endangered species and rapid detection of poaching activities. Satellite data analysis enhanced by AI offers comprehensive monitoring of deforestation, desertification, and ecosystem changes, enabling more targeted and effective conservation strategies.

AI transforms agricultural practices through precision farming techniques that optimise resource usage while minimising environmental impact. The technology processes complex datasets including soil conditions, weather patterns, and crop health indicators to enable more efficient land management. Satellite imagery analysis helps farmers make informed decisions about land use while ensuring compliance with environmental regulations. The United States Department of Agriculture (USDA) is increasingly leveraging AI across various aspects of its mission, including crop and forest health monitoring, wildfire prediction and assessments, disaster damage assessment, and crop identification.[20]

AI advances waste management through route optimisation and improved recycling processes, promoting circular economy principles. In water resource management, AI-powered systems monitor quality, optimise distribution, and predict supply needs while providing early warning of contamination events. Air quality monitoring benefits from AI analysis of sensor networks, enabling rapid response to pollution events through traffic management and industrial adjustments.

Despite its transformative potential, AI deployment in environmental applications requires careful consideration of energy consumption and ethical implications. The computational demands of AI systems can contribute significantly to energy usage, highlighting the importance of powering these systems with renewable energy sources. Additionally, the management and application of AI-driven environmental data must be governed by strong ethical frameworks to prevent misuse and ensure equitable outcomes. A compelling example comes from the use of AI in environmental reclamation projects, such as Microsoft's AI for Earth initiative, which supported the TerrAdept system. TerrAdept uses machine learning models to analyse satellite imagery and ecological data in real time to monitor habitat conditions, detect environment degradation, and guide conservation efforts. In regions like the Amazon basin and the Himalayas, the system has been used to prioritise restoration sites and manage land use more sustainably, helping to restore degraded ecosystems while supporting biodiversity.

This comprehensive integration of AI in environmental protection demonstrates both its tremendous potential for positive impact and the importance of responsible implementation to maximise benefits while minimising unintended consequences.

AI in Public-Sector Sustainability: A Framework for Impact and Governance

The integration of AI into public-sector decision-making presents both opportunities and challenges for sustainability. Let's examine the complex relationship between AI and public-sector sustainability and outline an effective governance framework.

Public-sector AI applications deliver significant sustainability benefits through enhanced policy effectiveness and environmental management.

In Nijmegen, Netherlands, AI-powered people counting systems inform evidence-based policies for traffic management and economic development. Such implementations enable governments to craft more targeted and effective sustainability initiatives.

Environmental monitoring capabilities have been transformed through AI applications. For example, the Queensland government uses machine learning and computer vision systems that automatically analyse satellite imagery for land use classification, improving disaster response and biosecurity management.[21]

AI's potential impact on climate change is particularly noteworthy, with projections in a recent EY report suggesting a 1.5 to 4 per cent reduction in global greenhouse gas emissions by 2030 through AI-enabled solutions.[22]

To fully realise the benefits of AI while managing its risks, public-sector organisations must adopt a robust, adaptable governance framework. The core challenge is balancing innovation, through experimentation and rapid implementation, with the need for clear objectives, effective oversight, transparency, and public accountability.

A coordinated, government-wide approach is essential. It ensures consistent standards for the procurement and deployment of AI technologies, aligns innovations with core public values and sustainability goals, and facilitates integration across departments and jurisdictions. Protocols must be established to ensure data quality, security, privacy, and interoperability. Responsible data sharing between agencies, and alignment with broader AI strategies, requires careful management to promote transparency without compromising individual rights.

Equally important is embedding democratic participation throughout the AI lifecycle. Citizens should have accessible opportunities to provide input, supported by diverse oversight bodies and regular public consultations to ensure systems remain aligned with the public interest. While such measures may occasionally slow rapid innovation, they are essential for building legitimacy and public trust.

It is important to recognise that AI generates its own environmental footprint. Sustainability must therefore be embedded within AI governance. Organisations should assess both the direct impacts, such as energy consumption and computational demands, and the indirect effects, including resource extraction, lifecycle emissions, and rebound effects. This requires robust environmental impact frameworks, integrated alongside social, ethical, and economic evaluations.

Achieving this balance demands collaborative effort, across public agencies, private-sector partners, academic institutions, and civil society. Through shared responsibility and ongoing evaluation, AI can be harnessed to drive responsible innovation while maintaining ethical standards and public trust.

Regular assessments should track progress across key dimensions: sustainability, equity, efficiency, transparency, and the achievement of policy objectives. This dynamic model of governance enables the public sector to remain agile and forward-looking as AI continues to evolve.

With careful management and strong governance, AI can become a catalyst for sustainable, citizen-centred public services, delivering long-term benefits while safeguarding the values at the heart of democratic institutions.

AI Revolution in Tax Audits

AI systems are rapidly gaining prominence as tools that can assist tax authorities in preventing and fighting tax evasion and misuse of loopholes.

AI systems in tax audits can represent a step forward towards *tax equality among taxpayers*, as they enable large-scale verification that taxes are paid appropriately by all taxpayers in similar real situations. The use of AI systems can improve impartiality to ensure that taxpayers are fairly assessed. Furthermore, AI can play a significant role in preventing and combating tax evasion and avoidance. Tax authorities are starting to use the vast amount of data available to them to identify new indicators of tax evasion or avoidance that might escape human detection. The use of these systems must be balanced against fundamental protections such as the right to personal data protection, right of defence, and the right to a fair trial. These principles are highlighted in the EU AI Act.

If a tax authority decides to use an AI system to justify a tax assessment, the justification must comply with the 'rules of algorithmic decision legitimacy'. This refers to the requirement that the rules governing the system must be knowable and transparent to ensure full comprehensibility of the decision. In other words, for an algorithmic decision to be legitimate, it must reveal the underlying logic and rules of the system, and be accessible and understandable to those affected, while also taking into account the privacy implications of using such systems.

Box 2.1 – Case Study: Artificial Intelligence and Tax Assessment Procedures in Italy Using the AI Tool Ve.Ra.

Ve.Ra. is the acronym for Verification of Financial Relationships, a data analysis tool developed to support tax evasion risk analysis by using information from the Financial Relationships Archive. Its implementation follows the provisions of the 2020 Italian Budget Law (Article 1, paragraphs 681 to 686, Law No. 160 of 2019).

At the heart of the control process is the identification of the risk of tax errors or fraud. This risk identification step guides the algorithms used to select taxpayers from a broad pool, narrowing it down to a smaller group of individuals or businesses deemed to present a higher probability of tax evasion.

According to Article 2 of Italian Legislative Decree 13/24 (Rationalisation and Reorganisation of Regulatory Provisions Regarding Risk Analysis Activities), risk analysis is defined as:

> A process, consisting of one or more phases, aimed at maximising the effectiveness of actions to prevent and combat tax evasion, tax fraud, and misuse of tax law, as well as to encourage voluntary compliance. This process uses deterministic[23] or probabilistic[24] models and analysis techniques, in compliance with personal data protection regulations, and relies on information from the databases of the Financial Administration or publicly available data, including through interconnected sources. It links the probability of a specific tax risk with one or more selection criteria or indicators, and where possible, forecasts the potential consequences of that risk.[25]

The primary goal of risk analysis is to reduce violations of tax regulations and prevent actions that go against the principles of the tax system. The results support enforcement activities, promote voluntary compliance, and can also inform preventive controls.

To facilitate these tasks, Italian regulations allow the interconnection of databases from the Italian Revenue Agency (Agenzia delle Entrate) with other public records for risk analysis, control, compliance support, and taxpayer services.

According to an example provided by the Italian Revenue Agency, the taxpayer selection process using Ve.Ra. typically unfolds in the following phases:

- Initial selection: Businesses operating in sectors known for high-profit margins are selected based on predefined criteria set in the system.
- Use of the Financial Relationships Archive: The initial list is enriched with financial data retrieved from the Archive, adding more detail to each profile.
- Filtering justifiable cases: To improve efficiency, the algorithm identifies businesses from the initial list that can justify anomalies and excludes them.
- List preparation and distribution: The filtered list, now focused on entities with potentially high tax risk, is sent to provincial offices.
- Inspections and follow-up: Being included on this list does not automatically trigger a tax audit. The Revenue Agency may choose to:
    - send compliance letters encouraging voluntary resolution of anomalies;
    - launch formal verification activities, if deemed necessary.

The Agency emphasises that 'Statistical models do not automatically result in enforcement measures. Instead, they support control structures in managing flagged cases. The purpose of these models is to enhance the ability to identify high-risk subjects more accurately.' [26]

Ve.Ra. operates using supervised learning, meaning it learns from data that has been pre-classified by human experts. While the exact model used by the Italian Tax Administration is unknown, it is believed that decision trees may be employed. However, more sophisticated models like random forests or neural networks may also be in use.

This lack of transparency, referred to as information asymmetry, raises important concerns. Transparency and interpretability are crucial to ensure that human users understand and trust the system's outputs. Without this, the risk of errors or misuse increases, potentially leading to a rise in tax litigation.

The Italian experience with Ve.Ra. illustrates the growing importance of algorithmic transparency, data protection, and legal safeguards in tax administration. While advanced analytical tools can improve efficiency and targeting, their use must be carefully monitored to prevent abuse and maintain public trust.

A Vision for the Future

The integration of AI into public service delivery represents a fundamental shift in governance and the provision of public services. Imagine a world where governments anticipate citizen needs rather than reacting to them, where services are personalised, efficient, and equitable. Social workers equipped with AI insights can provide better support to vulnerable populations. Urban planners can design smarter, greener cities. Public health agencies can predict and prevent disease outbreaks before they escalate.

This vision is not just aspirational; it is within reach. Achieving it requires thoughtful implementation, ongoing collaboration, and a commitment to ethical principles. Governments must embrace AI as a tool for enhancing human potential, not replacing it. However, these benefits come with significant challenges from internal resistance, lack of available resources, divergence of IT systems, and internal and external scepticism.

Notes

1 Tony Blair Institute for Global Change (2024), *The Potential Impact of AI on the Public Sector Workforce: A Companion to the Economic Case for Reimagining the State*, https://institute.global/insights/economic-prosperity/the-potential-impact-of-ai-on-the-public-sector-workforce (accessed on 28 March 2025.
2 BBC (2025), Government can be more efficient, says Keir Starmer, www.bbc.com/news/articles/c74kep983x3o (accessed on 15 April 2025).
3 Ministry of Finance India (2025), India's DBT: Boosting welfare efficiency, www.pib.gov.in/PressReleasePage.aspx (accessed on 30 April 2025).
4 UCL Partners (2025), *AI in London Healthcare: The Reality Behind the Hype*, https://uclpartners.com/wp-content/uploads/UCLP-AI-in-London-healthcare-03.25-final.pdf (accessed on 15 April 2025).
5 Cogent Infotech (No date), Predictive policing using machine learning (with examples), www.cogentinfo.com/resources/predictive-policing-using-machine-learning-with-examples (accessed on 28 March 2025).
6 The World Bank Group (2015), What's proactive governance?, https://blogs.worldbank.org/en/governance/what-s-proactive-governance (accessed on 28 March 2025).
7 Hertie School Centre for Digital Governance (2023), *Proactive Public Services: The New Standard for Digital Governments*, https://info.nortal.com/hubfs/whitepaper_hertie-school_2023_onepager_eng%20(1).pdf (accessed on 28 March 2025).
8 Republic of Estonia Ministry of Justice and Digital Affairs (2024), Proactive government services, www.justdigi.ee/en/digital-communications-and-cyber/digital-services/proactive-government-services (accessed on 28 March 2025).
9 Government of the UK – HM Land Registry (2022), HM Land Registry Strategy 2022+, www.gov.uk/government/publications/hm-land-registry-strategy-2022/hm-land-registry-strategy-2022 (accessed on 28 March 2025).
10 Government of the UK – HM Land Registry (2024), Digital services roadmap, www.gov.uk/government/publications/hm-land-registry-digital-services-roadmap/digital-services-roadmap (accessed on 28 March 2025).

11 The company Bitfury Group Limited created the first-ever blockchain land-registry system in partnership with the Republic of Georgia's National Agency of Public Registry.
12 The Exonum platform is an open-source, enterprise-grade blockchain framework that helps businesses and governments securely bring blockchain projects to life.
13 Aadhaar registration refers to the process of enrolling for an Aadhaar number, a unique 12-digit identification number issued by the Unique Identification Authority of India (UIDAI) to residents of India. This process involves providing minimal demographic and biometric information, such as fingerprints, iris scans, and a facial photograph, along with proof of identity and address documents. The enrolment is free of cost and is a one-time process, ensuring that each individual receives a unique Aadhaar number that serves as a proof of identity and address, facilitating access to various government and non-government services across India.
14 The Economic Times (2025), Common Service Centres: Digital transformation of rural India for inclusive, sustainable growth, https://government.economictimes.indiatimes.com/news/digital-india/common-service-centres-digital-transformation-of-rural-india-for-inclusive-sustainable-growth/118334624 (accessed on 28 March 2025).
15 McKinsey & Company (2022), Driven by purpose: 15 years of M-Pesa's evolution, www.mckinsey.com/industries/financial-services/our-insights/driven-by-purpose-15-years-of-m-pesas-evolution (accessed on 28 March 2025).
16 O. del Torso (2019), *Mobile Payment Systems and Financial Inclusion: The Case of M-Pesa*, https://tesi.luiss.it/24994/1/212901_DEL%20TORSO_OTTAVIO.pdf (accessed on 28 March 2025).
17 Kenya AI (2024), Does M-Pesa currently use AI?, https://kenyaai.ke/does-m-pesa-currently-use-ai/ (accessed on 28 March 2025).
18 The Official Website of the City of New York (2023), Mayor Adams releases first-of-its-kind plan for responsible artificial intelligence use in NYC government, www.nyc.gov/office-of-the-mayor/news/777-23/mayor-adams-releases-first-of-its-kind-plan-responsible-artificial-intelligence-use-nyc#/0 (accessed on 22 February 2025).
19 New York City Economic Development Corporation (2025), *NYC's Artificial Intelligence Advantage: Driving Economic Growth and Technological Transformation*, https://edc.nyc/sites/default/files/2025-01/NYCEDC-NYC-AI-Advantage-2025-Report.pdf (accessed on 22 February 2025).
20 U.S. Department of Agriculture (No date), Inventory of USDA artificial intelligence use cases, www.usda.gov/about-usda/reports-and-data/data/usda-open-data-catalog/inventory-usda-artificial-intelligence-use-cases, (accessed on 30 April 2025).
21 OECD (2024), *Governing with Artificial Intelligence: Are Governments Ready?*, OECD Publishing, Paris.
22 EY (2024), AI and sustainability: Opportunities, challenges, and impact, www.ey.com/en_nl/insights/climate-change-sustainability-services/ai-and-sustainability-opportunities-challenges-and-impact#footnotes (accessed on 22 February 2025).
23 Deterministic analysis refers to 'the set of models and analytical techniques based on the comparison and processing of data, pertaining to one or more taxpayers or tax periods, aimed at verifying the occurrence of a tax risk through selective criteria based on non-probabilistic relationships, where the risk is wholly or partially definable before the analysis begins'.
24 Probabilistic analysis refers to 'the set of models and analytical techniques that, by leveraging artificial intelligence solutions or inferential statistics, enable the isolation

of tax risks, including those not known a priori, which, once identified, can be used to develop independent selective criteria, or allow for the assignment of a specific probability of occurrence to a known tax risk'.

25 Official Gazette of the Italian Republic, Legislative Decree No. 13 of February 12, 2024: 'Provisions regarding tax assessment and biennial preventive tax agreement', Effective date of the provision 22 February 2024.

26 Agenzia delle Entrate (No date), *Informativa sulla logica sottostante i modelli di analisi del rischio basati sui dati dell'archivio dei rapporti finanziari*, www.agenziaentrate.gov.it/portale/documents/20143/5316839/Documento+illustrativo+della+logica+degli+algoritmi.pdf/672a3ef3-8cbf-a442-3b19-de910e751666 (accessed on 27 December 2024).

Chapter 3

AI Principles and Strategies Around the World

AI principles and strategies have been adopted globally to guide the development and use of artificial intelligence (AI) across a wide range of sectors and institutions. From China's state-driven AI initiatives to the European Union's emphasis on trustworthy AI, the international community has developed markedly different strategies and frameworks for AI development. These differences reflect not only technical priorities but also deeper variations in how societies view the relationship between technology, government, and human rights.

While China has embraced AI as a driver of economic growth and social governance, implementing extensive facial recognition systems and social credit programmes, the European Union has positioned itself as a global leader in ethical AI regulation. The EU's AI Act represents the first comprehensive legal framework designed to regulate AI systems according to their potential risks to society.

Meanwhile, the United States has maintained a more market-driven approach, giving private companies significant freedom to innovate while gradually introducing targeted regulations for specific high-risk applications.

These divergent approaches underscore a fundamental debate: how to balance the pursuit of technological advancement with the need to safeguard ethical standards, privacy rights, and social stability.

DOI: 10.4324/9781003673897-5

An Overview of Global AI Principles and Strategies

The rapid advancement of AI capabilities has pushed governments worldwide to establish guiding principles that reflect deeper cultural and economic differences. Some nations prioritise rapid deployment and economic growth, while others focus on establishing ethical guidelines and protecting individual privacy, creating a complex global landscape of AI governance.

At present, more than 69 countries have national strategies governing the responsible use of AI, as shown in Figure 3.1.

The approaches taken vary from guidelines-based approaches to comprehensive AI regulations that align with existing data protection and cybersecurity regulations, such as the EU's AI Act.[1]

G7 Members' AI Principles and Strategies

G7 members continue to develop their AI principles and strategies, exploring pathways to harness the AI potential for innovation while minimising risks.[2]
Industry-specific principles for AI implementation or guidance are becoming more prevalent, yet they remain unevenly distributed across different sectors.

On 22 January 2025, President Trump unveiled a massive private-sector initiative called the Stargate Project. Because of its financial scale, the groundbreaking alliance between OpenAI, Oracle, SoftBank, and MGX marks a transformative moment in the evolution of AI and global technological infrastructure. This unprecedented partnership has pledged an investment of up to $500 billion over the next four years, with an initial injection of $100 billion, laying the foundation for the next era of AI-driven advancements.

Central to this ambitious initiative is the plan to construct up to ten state-of-the-art data centres strategically located across the United States. These facilities will

Figure 3.1 Countries with national strategies for responsible AI use

Source: OECD (no date), National AI policies and strategies, https://oecd.ai/en/dashboards/overview (accessed on 3 January 2025)

Table 3.1 G7 countries' AI strategies

Country	*AI Strategy*
United States	Outlined its plans in the National Artificial Intelligence Research and Development Strategic Plan 2023 Update, with a focus on research and development. The plan defines the major research challenges in AI to coordinate and focus federal R&D investments to ensure continued leadership in the development and use of trustworthy AI systems. It also aims to prepare the current and future workforce for the integration of AI systems across all sectors, as well as coordinating ongoing AI activities across all federal agencies.[3]
United Kingdom	Launched a National AI Strategy, which aims to invest and plan for the long-term needs of the AI ecosystem, support the transition to an AI-enabled economy, capture the benefits of innovation in the UK across all sectors and regions, and get the national and international governance of AI technologies right to encourage innovation, investment, and protect the public and the UK's fundamental values.[4]
Canada	Launched the Pan-Canadian AI Strategy in 2017, the first in the world, and introduced an AI and Data Act in 2022. The Pan-Canadian Artificial Intelligence Strategy has three pillars: i) translate AI research into commercial applications; ii) develop and adopt standards related to AI; iii) attract, retain, and develop academic research talent.[5]
France	Launched a National Strategy for AI in 2018 under the claim of *AI for Humanity*, which has six main lines of action: i) launch a plan to raise awareness and train the nation; ii) redirect French savings towards innovation and create a *France & AI* fund; iii) make France a major location for computing power; iv) facilitate access to data; v) experiment with an *AI exception* in public research; v) promote global governance of AI.[6]
Germany	Laid out its goals in a National AI Strategy that focuses on public research capabilities, technology transfers and commercialisation, societal challenges, and environmental challenges.[7]
Italy	Defined the Italian Strategy for Artificial Intelligence 2024–2026 aimed at harnessing AI technologies to drive innovation and productivity across various sectors with three paths: i) support the creation and adoption of AI applications to support management practices, production models, and innovation projects; ii) promote foundational and applied scientific research; iii) create favourable conditions to enhance the potential of AI in terms of value generation.[8]

(Continued)

Table 3.1 Continued

Country	*AI Strategy*
Japan	Detailed its intentions in the AI Guidelines for Business Ver 1.0 that provide guidance for developing, providing, and using AI to all entities (including public organisations such as governments and local governments) involved in these activities. The Guidelines aim to develop a framework to promote innovation and reduce risks by implementing common guiding principles for each AI business actor and AI governance.[9]

Source: Adapted from OECD (2024), *Artificial Intelligence and Tourism: G7/OECD Policy Paper*, OECD Publishing, Paris

not only serve as hubs of innovation and computational power but also represent a significant boost to the US economy. The scale of this effort has the potential to generate an estimated 100,000 new jobs, spanning roles in technology, construction, operations, and beyond.

The Stargate endeavour reflects more than just an investment in infrastructure; it signals a commitment to redefining the role of AI in shaping the US economy, driving economic growth, and reinforcing the United States' position as a leader in the global AI race.

While the 2022–2025 UK Government Digital and Data Roadmap established the groundwork for digital transformation across the UK public sector, stakeholders are now anticipating its successor. The new Government Digital & AI Roadmap, launched in autumn 2025, represents a critical evolution in the government's digital strategy.

This roadmap not only replaces the current framework but also serves as a key indicator of how seriously the government intends to scale its digital and AI initiatives. As departments and agencies implement this transition, the new roadmap will be scrutinised for its ambition, practicality, and ability to deliver meaningful change across public services.

The shift from *Digital and Data* to *Digital & AI* in the title alone signals the government's recognition of AI as a core component of future public-sector innovation, rather than merely an emerging technology to consider.

The CEO of Nvidia, the company whose chips and data centres underpin AI, has warned that the UK lacks the infrastructure needed to capitalise on AI's potential. Jensen Huang acknowledged that while the UK boasts world-class AI research and is making significant investments in the sector, it still trails the United States and China. The UK is currently developing an AI technology hub in Bristol, with a focus on robotics, and Nvidia is working with the Financial Conduct Authority to create a digital sandbox for testing AI-driven financial innovations. According to research from Stanford University in 2025, private AI investment in the UK stands at approximately $4.5 billion, compared with an estimated $109 billion in the US, around 24 times greater.[10] The AI boom is most likely to benefit the US and China. Between them they provide more than 90 per cent of the world's publicly available AI data centres.

The European Commission unveiled the AI Continent Action Plan on 9 April 2025, a bold and comprehensive roadmap designed to position Europe as a global leader in AI. It is centred on five strategic elements, as shown in Figure 3.2.

This initiative reflects a deep, long-term commitment to transforming Europe's digital capabilities, strengthening its technological sovereignty, and shaping the future of AI on its own terms. The action plan reflects Europe's willingness to build the foundational capabilities required to lead in the global AI era.

The ambition is to create AI gigafactories, each equipped with approximately 100,000 next-generation AI chips, a fourfold leap from current capabilities. These facilities are strategic assets, engineered to provide the massive computing power needed to train and scale complex AI systems across sectors. Backed by InvestAI, a platform seeking to mobilise €20 billion in public and private investment, this signals Europe's intention not merely to compete but to lead globally in the new AI era. With a call for consortia now open, the message is clear: Europe's AI future is not theoretical; it is under construction.

A note of caution is warranted. Current AI technologies require vast data processing capacity, which comes with significant energy demands. However, as

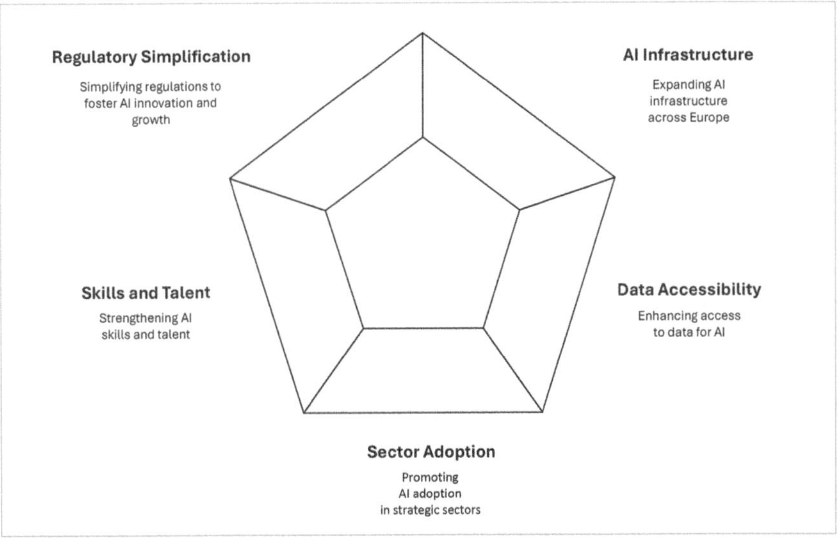

Figure 3.2 EU AI Continent Action Plan

Source: Authors' elaboration

processing efficiency continues to improve, these power requirements are likely to decline, perhaps following a trajectory similar to the rapid advances in electric vehicle technology.

Through the creation of data labs within AI factories, the European Commission aims to harness large volumes of high-quality, curated data from diverse sources, enabling their secure and efficient use across the innovation landscape. Set to launch in 2025, the Data Union Strategy will go even further, establishing a true internal market for data that breaks down silos and facilitates cross-border, cross-sectoral AI applications. This is not simply about moving data; it's about unlocking its full economic and technological value, enabling Europe to lead not just in AI development but in data-driven competitiveness and resilience.

With only 13.5 per cent of EU companies currently utilising AI, the forthcoming Apply AI Strategy is poised to close this gap by delivering tailored, sector-specific solutions that address practical challenges and deliver measurable value. By mobilising the strength of AI factories and European Digital Innovation Hubs (EDIHs), the strategy will do more than encourage uptake; it will catalyse a cultural and operational transformation, positioning AI as a core engine of productivity, innovation, and public service delivery. The EU is clearly making a declaration that AI is no longer optional but central to Europe's digital future and long-term economic resilience.

To meet the rising demand for advanced AI skills, the Commission is deploying a suite of programmes to attract, train, and retain world-class talent. Initiatives such as the Talent Pool, Marie Skłodowska-Curie Action, and the forthcoming AI Skills Academy are all designed to position Europe as a premier destination for top AI researchers and professionals. But this is about more than filling vacancies; it's about cultivating a deep, sustainable talent ecosystem, with education and training programmes in AI and generative AI that equip key sectors with the skills to thrive in a rapidly evolving technological landscape. In doing so, the EU is asserting that people, not just platforms, will define its leadership in the AI age.

To build trust in AI technologies and provide legal certainty, the Commission will launch the AI Act Service Desk, which will offer a central resource for companies navigating the Union's new regulatory framework, ensuring that AI deployment is both responsible and compliant. More than a help desk, this is a catalyst for innovation through clarity, empowering businesses of all sizes to integrate AI confidently and responsibly.

With public consultations on the Cloud and AI Development Act and the Apply AI Strategy open until 4 June 2025, and a third consultation on the Data Union Strategy that opened in May 2025, the Commission is actively inviting stakeholders to shape the policies that will define Europe's AI leadership. It is a clear signal that Europe's AI transformation will be built not in isolation but in partnership, with a shared vision, practical insight, and collective ambition.

Through strategic investments, inclusive governance, and a strong focus on talent, trust, and innovation, the EU is laying the groundwork for an AI ecosystem that is competitive, sovereign, and human centric. As these initiatives take shape, one thing is clear: Europe is not just preparing for the future of AI; it is determined to define it.

The G7's Hiroshima AI Process

In October 2023, G7 members reached a consensus on 11 guiding principles for the design, production, and deployment of advanced AI systems, alongside a voluntary Code of Conduct for AI developers.[11] This initiative, termed the Hiroshima AI Process, garnered support from EU leadership, aligning with the principles outlined in the EU AI regulation. It aims to enhance international AI governance through several key initiatives.

The Hiroshima AI Process established a Comprehensive Policy Framework (for further details, see the appendix) that comprises four main elements: i) an analysis of the priority risks, challenges, and opportunities posed by generative AI; ii) international guiding principles applicable to all AI actors; iii) an international code of conduct for organisations developing advanced AI systems; and iv) project-based cooperation designed to support responsible AI development.

The *Hiroshima Process International Guiding Principles* (HIGP) set out 11 principles aimed at ensuring the safe, secure, and trustworthy design, development, deployment, and use of advanced AI systems worldwide.[12] Complementing these principles, the *International Code of Conduct for Organisations Developing Advanced AI Systems* offers voluntary guidance specifically tailored for developers of advanced AI, including foundation models and generative AI. Moreover, the Hiroshima AI Process promotes international collaboration by engaging a broad spectrum of stakeholders, governments, private sector, academia, and civil society, and aligning its efforts with established international frameworks such as the UN Guiding Principles on Business and Human Rights and the OECD Guidelines for Multinational Enterprises.

The G7 is working closely with the Organisation for Economic Co-operation and Development (OECD) to create monitoring tools and mechanisms for advanced AI systems, with notable progress made in 2024. As part of this effort, the OECD initiated a pilot phase, from 9 July to 6 September 2024, to test a reporting framework that evaluates how organisations developing advanced AI systems align with the *Hiroshima Process International Code of Conduct for Organisations Developing Advanced AI Systems* (for further details, see the appendix). During this pilot, 20 entities from ten countries – Canada, Denmark, Germany, Israel, Japan, the Netherlands, Spain, Switzerland, the UK, and the US – participated. These groups represented a broad spectrum of stakeholders such as global technology companies, startups, research institutions, academic bodies, and firms specialising in AI compliance and auditing.

The draft reporting framework was developed with input from leading AI developers across the G7, under the support of the G7 Italian presidency. It features a set of questions derived from the Code of Conduct's 11 Actions, designed to enhance transparency and enable comparability in the measures taken to mitigate risks associated with advanced AI systems. Looking ahead, the G7 Digital and Tech Working Group, in collaboration with the OECD, is refining this framework. Their efforts include mapping existing AI reporting frameworks to avoid duplication, streamlining the language while ensuring alignment with the Code of Conduct, designing an adaptable online interface for easier data collection, and proposing a brand for those who voluntarily participate in the framework. The Reporting Framework was launched in February 2025.

This initiative represents a significant step towards establishing a robust monitoring mechanism for the Code of Conduct, underscoring the G7's commitment to promoting the safe, secure, and trustworthy development, deployment, and use of advanced AI systems.

The G7 has stated that it is dedicated to enhancing the principles and Code of Conduct within its Comprehensive Policy Framework, incorporating input from other nations, the OECD, the Global Partnership on AI (GPAI), and various stakeholders from academia, business, and civil society. By developing these frameworks and promoting international collaboration, the G7 Hiroshima AI Process is laying the groundwork for a more unified and effective approach to global AI governance that balances innovation with the responsible development and use of AI technologies.

International AI Governance Frameworks

In recent years, international AI governance has evolved rapidly, with a range of global initiatives and regional strategies emerging to address the challenges and opportunities posed by AI. Below is an overview of the current state of international AI governance.

The United Nations has made significant progress in establishing a global framework for AI governance. In September 2024, it introduced a proposed framework titled *Governing AI for Humanity*,[13] which is based on insights from over 2,000 participants worldwide and outlines principles for shaping new international AI governance institutions. A key recommendation from the report is the creation of an AI standards exchange, designed to bring together representatives from various stakeholders to address gaps in current AI governance frameworks (for further details, see the appendix). Additionally, the *United Nations System White Paper on AI Governance*,[14] prepared by the Inter-Agency Working Group on Artificial Intelligence and endorsed by the Chief Executive Board for Coordination, examines the UN system's institutional models and existing frameworks relevant to global AI governance (for further details, see the appendix).

The OECD has established AI principles that have gained broad recognition and endorsement across multiple international forums. These principles form the basis for numerous national and regional AI governance frameworks.

In 2019, the OECD adopted AI Principles to promote trustworthy and human-centric AI and provide policymakers with recommendations for effective AI policies; these principles were updated and adopted in 2024 to stay up to date with the rapid technological developments and to provide policymakers with recommendations for effective AI policies.

Countries use the OECD AI Principles and related tools to shape policies and create AI risk frameworks, building a foundation for global interoperability between jurisdictions. Today, the European Union, the Council of Europe, the United States, and the United Nations and other jurisdictions use the OECD's definition of an AI system and lifecycle in their legislative and regulatory frameworks and guidance. The principles, definition, and lifecycle are all part of the OECD Recommendation on Artificial Intelligence.

The 'values-based principles' focus on the major risks associated with the misuse of AI and highlight the importance of values such as inclusiveness, fairness, transparency, accountability, and respect for human rights, along with guidance on how to address these challenges. The recommendations for policymakers highlight the importance of AI investments and ecosystems, governance and policies, labour market transition, and international cooperation.

Regional AI Frameworks

The EU AI Act is recognised as one of the most extensive and ambitious regulatory frameworks for AI worldwide. Its key elements include a risk-based classification system for AI systems, stringent transparency and data governance requirements for AI providers, comprehensive compliance and monitoring procedures, and enforcement.

The US has taken a more decentralised, commercially driven approach, with a patchwork of federal, state, and industry frameworks. The new Trump administration's AI policy prioritises innovation, national security, and economic dominance by reducing regulatory barriers while tightening export controls on advanced AI technologies. This approach aims to bolster US leadership in AI, ensuring its strategic advantage in global competition, particularly against China.

The UK has no dedicated AI regulation but applies existing laws, such as data protection and consumer protection while following a sector-based approach.

Evaluating the Effectiveness of AI Governance Frameworks in Addressing Ethical Concerns

Current AI governance frameworks have made significant progress in addressing ethical concerns, but their effectiveness remains a work in progress. Here's an assessment of their current state.

The Strengths of Existing Frameworks

Many AI governance frameworks have established clear ethical principles that serve as a foundation for responsible AI development and deployment, as described in Figure 3.3.

Together, these principles contribute to addressing critical ethical concerns in the evolving AI landscape.

Regulatory frameworks, such as the EU AI Act, employ a risk-based approach, imposing stricter controls on high-risk AI applications while maintaining flexibility for lower-risk use cases. This balanced strategy aims to foster innovation while upholding essential ethical safeguards.

Strong AI governance frameworks prioritise the involvement of diverse stakeholders, including developers, users, policymakers, ethicists, and the public. This inclusive approach ensures that the regulations reflect a broad range of perspectives and effectively address key concerns.

Challenges and Limitations

Although many organisations acknowledge the significance of AI ethics, there remains a gap between commitment and implementation. The rapid advancement of AI makes it difficult for governance frameworks to stay aligned; they must be flexible and adaptable to tackle emerging ethical challenges. At present, the absence of standardised practices across sectors and jurisdictions results in inconsistent approaches to AI governance. This can lead to a fragmented landscape, with different entities adopting diverse ethical standards.

One of the key challenges is finding the right balance between encouraging innovation and enforcing essential controls. Excessive governance may hinder AI

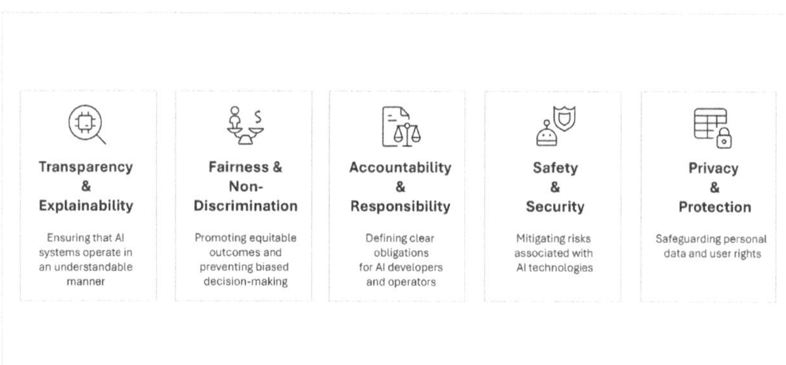

Figure 3.3 Pillars of AI governance frameworks

Source: Authors' elaboration

progress, significantly restrict implementation, and increase costs, while inadequate oversight could result in ethical violations and a general lack of confidence in AI-driven solutions. While many frameworks highlight fairness and non-discrimination, effectively addressing bias in AI systems remains a challenge. Further efforts are required to create and implement effective strategies for bias detection and mitigation.

Governance frameworks have made notable progress in addressing privacy concerns, often aligning with established data protection regulations such as the European General Data Protection Regulation (GDPR). However, the growing complexity of AI systems and data usage still presents ongoing challenges. GDPR also offers a warning of the risks and unintended consequences of overzealous regulation. A study by Oxford University economists in 2022 found that European businesses subject to GDPR experienced an average profit reduction of 8.1 per cent, with small and medium-sized enterprises (SMEs) facing an 8.5 per cent decline.[15] This suggests that compliance expenses and operational adjustments have significantly impacted profitability, particularly for smaller firms, increasing failure rates or reducing hiring and expansion. In the UK, there are an estimated 5.5 million SMEs,[16] making an average profit of £12,000.[17] SMEs' profits in total are around £66 billion a year; therefore, an 8.5 per cent profit reduction represents an annual cost of £5.6 billion. While regulators will want to control AI, they need to be cognisant of the downside when heavy-handed regulation hampers economic progress. Ill-conceived AI regulation risks having damaging or regressive effects.

Another recent example from the UK highlights the paradoxical balance between the efficiencies offered by AI and concerns over privacy. GPs are rapidly adopting Ambient Voice Technology (AVT), AI-driven software that records, transcribes, and summarises doctor–patient consultations. NHS England recently endorsed AVT's potential to reduce the administrative burden, enabling clinicians to focus more on patients rather than on note-taking. However, the technology has encountered resistance from some groups who argue that these systems may breach NHS data protection rules.

Beyond the immediate financial impact, over-regulation may also dampen innovation within the SME sector. Smaller firms, which often drive agile advancements in AI and digital technologies, could find themselves redirecting crucial resources from research and development to meeting complex compliance requirements. This shift not only diminishes their capacity to pioneer new technologies but may also discourage vital entrepreneurial risk-taking.

Moreover, the broader economic ecosystem stands to suffer if regulatory frameworks become overly burdensome. Stringent rules could deter international investors and partners, reducing foreign investment and collaborative opportunities essential for sustaining growth and technological progress. A balanced approach to AI regulation is vital, one that safeguards ethical and safe innovation while minimising adverse economic impacts. Policymakers must consider strategies that protect public interests without sacrificing the agility and competitive edge that drive global technological leadership.

Although transparency is a core principle in most legislative frameworks, achieving genuine explainability in complex AI systems remains a technical challenge. It should be remembered that AI is now widely incorporated into business, particularly in the financial sector, and its many applications are operating very effectively embedded within existing data systems. Additional research and development are needed to make AI decision-making processes more understandable.

While frameworks are placing greater emphasis on accountability, determining clear lines of responsibility for AI outcomes can be complex, particularly in systems involving multiple stakeholders or autonomous decision-making capabilities.

Advancing AI Governance: Addressing Ethical Challenges and Future Directions

In summary, current AI governance frameworks have laid important groundwork for addressing ethical concerns, but their effectiveness is still evolving. While they have successfully established key ethical principles and raised awareness of AI ethics, challenges persist in implementation, standardisation, and keeping pace with technological advancements. To improve their effectiveness, future developments in AI governance should focus on bridging the gap between principles and practice, creating more adaptive and flexible frameworks, fostering international collaboration for standardised approaches, and investing in research to tackle technical challenges in areas such as explainability and bias mitigation. As AI continues to evolve, governance frameworks will need to adapt and become more robust to effectively address emerging ethical challenges while supporting responsible innovation.

Emerging Trends

In 2025, several key trends are shaping the global AI landscape.

AI is advancing rapidly, transforming industries and reshaping global dynamics. Sophisticated models now exhibit human-like reasoning, enhancing applications in science, coding, medicine, and law. Improved data curation and training are further boosting performance.

AI agents with memory, reasoning, and multimodal abilities autonomously manage complex tasks, with users leveraging AI assistants for improved efficiency and client service. AI is also evolving to process text, images, audio, and video, enabling richer, more intuitive human–AI interactions, with multisensory capabilities on the horizon.

Generative AI (AI that can generate original content, such as text, images, audio, and video) is experiencing a major boom, and a huge number of organisations are exploring its applications, making it a foundational capability across industries. AI-driven research is accelerating discoveries in biomolecular science, drug development, climate solutions, and more. Meanwhile, nations are investing in AI self-sufficiency to reduce dependence on foreign technology, drive innovation, and enhance global competitiveness.

Artificial General Intelligence (AGI) refers to systems that can reason, learn, communicate, and adapt across diverse tasks without the need for task-specific programming, and that are capable of solving unfamiliar problems and transferring knowledge across domains in a human-like way. When AGI will progress beyond the experimental stage remains uncertain, with opinions ranging from imminent breakthroughs to deep scepticism. There is also little agreement on what 'human-level' truly means – whether it refers to average or expert performance, or which capabilities an AI model must demonstrate. New AI models are offering glimpses of what may be possible, showing early signs of general reasoning and agentic behaviour through the use of tools and strategic planning towards complex goals.[18]

AI is rapidly reshaping cybersecurity, bringing powerful capabilities to detect threats, automate responses, and analyse data at scale. At the same time, malicious actors are exploiting these advancements to craft adaptive malware, launch automated phishing campaigns, and generate realistic deepfakes. These AI-driven threats evolve quickly, often outpacing traditional defences. Vulnerabilities within AI systems, such as exposure to adversarial inputs or data tampering,[19] pose additional risks. As AI becomes more capable and widespread, cybersecurity must evolve in parallel, navigating a complex landscape of innovation and emerging threats.

Conclusion

AI governance frameworks have made important progress in establishing ethical principles and regulatory measures, yet the global landscape remains complex and rapidly evolving. Countries continue to pursue different strategies, reflecting distinct cultural, economic, and political priorities.

While there is growing recognition of the need for international cooperation, balancing innovation with effective risk management remains a critical challenge. The gap between regulation and the rapid advancement of AI technologies presents serious risks, and debates persist regarding the role of open-source versus proprietary models in promoting innovation while upholding principles of good governance.

To meet these challenges, AI governance must remain flexible, adaptive, and inclusive. It should prioritise ethical standards, privacy protection, and the broader well-being of society. Looking ahead, sustained international collaboration and investment in research will be essential to build a responsible and sustainable AI future.

Notes

1 Future of Life Institute (No date), The EU Artificial Intelligence Act: Up-to-date developments and analyses of the EU AI Act, https://artificialintelligenceact.eu (accessed on 3 January 2025).

2 OECD (2024), Artificial Intelligence and Tourism: G7/ OECD Policy Paper, OECD Publishing, Paris.

3 National Science and Technology Council (2023), National Artificial Intelligence Research and Development Strategic Plan 2023 Update, www.nitrd.gov/pubs/National-Artificial-Intelligence-Research-and-Development-Strategic-Plan-2023-Update.pdf (accessed on 3 January 2025).

4 Government of the United Kingdom (2021), National AI Strategy, www.gov.uk/government/publications/national-ai-strategy/national-ai-strategy-html-version (accessed on 3 January 2025).

5 Government of Canada (2021), Pan-Canadian Artificial Intelligence Strategy, https://ised-isde.canada.ca/site/ai-strategy/en (accessed on 3 January 2025).

6 France Artificial Intelligence Commission (2024), Our AI: Our Ambition for France, www.info.gouv.fr/upload/media/content/0001/09/02cbcb40c3541390be391feb3d963a4126b12598.pdf (accessed on 3 January 2025).

7 Ministry for Education and Research, Germany (2018), Strategy on Artificial Intelligence of the German Government.

8 Department for Digital Transformation, Italy (2024), Italian Strategy for Artificial Intelligence 2024–2026, www.agid.gov.it/sites/agid/files/2024-07/Italian_strategy_for_artificial_intelligence_2024-2026.pdf (accessed on 3 January 2025).

9 Ministry of Internal Affairs and Communications; Ministry of Economy, Trade and Industry, AI Guidelines for Business Ver1.0, 19 April 2024, www.meti.go.jp/shingikai/mono_info_service/ai_shakai_jisso/pdf/20240419_9.pdf, (accessed on 3 January 2025).

10 Financial Times (2025), Nvidia chief says UK lacks digital infrastructure as Keir Starmer pledges £1bn for AI, www.ft.com/content/cc04adfb-81b2-477f-b85c-ce042e8f83a8 (accessed on 15 June 2025).

11 European Commission (2023), Hiroshima Process International Code of Conduct for Advanced AI Systems, https://digital-strategy.ec.europa.eu/en/library/hiroshima-process-international-code-conduct-advanced-ai-systems (accessed on 28 December 2024).

12 European Commission (2023), G7 Leaders' Statement on the Hiroshima AI Process, https://digital-strategy.ec.europa.eu/en/library/g7-leaders-statement-hiroshima-ai-process, (accessed on 28 December 2024).

13 United Nations (2024), Governing AI for Humanity, www.un.org/sites/un2.un.org/files/governing_ai_for_humanity_final_report_en.pdf (accessed on 27 December 2024).

14 UNESCO (2024), United Nations System White Paper on Artificial Intelligence Governance: An Analysis of Current Institutional Models and Related Functions and Existing International Normative Frameworks within the United Nations System That Are Applicable to Artificial Intelligence Governance, https://unsceb.org/sites/default/files/2024-11/UNSystemWhitePaperAIGovernance.pdf (accessed on 27 December 2024).

15 Center for Data Innovation (2022), A new study lays bare the cost of the GDPR to Europe's economy: Will the AI Act repeat history?, https://datainnovation.

org/2022/04/a-new-study-lays-bare-the-cost-of-the-gdpr-to-europes-economy-will-the-ai-act-repeat-history/ (accessed on 3 January 2025).

16 Statista (2024), Number of small and medium-sized enterprises (SMEs) in the United Kingdom from 2010 to 2024 by size, www.statista.com/statistics/880155/number-of-smes-in-united-kingdom-uk/ (accessed on 3 January 2025).

17 BVA BDRC (No date), SME Finance Monitor Q4 2023 Report, www.bva-bdrc.com/wp-content/uploads/2024/03/BVABDRC_SME_FM_Q423_Full_Report.pdf (accessed on 3 January 2025).

18 E. Mollick (2025), On Jagged AGI: o3, Gemini 2.5, and everything after, www.oneusefulthing.org (accessed on 22 April 2025).

19 Data tampering is the unauthorised modification, deletion, or manipulation of data, often by cybercriminals for malicious purposes like financial gain, espionage, or sabotage.

Chapter 4

The Regulatory Landscape

Nations have responded with distinctly different approaches to artificial intelligence (AI) regulation and development. While the United States has largely embraced a market-driven approach that emphasises innovation and commercial applications, the European Union has positioned itself as a pioneer in ethical AI governance, implementing comprehensive frameworks like the AI Act to protect individual rights and ensure responsible AI development.

Artificial Intelligence Regulations Around the World

AI is becoming increasingly embedded across industries and public life, prompting governments around the world to introduce regulatory frameworks to govern its development and use. These efforts aim to ensure that AI is implemented in a responsible, ethical, and transparent manner while addressing risks related to privacy, bias, and misuse.

AI regulations are evolving rapidly, with several major developments shaping the global landscape. This chapter examines the key international approaches and explores the tensions between innovation, control, and accountability that define the emerging regulatory environment.

European Union Artificial Intelligence Act

In the European Union, the EU AI Act is landmark legislation, which took full effect in 2025. Its aim is to ensure the safety and fundamental rights protection in the development and use of AI systems across the EU. The rules establish obligations for providers and developers of AI systems marketed or used within the EU, tailored to

DOI: 10.4324/9781003673897-6

the systems' risk level, to ensure the safety and protection of fundamental rights in relation to how these systems are used.

The Current Landscape of AI Regulation in the United States

The United States issued an Executive Order on AI in October 2023, amended in January 2025, which implemented new rules to create a global licensing regime for the export of advanced AI chips and model weights (essentially an element of how AI models learn). On his first day in office, President Trump repealed President Biden's 2023 AI executive order.

Trump's approach to AI policy reflects a strategic alignment of innovation, national security, and economic dominance. By prioritising the reduction of regulatory barriers, the administration aims to create an environment that fosters rapid advancements in AI technologies. This emphasis on innovation is not just an economic strategy but a calculated effort to position AI as a critical tool in the geopolitical competition with China, a nation that has aggressively invested in AI to assert global leadership.

Central to this policy framework is the recognition of AI's dual role as both an economic catalyst and a national security imperative. The administration has shown a clear intent to tighten export controls on AI technologies, ensuring that sensitive innovations remain within US borders to prevent adversaries from gaining a technological edge. At the same time, efforts to encourage deeper collaboration between American companies and defence initiatives highlight the integration of private-sector ingenuity with military strategy, solidifying AI's role as a cornerstone of modern warfare and security operations. How effective this will be is an open question following China's launch of DeepSeek. The Chinese large language model (LLM) is developing rapidly and appears to be as powerful as US models. The developers claim to have produced their AI model at a fraction of the US cost and without access to the latest Nvidia chips.

President Trump's Department of Government Efficiency (DOGE) has made numerous statements about the use of AI as a tool for greater efficiency. America's AI-First Strategy has DOGE taking a central role in encouraging AI adoption, as well as using AI to analyse agency operations. In fact, DOGE has a key goal of automating government operations, with some officials suggesting the 'end goal is replacing the human workforce with machines'. Other applications of AI by DOGE include fraud detection, analysing employee productivity, and, controversially, scanning for DEI references. DOGE's fast-moving approach is an anathema to public agencies and there have been concerns about privacy violations, a lack of transparency, the potential for misuse of data, security risks, and the erosion of due process. Many of these criticisms are exactly what other international agencies are seeking to manage through carefully drafted legislation.

The US approach also grapples with the delicate balance between accelerating innovation and safeguarding national interests. By promoting policies that encourage technological growth while maintaining stringent oversight, the administration seeks to ensure that AI advancements do not inadvertently compromise US security or economic stability. This calculated strategy not only aims to preserve the nation's leadership in AI but also underscores the intricate interplay between innovation and strategic policy in shaping the future of global power dynamics.

As the AI landscape continues to evolve at a rapid pace, the policies of the Trump administration are poised to play a pivotal role in shaping the development and regulation of AI technologies both within the United States and on the global stage.

The Global Perspective

China introduced an Algorithm Registry in December 2022, focusing on regulating AI algorithms. As of June 2025, the United Kingdom was developing specific AI regulations; however, various existing laws apply to AI, including data protection, consumer protection, and equality laws. Canada, Australia, Brazil, and Singapore have proposed or enacted AI-specific regulatory frameworks that align with the EU's risk-based approach.

As AI continues to evolve, countries and international organisations are working to balance innovation with risk management, emphasising shared principles of transparency, fairness, and accountability in the development and deployment of AI.

The European Union Artificial Intelligence Act

In March 2024, the European Parliament passed the Regulation (EU) 2024/1689, commonly known as the EU Artificial Intelligence Act.[1] This is the first comprehensive regulatory package for AI, setting EU-wide requirements for the development, deployment, and use of AI systems.

The Regulation was published in the *Official Journal of the European Union* in July and has been in effect since August 2024. This regulation will gradually come into force in the European Union, as shown in Figure 4.1.

In this section, we explore key provisions of the EU AI Act in detail, given its wide-ranging implications across the EU and its potential as a template for other countries developing similar legislation.

According to the Regulation, AI can be prohibited, permitted, or conditionally approved based on the potential level of risk it poses to fundamental human rights. Public authorities must comply with the Regulation by the end of 2030 or within six years of its enactment, ensuring public accountability and a smooth transition.

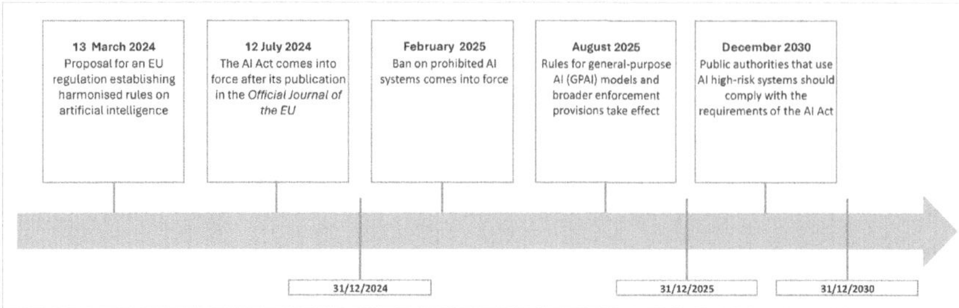

Figure 4.1 AI Act timeline

Source: Authors' elaboration from the *Official Journal of the European Union*, 2024/1689, Regulation (EU) 2024/1689 of the European Parliament and of the Council of 13 June 2024 laying down harmonised rules on artificial intelligence and amending Regulations (EC) No 300/2008, (EU) No 167/2013, (EU) No 168/2013, (EU) 2018/858, (EU) 2018/1139 and (EU) 2019/2144 and Directives 2014/90/EU, (EU) 2016/797 and (EU) 2020/1828 (Artificial Intelligence Act), Effective date of the provision 12 July 2024

The AI Act is expected to have an impact beyond EU borders due to its potentially large fines and its broad extraterritorial reach, requiring even non-EU organisations to comply when their AI systems affect EU users or markets.

The Six Ethical Principles

The EU AI Act is built around six distinct ethical principles outlined for AI systems in Recital 27 ('accountability' is mentioned as a seventh principle but is not examined). Each principle aligns with a key aspect of the responsible and safe development, deployment, and use of AI, and the Act states that these principles should be reflected in the design and implementation of AI models. Every ethical principle outlines a core aspect of responsible AI, closely aligning with the risk pillars (see Table 4.1).

The implementation of these principles should be reflected in the design and use of AI models and may be used to create codes of conduct, voluntary best practices, and standards.

The Purpose and Scope of the EU AI Act

As stated in Article 1 of the legislation:

> The purpose of this Regulation is to improve the functioning of the internal market and promote the uptake of human-centric and trustworthy

Table 4.1 The six ethical principles of the EU AI Act

Ethical Principle	*Definition*	*Technical Requirement*
Human agency and oversight	'AI systems are developed and used as a tool that serves people, respects human dignity and personal autonomy, and that is functioning in a way that can be appropriately controlled and overseen by humans.'	This principle defines the societal and systemic informational needs for deploying AI systems, emphasising their broader impact while not imposing specific technical standards on the foundational models that make up these systems.
Technical robustness and safety	'AI systems are developed and used in a way that allows robustness in the case of problems and resilience against attempts to alter the use or performance of the AI system so as to allow unlawful use by third parties, and minimise unintended harm.'	Drawing from subsequent sections of the EU AI Act, it is possible to identify three core technical requirements for foundation models under this ethical principle: i) robustness and predictability, ii) resilience to cyberattacks, and iii) corrigibility (accept correction, oversight, or shutdown by human operators).
Privacy and data governance	'AI systems are developed and used in accordance with privacy and data protection rules, while processing data that meets high standards in terms of quality and integrity.'	From this ethical principle, it is possible to collect all the requirements that concern the training data of an AI model: i) training data suitability, ii) avoiding copyright infringement, iii) user privacy protection.
Transparency	'AI systems are developed and used in a way that allows appropriate traceability and explainability, while making humans aware that they communicate or interact with an AI system, as well as duly informing deployers of the capabilities and limitations of that AI system and affected persons about their rights.'	The regulatory and technical requirements linked to this principle are: i) capabilities, performance, and limitations; ii) interpretability; iii) disclosure of AI presence; iv) traceability; v) summary of risks; vi) summary of evaluations; vii) general description.

(Continued)

Table 4.1 Continued

Ethical Principle	*Definition*	*Technical Requirement*
Diversity, non-discrimination, and fairness	'AI systems are developed and used in a way that allows appropriate traceability and explainability, while making humans aware that they communicate or interact with an AI system, as well as duly informing deployers of the capabilities and limitations of that AI system and affected persons about their rights.'	From this it is possible to highlight the following regulatory requirements: i) avoiding 'unfair biases' (avoidance of creating biased/stereotypical representations of specific groups), and ii) avoiding 'discriminatory impacts' (evaluating the model's discriminatory impacts when applied in specific end-to-end scenarios where its outputs are expected to directly affect individuals). These two requirements are interconnected, as a biased model can result in discriminatory impacts during deployment, while an unfair model may reflect deeper, systemic biases.
Social and environmental well-being	'AI systems are developed and used in a sustainable and environmentally friendly manner as well as in a way to benefit all human beings, while monitoring and assessing the long-term impacts on the individual, society and democracy.'	This ethical principle can be divided into two components: i) the environmental sustainability or impact of the AI system, including its development process, and ii) the social impact of the AI system, particularly its potential for generating harmful or toxic content, categorised as iii) environmental impact and iv) harmful content and toxicity.

Source: Authors' elaboration from the *Official Journal of the European Union*, 2024/1689, Regulation (EU) 2024/1689 of the European Parliament and of the Council of 13 June 2024 laying down harmonised rules on artificial intelligence and amending Regulations (EC) No 300/2008, (EU) No 167/2013, (EU) No 168/2013, (EU) 2018/858, (EU) 2018/1139 and (EU) 2019/2144 and Directives 2014/90/EU, (EU) 2016/797 and (EU) 2020/1828 (Artificial Intelligence Act), Effective date of the provision 12 July.2024

artificial intelligence (AI), while ensuring a high level of protection of health, safety, fundamental rights enshrined in the Charter, including democracy, the rule of law and environmental protection, against the harmful effects of AI systems in the Union and supporting innovation. This Regulation lays down:

a) Harmonised rules for the placing on the market, the putting into service, and the use of AI systems in the Union.
b) Prohibitions of certain AI practices.
c) Specific requirements for high-risk AI systems and obligations for operators of such systems.
d) Harmonised transparency rules for certain AI systems.
e) Harmonised rules for the placing on the market of general-purpose AI models.
f) Rules on market monitoring, market surveillance, governance and enforcement.
g) Measures to support innovation, with a particular focus on SMEs, including startups.

Article 2 states that 'the legislation is applicable to':

a) Providers placing on the market or putting into service AI systems or placing on the market general-purpose AI models in the Union, irrespective of whether those providers are established or located within the Union or in a third country.
b) Deployers of AI systems that have their place of establishment or are located within the Union.
c) Providers and deployers of AI systems that have their place of establishment or are in a third country, where the output produced by the AI system is used in the Union.
d) Importers and distributors of AI systems.
e) Product manufacturers placing on the market or putting into service an AI system together with their product and under their own name or trademark.
f) Authorised representatives of providers, which are not established in the Union.
g) Affected persons that are located within the Union.

This Regulation does not apply to AI systems for military, defence, or national security purposes; to public authorities in a third country or to international organisations falling within the scope of the Regulation; or to AI systems or models used for scientific research and development.

The Definition of AI and the Definition of Deployer

Article 3 of the Regulation defines, in a rather legalistic way, what is an AI system:

> "*AI system*" means a machine-based system that is designed to operate with varying levels of autonomy and that may exhibit adaptiveness after deployment, and that, for explicit or implicit objectives, infers, from the input it receives, how to generate outputs such as predictions, content, recommendations, or decisions that can influence physical or virtual environments.

The same article defines what is a deployer: 'a natural or legal person, public authority, agency or other body using an AI system under its authority except where the AI system is used in the course of a personal non-professional activity'.

Given the rapid developments in AI, the European Union wanted to define what AI means, what is subject to regulation, who are the actors in this ecosystem, and what rules apply to them.

Risk Categorisation

The AI Act classifies AI systems into four risk levels: minimal, limited, high, and unacceptable (see Table 4.2).

As outlined in Article 71, the EU aims to create a publicly accessible online register that lists all deployed high-risk AI systems, their use cases, and foundation models available on the market; law enforcement agencies, such as the police and migration control, are allowed to register their systems privately, with access restricted to an independent supervisory authority.

The classification of AI systems as high risk under the EU AI Act was among the most debated aspects, as it places a substantial burden on businesses and different entities.

As the AI Act is rather complex to understand, different companies offer compliance assessment and consultancy services to help businesses to identify the risk level classification of their AI use case and which obligations the company must follow.

Prohibited AI Practices Under the AI Act

On 4 February 2025, two days after the EU AI Act banned AI systems utilising prohibited practices, the European Commission released a draft version of the Commission Guidelines on Prohibited Artificial Intelligence Practices.[2]

These Draft Guidelines offer further clarification and context regarding AI practices prohibited under the Act, and they aim to guide i) the surveillance authorities in enforcing the regulations and ii) deployers and providers in ensuring compliance with the AI Act.

Table 4.2 EU AI Act risk categories

EU AI Act Risk Categories	*Definition*
Minimal risk	The EU AI Act defines the lowest level of risk as minimal risk. This category includes AI systems that do not fall into the higher-risk classifications, such as spam filters. Minimal-risk AI systems are not subject to restrictions or mandatory requirements. However, it is recommended that they adhere to general principles, including human oversight, non-discrimination, and fairness.
Limited risk	The second level of risk is classified as limited risk and includes AI systems that may pose risks of manipulation or deception. AI systems in this category must ensure transparency, meaning users should be informed when interacting with the AI, unless it is self-evident. Additionally, any deepfakes must be clearly identified as such. For instance, chatbots are considered limited-risk systems. This requirement is particularly important for generative AI systems and the content they produce.
High risk	AI systems are the most heavily regulated category permitted in the EU market. This classification encompasses safety components of products already subject to regulation, as well as standalone AI systems in specific domains, which could adversely impact public health and safety, fundamental rights, or the environment. These systems carry the potential for significant harm if they malfunction or are misused. Under Article 6 of the Regulation an AI system is considered high risk if it meets two conditions: • the system must either serve as a safety component of a product or be a product itself, as defined by the European Union harmonisation legislation (as shown in Annex I of the EU AI Act) • the product incorporating the safety component or the AI system as a standalone product must undergo a third-party conformity assessment under the relevant Union harmonisation legislation before being placed on the market or put into service. Annex III of the AI Act identifies areas which would classify standalone AI systems as high risk. These include: • biometric and biometrics-based systems • management and operation of critical infrastructure

(Continued)

Table 4.2 Continued

EU AI Act Risk Categories	*Definition*
	• education and vocational training • employment and workers management • access to essential private and public services and benefits • law enforcement • migration, asylum and border control management • administration of justice and democratic processes
Unacceptable risk	Unacceptable risk is the highest level of risk, and it can be divided into eight AI application types that are incompatible with EU values and fundamental rights: • subliminal manipulation • exploitation of the vulnerabilities of persons resulting in harmful behaviour • biometric categorisation of persons based on sensitive characteristics • general-purpose social scoring • real-time remote biometric identification in public spaces • assessing the emotional state of a person • predictive policing • scraping facial images AI systems related to these areas will be prohibited in the EU.
Exceptions	Law enforcement authorities may use high-risk systems related to public security without undergoing a prior conformity assessment with judicial authorisation.

Source: Authors' elaboration from the *Official Journal of the European Union*, 2024/1689, Regulation (EU) 2024/1689 of the European Parliament and of the Council of 13 June 2024 laying down harmonised rules on artificial intelligence and amending Regulations (EC) No 300/2008, (EU) No 167/2013, (EU) No 168/2013, (EU) 2018/858, (EU) 2018/1139 and (EU) 2019/2144 and Directives 2014/90/EU, (EU) 2016/797 and (EU) 2020/1828 (Artificial Intelligence Act), Effective date of the provision 12 July 2024

Although not legally binding or authoritative, the Draft Guidelines are designed to encourage uniform application of the EU AI Act across the European Union. While they have been approved by the European Commission, they have not yet been formally adopted.

The Draft Guidelines seek to enhance clarity and offer insight into the Commission's interpretation of Prohibited Practices under Article 5 of the AI Act. For each prohibited practice listed in Article 5 of the Act, the Draft Guidelines offer an overview of key elements, practical examples, and clarification on practices that fall outside the scope of the prohibitions. They also suggest measures to help avoid developing or using AI systems in ways that may be prohibited. Additionally, the Draft Guidelines highlight areas where these prohibitions intersect with or relate to other Union legal acts. Although not exhaustive, the Draft Guidelines serve as a useful tool for evaluating whether an AI system falls under the AI Act's prohibitions.

While extensive, the Draft Guidelines remain in draft form and will remain non-binding even after finalisation. Any guidance they provide is subject to the formal requirements outlined in the AI Act.

General-Purpose AI Systems

The risk classification under the EU AI Act is determined by the application of general-purpose AI (GPAI) systems to specific use cases. The Act distinguishes between two risk categories: non-systemic and systemic risk, based on the computing power required to train the model. While all foundational models are subject to transparency requirements, those classified as systemic risks face significantly stricter obligations. Additionally, GPAI developers are required to provide necessary information to downstream providers, those seeking to integrate a third-party GPAI model into their products or AI systems, and those utilising these models in high-risk applications.

A GPAI model is classified as a systemic risk if it exhibits 'high capabilities' determined by factors such as the cumulative computing power used during its training. The AI Act designates a GPAI model as posing systemic risk based on various criteria, including the model's complexity (e.g. the number of parameters), its input/output modalities, and its level of adoption among businesses and consumers (as outlined in Annex XIII of the EU AI Act).

The AI Act imposes additional obligations on models classified as systemic risk. Providers of systemic risk GPAI models must promptly inform the European Commission for inclusion in the public database, similar to the requirements for high-risk AI systems, and report any significant incidents, along with the corrective actions taken. They must also conduct comprehensive risk assessments, implement cybersecurity and infrastructure security measures, and establish a code of practice to demonstrate compliance with the AI Act. Documentation requirements are further expanded to include detailed descriptions of model evaluation strategies and results, adversarial testing conducted, and the system architecture, which explains how software components interact and integrate into the overall processing system. All providers are required to comply with transparency obligations and inform users when they are interacting with an AI system, such as a generative AI chatbot, and to label all AI-generated content.

Each GPAI model, along with its training and testing processes and the results of its evaluation, must be thoroughly documented (see Annex XI of the EU AI Act). This documentation must be kept current and accessible to downstream providers to help them comply with their obligations under the AI Act (see Annex XII of the EU AI Act).

GPAI providers are also required to make a publicly accessible and detailed summary of the content used to train their models. Providers based outside the EU who place their models on the Union's market must appoint an authorised representative within the EU. This representative is responsible for verifying the technical documentation and providing the necessary information to authorities, among other duties.

The Complexities of a High-Risk AI System

Article 11 'Technical documentation' of the EU AI Act states that:

> the technical documentation of a high-risk AI system shall be drawn up before that system is placed on the market or put into service and shall be kept up-to date. The technical documentation shall be drawn up in such a way as to demonstrate that the high-risk AI system complies with the requirements set out in this Section and to provide national competent authorities and notified bodies with the necessary information in a clear and comprehensive form to assess the compliance of the AI system with those requirements. It shall contain, at a minimum, the elements set out in Annex IV.

Furthermore, there are other Annexes related to AI systems: i) Annex VIII 'Information to be submitted upon the registration of high-risk AI systems in accordance with Article 49', and ii) Annex IX 'Information to be submitted upon the registration of high-risk AI systems listed in Annex III in relation to testing in real world conditions in accordance with Article 60'.

The main challenge for any entity seeking to deploy a high-risk AI system lies in interpreting regulatory requirements and translating them into measurable technical criteria. This task is particularly complex because the regulations are written in legal language, emphasising high-level objectives rather than detailed technical specifications. There is significant ambiguity regarding which specific metrics should be used, as well as potential requirements that lack established evaluation standards or methods. The difficulty stems from the vague and technically challenging nature of the regulatory language, which often implies technical specifications that cannot be effectively assessed. Regulators and the AI community are encouraged to invest in efforts to make these rules more practical and easier to implement. Ironically, AI is very efficient at reading complex rules and interpreting them.

Navigating the Challenges of Public-Sector Compliance with the EU AI Act

The introduction of the EU AI Act brings a transformative yet demanding regulatory framework, for every business and particularly for the public sector, which faces unique challenges in its implementation. Automated decision-making processes and the administrative procedures required for binding single-case decisions lie at the heart of these challenges. Public authorities are typically classified as 'users' under the EU AI Act but may also be 'providers' when they develop AI systems in-house or commission custom-built solutions. This dual role significantly heightens the complexity of compliance, demanding a careful balance between innovation and regulation.

A key concern for the public sector is the uncertainty surrounding the AI Act requirements. Translating its broad, sometimes ambiguous provisions into actionable solutions is challenging. The public sector must interpret how to categorise AI systems into high-risk, limited-risk, or minimal-risk categories and conduct rigorous impact assessments for high-risk systems before deployment. Furthermore, to meet compliance obligations they face the challenge of finding resources and expertise to handle these sensitive and intensive tasks. To give an indication of the scale of the compliance challenge, consider just one of the many organisations likely to be impacted by the EU AI Act: the Financial Conduct Authority (FCA) in the UK. The FCA, which manages risk and compliance in the financial sector, employs over 5,000 full-time staff, many of whom will need to be trained to understand these developing AI regulations.

The AI Act mandates transparency in AI-driven decision-making, requiring the public sector to inform citizens and provide clear explanations about AI's role in administrative procedures. However, achieving this level of transparency across diverse AI applications necessitates interdisciplinary expertise. Legal, ethical, and technical considerations must converge seamlessly to design systems that align with regulatory expectations while maintaining usability and fairness.

Another pressing challenge is the creation of robust oversight mechanisms to evaluate new AI implementations. Authorities must address persistent hurdles in data sharing, quality assurance, and privacy protection, which are areas critical for ensuring compliance. Monitoring systems must be established for high-risk AI applications, and the legal framework must adapt continuously to keep pace with rapid technological advancements.

The compliance journey is not without trade-offs. Stricter regulations may result in longer development cycles, delaying the deployment of AI solutions and potentially limiting their functionality. Some AI features might need to be disabled or restricted to meet the stringent requirements, slowing the modernisation of public services. Yet, this regulatory push also creates opportunities to build public trust in AI and lay the groundwork for ethical and effective innovation. The appendices provide examples of the EU AI Act Compliance Checklist, Audit Checklist, and Transparency Checklist to help organisations effectively align with the regulation's requirements.

In conclusion, while the EU AI Act introduces significant challenges for public sector compliance, it also provides a pathway to modernisation and enhanced public services. To succeed, public authorities must act swiftly and decisively, understanding their obligations, identifying high-risk systems, and implementing necessary changes. With the right strategies, the public sector can harness the transformative potential of AI within a framework that prioritises transparency, fairness, and accountability.

Comparing the US AI Bill of Rights and the EU AI Act

As of March 2025, the United States lacks comprehensive federal legislation specifically governing AI, but efforts to address AI regulation are progressing at both federal and state levels. Federally, the White House released a Blueprint for an AI Bill of Rights in October 2022, establishing principles for designing and deploying automated systems. In October 2023, President Biden issued an executive order outlining priorities for safe and trustworthy AI development. The Algorithmic Accountability Act of 2023, currently under consideration, would empower the Federal Trade Commission to regulate AI systems that handle consumers' personal data.

In January 2025, President Donald Trump rescinded the Biden administration's comprehensive executive order on AI regulation, signalling a major shift in federal oversight of AI technology. This decision immediately halted the enforcement of key safety and transparency requirements, such as mandatory sharing of safety test results and critical information about advanced AI systems with the federal government.

The Trump administration is expected to adopt a less restrictive approach, focusing on reducing regulatory barriers to stimulate AI innovation and reinforcing America's leadership in AI, particularly in innovation, defence, and national security. This shift in policy underscores the need for stakeholders to adapt to a regulatory environment that prioritises innovation over prescriptive oversight.

While federal regulation is undergoing a transformation, state-level efforts remain active. States – including Colorado, Utah, and Tennessee – are enforcing separate AI-related legislation, and Texas is considering introducing the Texas Responsible Governance Act (TRAIGA), although this has not yet passed into law. These patchworks of regulatory initiatives contain the familiar themes of protecting privacy, preventing misuse, and avoiding discrimination. Existing federal laws addressing areas like privacy and intellectual property are also being applied to oversee AI technologies.

Despite the lack of a dedicated federal AI regulator, multiple agencies continue to monitor AI within their respective domains, addressing critical issues such as safety, fairness, and privacy. Meanwhile, US businesses developing AI for the European market must still comply with the EU's AI Act, which continues to influence global AI governance.

The key difference between the EU AI Act and the US approach lies in their regulatory structures. The EU AI Act provides a comprehensive and legally binding framework for AI regulation. In contrast, as of March 2025, the US follows a fragmented approach, relying on existing laws and regulations rather than a dedicated federal AI law. This highlights the EU's proactive and cohesive approach to AI governance, in contrast to the US's more adaptable, sector-specific regulatory model. The EU AI Act seeks to establish a global benchmark for AI regulation, which may shape the future direction of US AI policies.

UK AI Regulation and Its Differences from the EU AI Act

In January 2025, the UK government announced its commitment to implement all 50 recommendations set out in the AI Opportunities Action Plan by the UK government adviser on AI, Matt Clifford.[3] This ambitious plan aims to strengthen the UK's global competitiveness in AI development and adoption.

The AI Opportunities Action Plan is a comprehensive blueprint designed to position the UK as a global leader in AI development and adoption. The plan focuses on critical areas such as improving data access, fostering AI talent, reforming regulation, and driving AI integration across both public and private sectors. Figure 4.2 explains the scope of the plan.

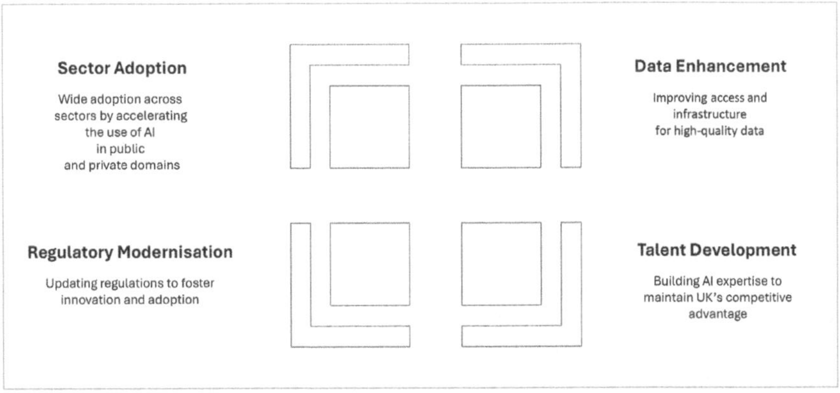

Figure 4.2 UK AI Opportunities Action Plan

Source: Authors' elaboration

The regulatory approach is completely different from the EU AI Act. The plan emphasises a shift in the role of UK regulators, who are expected to promote AI innovation within their sectors rather than focusing solely on risk analysis and enforcement. Furthermore, regulators are required to publish annual reports on how they have enabled AI-driven innovation and growth in their sectors.

As stated earlier, there is currently no specific AI regulation in the UK. Various existing laws apply to AI, including data protection, consumer protection, and equality laws. The UK is adopting a sector-based approach to regulation, with regulators required to consider six cross-sector principles:

- Safety.
- Security and robustness.
- Appropriate transparency and explainability.
- Fairness.
- Accountability and governance.
- Contestability and redress.

The UK's AI regulatory framework is centred on six core principles designed to guide the responsible development and use of AI across all sectors. These principles emphasise safety, security, and robustness, requiring AI systems to operate reliably and minimise harmful consequences. Transparency and explainability are also prioritised, ensuring that AI systems provide clear insights into their decision-making processes, capabilities, and limitations. Fairness is a key consideration, mandating that AI systems treat all individuals and groups equitably, without discrimination. The framework highlights accountability and governance, requiring organisations to take responsibility for the impacts of their AI systems and implement effective oversight. Lastly, contestability and redress are essential, providing mechanisms for individuals to challenge AI-driven decisions and seek remedies when necessary. This principles-based approach relies on existing regulators within specific sectors rather than new legislation, aiming to promote innovation while addressing risks and ensuring the framework remains adaptable to future developments.

Prime Minister Keir Starmer has stated that Britain will pursue its own path on AI regulation, distinct from the EU's approach.[4] This UK approach aims to balance innovation with risk management, focusing on regulating the most advanced AI models while promoting growth in the AI sector.

The UK's approach to AI regulation contrasts with the EU's AI Act in several fundamental ways. The UK employs a principles-based, flexible framework that relies on existing sector-specific regulatory bodies and avoids comprehensive AI-specific legislation. In contrast, the EU adopts a prescriptive, top-down legal framework with the AI Act, introducing new regulatory bodies like the European AI Office and applying horizontal regulations across sectors.

The UK focuses on regulating outcomes of specific AI applications without assigning risk levels to entire sectors or technologies; the EU AI Act categorises AI systems into risk levels, banning those deemed unacceptable. Compliance requirements in the UK are less prescriptive, emphasising adaptability and fostering innovation, while the EU imposes stringent obligations, particularly on high-risk systems, with rigorous risk management and transparency standards.

The Tony Blair Institute has highlighted two forthcoming UK legislative efforts, focused on data usage and copyright, that could jeopardise the AI vision by placing overly restrictive limits on AI innovation within the country.

The UK's proposed Data (Use and Access) Bill seeks to improve transparency around data practices but does so by introducing strict disclosure requirements that could force AI developers to reveal training data containing trade secrets. The bill may also extend UK liability to globally trained AI systems, potentially complicating their deployment for domestic use, whereas other countries typically exempt foreign-trained models from local compliance burdens.[5]

The UK's approach to copyright and intellectual property involves a proposed commercial text- and data-mining exemption with opt-outs for rights-holders, aligning broadly with the EU; however, the debate is framed in adversarial terms, with rights-holders positioned against AI developers, unlike in other regions where more integrative models are being explored to balance innovation with content protection.[6]

Box 4.1 – Case Study: Anna's Archive and Library Genesis

The story of Anna's Archive and Library Genesis (LibGen) illustrates the immense and controversial scale of information accessible to LLMs.

Anna's Archive, launched in 2022 after law enforcement targeted Z-Library, aggregates metadata from major shadow libraries, including LibGen, Sci-Hub, and Z-Library, claiming to be 'the largest truly open library in human history' and aiming to catalogue all books in existence. LibGen has evolved into a vast repository of scholarly articles, books, and media, frequently operating in defiance of copyright law. These shadow libraries have become crucial data sources for AI companies building massive training datasets, with Anna's Archive offering high-speed access to its entire collection in exchange for payments or data contributions.

The scale of these collections is extraordinary: as of January 2025, Anna's Archive had indexed over 40 million books and nearly 100 million papers, with its torrent list nearing a petabyte. Despite ongoing legal and technical challenges, LibGen continues to host millions of books and tens of millions of journal articles. This unprecedented availability of digital content has empowered companies like Meta to train AI models on an unsurpassed breadth of material. Court documents and investigative reports reveal that Meta downloaded and utilised the LibGen database, including millions of copyrighted works, to train its flagship Llama 3 model, fully aware of the legal risks. These practices have sparked lawsuits and strong backlash from authors and publishers, who argue that their intellectual property is exploited without permission or compensation.

The reliance on these illicit databases by LLM developers raises significant concerns about data security and privacy. Many AI models are trained on unprotected or sensitive data, heightening risks of regulatory breaches, data leaks, and unintended disclosure of confidential information. The absence of rigorous safeguards or anonymisation protocols means that sensitive personal or proprietary data can be memorised and reproduced by LLMs, creating legal and ethical dilemmas. Furthermore, the rapid, largely unregulated growth of AI training pipelines has outpaced the development of effective mitigation measures, leaving organisations exposed to compliance failures and security vulnerabilities.

In short, the convergence of shadow libraries like Anna's Archive and LibGen with LLM development exemplifies both the massive information fuelling AI advances and the profound challenges posed for data security, privacy, and intellectual property rights. As the AI sector accelerates, often sidestepping legal and ethical constraints, the risks linked to the use of these vast, frequently illegal, datasets remain unresolved.

These proposals risk concentrating compliance burdens on small AI firms and researchers, advantaging large technology companies with the resources to navigate complex regulation; this diverges from models in more innovation-centric jurisdictions, where regulatory frameworks are calibrated to support a diverse ecosystem of developers and academic institutions.

Internationally, the UK aligns with global frameworks and leans towards a 'pro-innovation' stance, possibly influenced by US approaches, while the EU extends its regulations extraterritorially to companies operating within or selling to the EU. The UK maintains a 'hold and wait' regulatory approach with potential future legislation, contrasting with the EU's AI Act, which requires full implementation by 2026. This divergence highlights the UK's prioritisation of flexibility and innovation versus the EU's structured and comprehensive regulatory approach, posing challenges for businesses operating across both jurisdictions.

Global Approaches to AI Regulation

Across the globe, nations are actively developing regulatory frameworks to govern AI, reflecting diverse strategies tailored to regional priorities and values. These efforts emphasise promoting responsible AI innovation while mitigating risks and ethical concerns.

China has been a leader in implementing AI-specific regulations, particularly in generative AI. The 2023 Interim Measures for the Management of Generative Artificial Intelligence Services regulate AI services offered in mainland China. This framework mandates content alignment with core socialist values, real-name verification for users, and security assessments for AI models before public release.

Canada is advancing the Artificial Intelligence and Data Act (AIDA), aiming to establish a comprehensive regulatory framework for AI. AIDA proposes prescriptive, ex-ante requirements for AI development and deployment, introduces new AI regulators, and includes provisions for extraterritorial application.

Japan has balanced innovation with risk mitigation, initially emphasising voluntary guidelines before advancing towards more stringent laws to address specific AI-related harms. This dual approach reflects Japan's strategy of fostering innovation while safeguarding against potential risks.

Singapore has developed an AI governance framework that blends ethical principles with sector-specific regulations. This approach promotes responsible AI innovation while maintaining public safety and ensuring compliance with ethical standards.

India is gradually shaping its AI regulation, focusing on sector-specific initiatives in areas such as finance and healthcare. Its evolving framework seeks to balance the encouragement of AI development with necessary safeguards against potential risks.

Brazil is in the process of crafting its AI regulatory framework, with proposed legislation under review. The framework aims to combine ethical considerations with innovation, emphasising compliance and risk management.

These regulatory efforts highlight a global trend towards adopting risk-based approaches, prioritising high-risk AI applications, and promoting principles such as transparency, accountability, and human oversight. While each country tailors its strategy to local contexts, the overarching goal remains consistent: fostering AI's transformative potential while addressing its inherent challenges responsibly.

A Vision for the Future: Reconciling Innovation and Regulation in the AI Era

As the world confronts the complexities of the AI era, achieving a workable balance between innovation and regulation remains both essential and challenging. The European Union's AI Act reflects a proactive approach, placing strong emphasis on ethical safeguards and institutional accountability. In contrast, the United Kingdom's evolving regulatory framework aims to balance flexibility with oversight, creating conditions for innovation while maintaining public trust.

Within the public sector, AI offers significant potential to improve service delivery, streamline operations, and enhance decision-making. Across domains such as healthcare, transport, education, and social welfare, AI's capacity to process large datasets and generate actionable insights is already influencing how governments operate. However, its deployment in these areas raises pressing questions about accountability, fairness, and individual privacy. Ensuring that AI is used responsibly in contexts that directly affect citizens' lives must remain a priority for policymakers, underlining the need for clear, transparent, and ethically grounded regulation.

These trends highlight the growing urgency for global dialogue on AI governance, one that transcends political divisions and national interests. A coordinated approach is needed to address the shared risks and opportunities posed by this transformative technology. By aligning innovation with appropriate regulation, and by responsibly integrating AI into both public and private sectors, it is possible to shape a future in which technology enhances human capability without compromising core democratic values.

The path forward will require collaboration, vision, and the collective determination to navigate this pivotal moment with foresight and responsibility.

Notes

1 *Official Journal of the European Union*, 2024/1689, Regulation (EU) 2024/1689 of the European Parliament and of the Council of 13 June 2024 laying down harmonised rules on artificial intelligence and amending Regulations (EC) No 300/2008, (EU) No 167/2013, (EU) No 168/2013, (EU) 2018/858, (EU) 2018/1139 and (EU) 2019/2144 and Directives 2014/90/EU, (EU) 2016/797 and (EU) 2020/1828 (Artificial Intelligence Act), Effective date of the provision 12 July 2024.

2 European Commission (2025), Commission publishes the Guidelines on prohibited artificial intelligence (AI) practices, as defined by the AI Act, https://digital-strategy.ec.europa.eu/en/library/commission-publishes-guidelines-prohibited-artificial-intelligence-ai-practices-defined-ai-act (accessed on 6 February 2025).

3 Government of the UK (2025), AI Opportunities Action Plan, www.gov.uk/government/publications/ai-opportunities-action-plan/ai-opportunities-action-plan (accessed on 2 February 2025).

4 Reuters (2025), UK's Starmer says Britain will go its own way on AI regulation, www.reuters.com/world/uk/uks-starmer-says-britain-will-go-its-own-way-ai-regulation-2025-01-13/ (accessed on 2 February 2025).

5 UK Parliament (2025), Data (Use and Access) Bill [HL], https://bills.parliament.uk/bills/3825 (accessed on 15 April 2025).

6 Government of the UK (2022), Artificial intelligence and IP: Copyright and patents, www.gov.uk/government/consultations/artificial-intelligence-and-ip-copyright-and-patents (accessed on 15 April 2025).

Part II

The Human Impact of Automation

Chapter 5

The Automation Threat

Administrative Jobs at Risk

In the previous chapter, we examined the growing number of government consultations, draft regulations, and legislative measures aimed at managing the widespread adoption of artificial intelligence (AI). The advance of AI across the landscape of public administration is both promising and unsettling. While it holds the potential to transform how governments deliver services, it also poses a direct threat to the livelihoods of millions of public-sector employees.

Clerical, administrative, and middle-management roles, which have long provided stability within the public workforce, are especially vulnerable to automation. The efficiency and cost savings that AI can offer are considerable, but they raise important concerns around employment, equity, and the broader social contract between governments and the citizens they serve.

Public administration has traditionally been viewed as a dependable source of secure employment. For decades, administrative roles have provided financial stability, job security, and clear career progression. With the increasing use of AI, however, many of the core functions of these positions, such as data entry, compliance monitoring, and routine decision-making, are now being handled by automated systems.

Governments eager to realise the benefits of AI must also confront the disruptions these technologies may bring, not only to their internal operations but also to the communities that rely on public employment.

DOI: 10.4324/9781003673897-8

Systemic Risks of Automating Administrative Tasks

While the allure of AI lies in its promise of efficiency, it also introduces systemic risks that governments must address to ensure successful implementation. Chief among these risks are the reliance on outdated datasets, insufficient oversight mechanisms, and the erosion of human accountability. In addition, we must be mindful of the increasing number of cyberattacks focused on large datasets.

Reliance on Outdated Datasets

AI systems are only as good as the data on which they are trained on. Many government databases are outdated, incomplete, or inconsistent, factors that can compromise the effectiveness of automated systems. For example, in welfare administration, reliance on outdated socio-economic data could lead to erroneous eligibility decisions, depriving vulnerable individuals of much-needed support. Similarly, AI systems in tax agencies may disproportionately target low-income earners if training datasets reflect historical biases.[1]

Historical inequities embedded in these datasets risk perpetuating systemic biases. For instance, if a dataset reflects underfunded programmes in marginalised communities, AI systems might prioritise resources inequitably, reinforcing rather than addressing disparities. Addressing this challenge requires rigorous, ongoing reviews and updating of datasets to ensure accuracy, inclusivity, and fairness.

Insufficient Oversight and Accountability

As AI takes on more complex tasks, the potential for errors or misuse grows. Without sufficient human oversight, automated systems can make decisions that are difficult to explain or correct. Consider an AI system used to process unemployment claims: if an algorithm mistakenly flags a claim as fraudulent, the claimant may face lengthy delays or denial of benefits without understanding why the decision was made. Such cases can undermine public trust and satisfaction in government services.

Effective oversight mechanisms are crucial to mitigating these risks. Governments must establish clear protocols for human intervention, conduct regular audits of AI systems, and maintain transparency in decision-making processes. Public servants must be equipped with the skills to manage and interpret AI outputs, balancing efficiency with accountability and fairness.

The UK Post Office Horizon scandal stands as a stark warning about blind faith in technology and institutional power.[2] Between 1999 and 2015, the UK Post Office prosecuted over 700 sub-postmasters based solely on data from the flawed Fujitsu Horizon IT system. Ultimately, 236 postmasters were convicted and approximately 60 to 70 people were sent to prison for crimes they never committed. Effective oversight mechanisms were notably absent, allowing a blind faith in technology to mask errors that cascaded into a serious miscarriage of justice. What makes this case particularly egregious was the Post Office's unwavering defence of the computer system despite mounting evidence of its flaws. The case highlights how a toxic institutional culture and incompetent leadership, combined with dehumanised decision-making, can lead to great injustice. Lives were destroyed as honest workers lost their livelihoods, homes, and reputations; some were driven to bankruptcy, while others took their own lives under the unbearable weight of false accusations. Without doubt, the scandal also increased public scepticism about the reliability of computer software.

The Horizon scandal underscores the critical need for robust governance frameworks surrounding technological systems. Governments must establish clear protocols for human intervention, conduct regular audits of complex systems like Horizon, and maintain transparency in decision-making processes that affect citizens' lives. Organisations must develop processes where technology-based evidence can be meaningfully challenged, especially when serious accusations are involved. Furthermore, public servants must be equipped with the skills to properly understand, manage, and interpret system outputs, balancing efficiency with accountability and fairness. The Post Office's failure teaches us that technological systems are only as reliable as the human teams that implement and manage them, and that justice requires both humility about the fallibility of our machines and the courage to question automated decisions when human welfare is at stake.

Overcoming the Complexities: Implementation Challenges in AI Systems

Implementing AI systems presents a range of complex challenges that span technical, organisational, and human factors. One of the primary difficulties is ensuring data quality and accessibility. AI systems rely heavily on high-quality, structured data for training and decision-making, yet many organisations face issues with fragmented, outdated, or inconsistent datasets. Problems such as biased data or incomplete information can lead to inaccurate predictions and ethical concerns, particularly in sensitive areas like healthcare and recruitment. Overcoming these challenges requires not only significant upfront investment but strong data governance, automated data cleaning tools, and investments in synthetic data to address gaps and ensure reliability.

Legacy Systems

Another significant challenge is integrating AI with legacy systems. Many organisations still operate with outdated infrastructure that is not compatible with modern AI technologies, resulting in delays and inefficiencies during deployment. The UK's *State of Digital Government Review* in 2025 found that 28 per cent of central government's technology is considered as 'legacy'. Despite spending £26 billion annually on IT, the report found a notable proportion of its technology remains outdated, and service reliability is too low. Legacy tech is defined as 'an end-of-life product, out of support from the supplier, impossible to update, no longer cost-effective or otherwise above the acceptable risk threshold'.[3] A notable example occurred in May 2024 when an incident at the UK's HMRC left half a million people without their child benefit payments.

There is an even starker example of the challenges posed by legacy data. In 2010, the UK Home Office began destroying paper records of immigrants who had arrived in the UK between the late 1940s and early 1970s. These records had not been digitised, and thus vital proof of the right to remain in the UK was lost. Thousands of people were affected, resulting in job losses, denial of healthcare, and detention. This raises the critical question of how many other important databases remain in paper format and are consequently outside the scope of any advantages of AI technology.

Solutions including custom APIs (application programming interfaces that allow different software programs to communicate and exchange data), middleware, and scalable cloud platforms can help bridge the gap between legacy systems and AI applications. Additionally, upgrading computational resources and optimising data storage, are crucial for meeting the processing demands of AI models.

Human factors also play a critical role in the successful implementation of AI. Resistance from management, employees, and unions, a shortage of skilled professionals, and a lack of understanding of AI's strategic benefits can hinder progress. To address these challenges, upskilling existing staff through training programmes and fostering a culture of innovation are clearly important.

Finally, and of relevance in these budget-constrained times, upfront costs are another obvious barrier to AI adoption. The significant investment associated with infrastructure upgrades, talent acquisition, and ongoing maintenance can be a significant burden, particularly for smaller agencies. Cloud-based solutions with flexible pricing models or focusing on pilot projects can help mitigate financial risks while demonstrating the value of AI. By strategically addressing these challenges and continuously refining the implementation process, organisations can unlock the transformative potential of AI while effectively navigating its complexities.

Challenges of Ensuring Fairness and Inclusivity in Automation

While automation holds the promise of streamlining public services, it also risks excluding marginalised communities and exacerbating existing inequalities. Governments must take proactive steps to ensure that AI-driven systems promote fairness and inclusivity rather than reinforcing systemic biases.

Accessibility for Marginalised Communities

Marginalised communities, including low-income populations, people with disabilities, and individuals in remote areas, often face barriers to accessing government services. Automation can either alleviate or worsen these barriers, depending on how it is implemented. For instance, an AI-powered chatbot designed to handle citizen inquiries may struggle to understand non-standard dialects or accents, excluding individuals who do not speak the dominant language fluently. Saying that, AI is making remarkable advances in understanding multiple languages with extraordinary accuracy.

Moreover, the shift to digital-first service delivery risks alienating individuals without reliable internet access or adequate digital literacy. Internet accessibility remains a challenge for many households. In the United States in 2023, an estimated 6.87 million households did not have internet access. In the UK in 2025, around 2.8 million people, 5 per cent of the UK population, do not have internet access at home.

In both the US and UK, public libraries provide an important public service in the digital age, offering free internet access and often expert guidance on using the technology. In the UK, budget cuts have resulted in the closure of about 800 libraries since 2010, and many more have reduced open hours. The US is seeing similar pattern of diminishing library funding. As more services move online, public accessibility will be increasingly important.

Programmes like India's Common Service Centres (CSCs) highlight the importance of bridging the digital divide to ensure equitable access to AI-enabled services. These centres provide rural citizens with access to digital platforms, allowing them to interact with automated systems through human intermediaries.

Algorithmic Bias and Discrimination

Algorithmic bias is another challenge in ensuring fairness. AI systems trained on biased data can produce discriminatory outcomes, even if unintentional. For instance, in hiring processes, algorithms trained on historical employment data may prioritise candidates from traditionally privileged groups, perpetuating inequality. In public administration, such biases could result in unequal treatment of citizens based on race, gender, or socio-economic status.

A striking example of this occurred in Michigan between 2013 and 2015 when the state implemented an algorithm known as MiDAS[4] to detect unemployment fraud.[5] The system wrongly accused over 40,000 people of fraudulently claiming benefits, leading to severe consequences such as heavy fines, bankruptcy, and home foreclosures. The errors stemmed from poor system design and a lack of human oversight, as decisions were based on incorrect or mismatched data. Vulnerable populations relying on unemployment benefits were disproportionately affected, demonstrating the risks of flawed algorithmic decision-making.

A similar case took place in the Netherlands, where tax authorities used an algorithm to detect childcare benefit fraud.[6] The system disproportionately flagged low-income parents, single parents, and individuals with foreign nationalities as high risk, leading to thousands of families being wrongly accused of fraud. As a result, many suffered financial hardship. The algorithm relied on discriminatory assumptions based on nationality and socio-economic status, exacerbating existing inequalities. This case underscores how biased algorithms, when used without adequate oversight, can reinforce systemic discrimination and cause widespread societal harm.

Governments must prioritise diversity in data collection and involve marginalised groups or their representatives in the design and testing of AI systems. Regular audits of algorithms for bias and fairness, along with independent oversight, are essential to maintaining public confidence in AI-driven systems.

Economic and Social Implications of Job Displacement

The economic ramifications of AI-driven job displacement are vast. For individual workers, the loss of stable government jobs, particularly for older workers, can have devastating consequences. Public-sector employment has traditionally been a source of economic security, offering reliable income, benefits, and opportunities for advancement. As automation eliminates these positions, affected workers may struggle to find comparable employment, particularly in regions where public administration forms the backbone of local economies.

Regional and Cultural Variations Affecting Impact

The impact of automation varies significantly by socio-economic and cultural context. In high-income countries, public-sector employees may have greater access to retraining programmes and alternative employment opportunities. By contrast, in emerging economies, public administration often serves as a vital source of employment, particularly in rural areas. For example, India's sprawling bureaucratic system employs millions of clerical workers who could be displaced by automation, creating severe economic and social disruptions.

Cultural factors also influence how governments approach automation. In collectivist societies like Japan and South Korea, where employment stability is deeply valued, governments may prioritise redeployment over displacement, retraining workers for roles that complement AI systems. In more individualistic societies, efficiency gains often take precedence, accelerating the pace of job elimination.

For example, South Korea's Ministry of Employment and Labor has introduced programmes to help administrative workers transition to roles focused on monitoring and managing AI systems. This approach balances efficiency with social responsibility, minimising the negative impact of job displacement.

The U.S. Department of Government Efficiency (DOGE), established in 2025 under President Trump and led at the time by Elon Musk, was tasked with streamlining federal operations through aggressive cost-cutting and rapid technological modernisation. The impact of DOGE's efforts act as a warning of the risks involved in rapid AI rollout. While DOGE's stated aim was to improve efficiency, the reality has been far more complex. The sweeping reforms initiated under DOGE have triggered systemic disruptions, large-scale workforce reductions, funding withdrawals, and controversial IT overhauls. These measures have also led to ongoing legal battles and raised serious questions about the long-term sustainability and governance of such interventions.

Among the most notable cuts, over 6,800 Internal Revenue Service jobs were eliminated,[7] weakening tax enforcement, while the U.S. Agency for International Development (USAID) faced a planned 90 per cent workforce reduction alongside layoffs in nuclear security agencies.[8] Diversity, Equity, and Inclusion (DEI) programmes were dismantled, leading to mass firings and content purges. Climate and science funding also suffered, with grants for climate research and wildfire preparedness slashed and National Oceanic and Atmospheric Administration (NOAA) staff linked to DEI initiatives removed. Additionally, rapid IT modernisation efforts introduced cybersecurity risks due to insufficient data access controls.

These cuts have had widespread economic, operational, and social consequences. Local economies, such as Oklahoma City, have struggled due to reduced federal worker spending. Service delays have affected tax refunds, veterans' benefits, and national park access. Safety risks have emerged from understaffed nuclear security teams and underfunded disaster response programmes. The erosion of institutional trust has also deepened, fuelled by politicised audits and whistleblower reports.

Legally, DOGE faces mounting challenges. Lawsuits argue that its leaders, including Musk, bypassed Senate confirmation, violating the Appointments Clause. Congress has accused the agency of breaching the Impoundment Control Act by illegally withholding funds, such as foreign aid. DOGE's $40 million budget, sourced from other agencies via the Economy Act, has been scrutinised for sidestepping congressional appropriations.[9] Court rulings remain divided: some have blocked layoffs and data access changes, while others have upheld the cuts, citing presidential authority under the unitary executive theory. While DOGE claims efficiency gains, its methods have sparked fierce legal and public backlash. Ultimately, the courts will determine whether its actions comply with constitutional limits, setting significant precedents for the future of federal restructuring.

DOGE serves as a cautionary example of what can happen when transformation is driven by ideology and speed rather than strategic planning and consultation. Its ad hoc and poorly coordinated implementation underscores the risks of introducing technology, especially AI, without adequate oversight, testing, and stakeholder engagement. Rather than achieving coherent reform, DOGE's approach has revealed the potential for chaos when ambitious innovation outpaces the frameworks needed to support it.

Psychological and Social Impacts

For many individuals, administrative roles provide not only financial stability but also a sense of identity and purpose. Losing these roles to automation can lead to feelings of obsolescence and alienation. On a societal level, widespread job displacement risks fuelling resentment towards AI adoption, particularly if the benefits are perceived to accrue disproportionately to governments and corporations at the expense of workers.

Governments must address these broader societal impacts, ensuring that displaced workers have access to resources, support systems, and opportunities for meaningful reemployment.

Opportunities Amid Disruption

Alongside the challenges posed by automation lies the opportunity to reimagine public service delivery. By addressing systemic risks and prioritising fairness, governments can harness AI to create more responsive, inclusive, and equitable systems.

Redefining Public-Sector Roles

Automation can liberate employees from repetitive, low-value tasks, enabling them to focus on more meaningful and impactful roles. For example, as AI systems handle routine permit approvals, human workers can be reassigned to roles that involve engaging with citizens, addressing complex issues, or ensuring ethical compliance in AI decision-making.

This is amplified with the application of emerging technologies in human–AI interaction, for example replacing typed queries with natural, speech-based communication. By combining cutting-edge speech recognition, natural language processing, and text-to-speech technologies, these AI models are capable of comprehending spoken language, preserving context throughout multi-turn conversations, and delivering responses with realistic, adaptive voices that reflect tone, rhythm, and emotion. This advancement may significantly improve user experience and expands accessibility, enabling seamless hands-free interactions in diverse settings such as customer service and personal assistance. At its core, incorporating speech capabilities into large language models (LLMs) is transforming human–AI interaction by emphasising ease of use, natural dialogue, and emotional awareness. This progression is establishing voice as the dominant interface for interacting with technology. Despite its benefits, the integration of speech into LLMs also introduces significant risks, including potential misuse through voice cloning, privacy concerns from continuous audio data collection, the spread of misinformation via convincing synthetic speech, and user frustration when the AI cannot provide relevant answers to queries or service requests. Ensuring ethical use and robust safeguards is essential to mitigate these challenges as voice-driven AI becomes more prevalent.

Creating New Opportunities in Data Governance

The rise of AI also creates new roles in data governance, algorithm auditing, and ethical oversight. These positions are critical to ensuring that automated systems align with public values and serve the common good. Data ethics officers, for instance, can identify and mitigate biases in AI systems, while algorithm auditors ensure compliance with transparency and accountability standards.

Preparing for a Fair and Inclusive Future

To navigate the complexities of automation, governments must adopt a proactive, citizen-centric approach. This involves:

- Investing in data quality: Ensuring datasets are accurate, diverse, and representative of the populations they serve.
- Engaging stakeholders: Involving public servants, civil society groups, and marginalised communities in the design and implementation of AI systems.
- Prioritising transparency: Clearly communicating how AI systems make decisions and what safeguards are in place to protect citizens.
- Providing support for transition: Establishing retraining programmes and career transition support for displaced workers.
- Audit and feedback: Building into system design constant evaluation of outcomes and establishing a feedback mechanism to reduce errors and anomalies.

Continuous Evaluation and Feedback: Ensuring Accuracy and Accountability in System Design

Continuous evaluation and feedback are essential for ensuring the accuracy and accountability of AI systems. As AI increasingly shapes critical sectors like healthcare, finance, and governance, it's crucial to maintain both reliability and ethical alignment. This begins with establishing performance metrics that act as benchmarks for tracking improvements or detecting issues over time. These metrics should be tailored to the specific objectives of the AI application, whether it's accuracy in medical diagnostics or user engagement in recommendation systems. Alongside this, a dynamic feedback loop compares real-world outcomes with system outputs, enabling adjustments to address issues like data drift or bias.

Transparency is key to accountability. Tools like explainable AI (XAI),[10] a set of processes and methods that allows human users to comprehend and trust the results and output created by machine learning algorithms, allows stakeholders to understand and justify AI decisions. Regular audits conducted by multidisciplinary teams, including data scientists, ethicists, and domain experts, help identify biases, security concerns, and ethical issues while ensuring compliance with regulatory standards. Real-time monitoring tools track key performance indicators, detecting anomalies early and enabling timely intervention.

Equally important is the role of data. Continuous learning from new data ensures that AI systems stay adaptive to changing conditions, but this requires rigorous data validation to maintain integrity and relevance. Before deployment, updates to models and infrastructure must undergo thorough testing to prevent errors.

By integrating practices like baseline metrics, feedback loops, explainability, audits, and continuous learning, AI systems can maintain accuracy and accountability. This ongoing process enhances performance and builds trust among users, ensuring that AI technologies are deployed responsibly in ever-changing environments.

A Vision for Equitable Automation

The automation of administrative tasks presents both a challenge and an opportunity for public service delivery. If governments can address systemic risks, prioritise inclusivity, and foster public trust, automation can strengthen rather than weaken the social contract. Achieving this will require a sustained commitment to fairness, transparency, and the principle that technology must serve people, not the other way round.

The next chapter will examine why certain administrative roles are especially vulnerable to automation. It will explore the dynamics of job displacement in greater detail and consider strategies to mitigate its social and economic effects.

Notes

1 Bloomberg (2024), Biased IRS predictive algorithm is cautionary tale for employers, https://news.bloombergtax.com/tax-insights-and-commentary/biased-irs-predictive-algorithm-is-cautionary-tale-for-employers (accessed on 29 March 2025).
2 BBC (2024), Post Office Horizon scandal: Why hundreds were wrongly prosecuted, www.bbc.com/news/business-56718036 (accessed on 29 March 2025).
3 UK Department for Science, Innovation & Technology (2025) *State of Digital Government Review. A Review of Technology and Data in the Public Sector: Successes, Challenges and Root Causes*, https://assets.publishing.service.gov.uk/media/678a47649752f24aa1573589/state-of-digital-government.pdf (accessed on 29 March 2025).
4 The Michigan Integrated Data Automated System (MiDAS) was an automated system implemented by Michigan's Unemployment Insurance Agency (UIA) in 2013 to modernise unemployment insurance processing.
5 The Greenlining Institute (No date), *Algorithmic Bias Explained: How Automated Decision-Making Becomes Automated Discrimination*, https://greenlining.org/wp-content/uploads/2021/04/Greenlining-Institute-Algorithmic-Bias-Explained-Report-Feb-2021.pdf (accessed on 29 March 2025).

6 The Parliament (2024), What can the EU learn from the Dutch algorithm scandal?, www.theparliamentmagazine.eu/news/article/ai-bias-will-europes-race-for-efficiency-reinforce-discrimination (accessed on 29 March 2025).
7 CNN (2025), DOGE proposes cutting IRS workforce by a total of nearly 20%, https://edition.cnn.com/2025/03/13/politics/doge-irs-workforce-cuts-downsizing/index.html (accessed on 29 March 2025).
8 CBC (2025), USAID workers pack belongings, as Trump administration targets 90% of foreign aid contracts, www.cbc.ca/news/world/usaid-layoffs-cuts-1.7469873 (accessed on 29 March 2025).
9 Government Executive (2025), DOGE's millions: As Musk and Trump gut the government, their ax-cutting agency gets a cash infusion, www.govexec.com/management/2025/02/doges-millions-musk-and-trump-gut-government-their-ax-cutting-agency-gets-cash-infusion/403197/ (accessed on 29 March 2025).
10 IBM (2025), What is explainable AI?, www.ibm.com/think/topics/explainable-ai (accessed on 29 March 2025).

Chapter 6

The Anatomy of Job Displacement

Why Administrative Roles Are Vulnerable

As noted in the introduction, the long-term shift from agricultural employment in the United States, where around 40 per cent of the workforce were employed in farming at the start of the twentieth century to less than 2 per cent a century later, illustrates the profound impact of technological change. This decline occurred gradually, over more than 100 years, and coincided with rapid population growth and economic diversification.

Over the past century, automation has steadily reduced the need for physical labour. Few in the early 1900s could have predicted the emergence of entire sectors such as medicine, software, and tourism. Today, as work becomes increasingly machine driven, humans will continue to play a vital role in oversight, decision-making, and contextual judgement.

However, if this transition is not managed carefully, it risks causing significant disruption and the obsolescence of many existing roles. Although artificial intelligence (AI) is unlikely to result in widespread job losses in the immediate term, ageing populations and restricted immigration in many high-income countries are already contributing to growing labour shortages.[1]

The rise of AI is fundamentally reshaping the workplace, and public administration is no exception. Administrative roles, traditionally viewed as stable and essential, are now among the most exposed to automation. These positions, which

DOI: 10.4324/9781003673897-9

depend on structured workflows, rule-based decision-making, and large volumes of predictable tasks, are increasingly being carried out by AI systems that can perform the same functions more quickly, more efficiently, and often with greater accuracy.

Although this transformation brings significant improvements in operational efficiency, it also reveals major vulnerabilities within public-sector employment. It raises urgent questions about economic stability, social equity, and the capacity of the workforce to adapt to a rapidly changing environment.

In the United Kingdom, the Tony Blair Institute (TBI) estimates that AI-driven automation could save around 20 per cent of public-sector workers' time by streamlining routine tasks. This could generate fiscal savings of approximately £41 billion per year, equivalent to a reduction of around 3.4 per cent in total government spending.

However, large-scale job cuts in the public sector may destabilise local economies that rely heavily on government employment. At the same time, productivity gains from AI could increase GDP growth by as much as one percentage point annually, but only if displaced workers are successfully retrained or absorbed into alternative roles.

The TBI also suggests that AI could reduce public-sector wage bills by 1.5 per cent of GDP; however, realising these savings requires significant upfront investments in AI infrastructure. The costs are estimated at £4–7 billion annually, along with efforts to improve data quality. However, if workforce transitions are poorly managed, increased welfare spending may counteract these benefits.[2]

The impact of AI on administrative employment is expected to materialise within the next five years, making the risk of displacement both immediate and substantial.

This chapter explores the characteristics of administrative roles that make them especially vulnerable to automation. It also examines the socio-economic and cultural factors that heighten these risks and sets out strategies to mitigate the effects of AI-driven job displacement.

Structural Vulnerabilities in Administrative Roles

Administrative roles are uniquely susceptible to automation because of their reliance on processes that are highly structured and codified. These roles often involve repetitive tasks that follow clearly defined rules, conditions where AI excels. Figure 6.1 shows AI automation in administrative roles.

Studies by the Brookings Institution, OpenAI, and Model Evaluation & Threat Research point to a fundamental limitation: AI systems struggle with unstructured, unpredictable tasks.[3] Their strength lies in processing clean data and executing repetitive, rule-based functions, such as data entry or routine customer service, with efficiency and scale. In contrast, roles requiring adaptability, nuanced judgement, or emotional intelligence remain less vulnerable to automation. This distinction explains why well-defined tasks are automated first.[4]

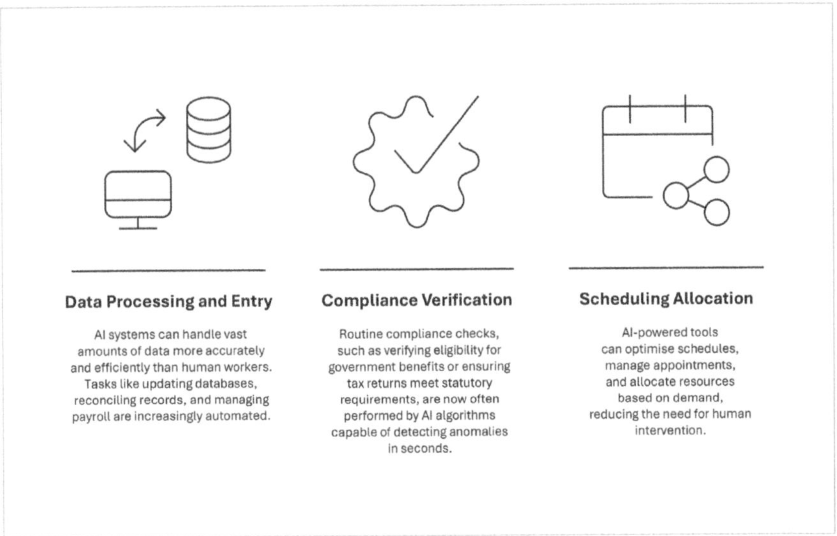

Figure 6.1 AI automation in administrative roles

Source: Authors' elaboration

As an example, Japan has adopted robotic process automation (RPA) in municipal offices to streamline tasks such as licence renewals and permit processing. This shift has significantly reduced the workload of administrative staff while improving service delivery times. However, it has also led to a decrease in demand for clerical positions.

The U.S. Treasury Department leverages AI for compliance and verification by detecting anomalies in tax filings and preventing fraudulent claims. AI algorithms analyse extensive datasets to uncover patterns and inconsistencies that may signal fraud or non-compliance. Machine learning models, for example, have helped recover $4 billion in fraudulent payments by identifying high-risk transactions, automating risk-based screenings, and flagging anomalies in real time.[5] This technology enables the government to efficiently ensure tax returns adhere to statutory requirements, significantly reducing the time and resources needed for manual audits.

The predictable and repetitive nature of these tasks means they can be encoded into algorithms with minimal human oversight. This contrasts with roles requiring creativity, empathy, or complex decision-making, which remain less likely to be affected by automation, at least at this stage of AI development.

Socio-economic and Cultural Contexts

The vulnerability of administrative roles to displacement by AI is not uniform; it varies significantly depending on socio-economic and cultural factors.

Understanding these differences is an important factor when designing effective strategies for mitigating job losses.

For instance, in high-income countries like the United States, AI-powered chatbots are increasingly replacing human customer service representatives in both public and private-sector call centres. It is worth noting that many of these jobs are already outsourced overseas, so the impact will be felt in countries well known for outsourcing services such as India, the Philippines, and South Africa. This shift is primarily driven by the need to cut labour costs and enhance efficiency. Workers, especially those with higher education or access to retraining programmes, may find better opportunities to transition into new roles through reskilling initiatives. However, job displacement can still have significant psychological effects, including reduced social participation and well-being, particularly for those accustomed to stable employment, and create financial hardship through the transition process.

In lower-income countries where customer service jobs are often outsourced due to lower labour costs, automation can have a more severe socio-economic impact. Many workers in these regions lack access to retraining programmes or social safety nets, making it more difficult to recover from job losses. Cultural factors, such as reliance on extended family for financial support, may help alleviate some economic pressures but can also intensify social stigma and psychological distress linked to unemployment.

This contrast underscores how socio-economic conditions, such as income levels and access to retraining, and cultural contexts, including societal attitudes towards unemployment, shape the impact of job displacement. Recognising these differences is important when developing targeted solutions, such as region-specific retraining initiatives and stronger social safety nets, to mitigate the negative effects of automation on administrative roles.

Economic Disparities and Automation Readiness

As highlighted in the previous section, in high-income countries, public-sector workers often have access to robust retraining programmes and alternative employment opportunities, which can mitigate the impact of automation. For example, in Denmark, government initiatives focus on transitioning displaced workers into new roles through comprehensive upskilling programmes.

The Danish adult apprenticeship and vocational training programme allows unemployed people without formal qualifications to pursue skilled vocational education while receiving unemployment benefits. Targeting unskilled workers and those with outdated skills, this programme enables participants to undertake up to two years of vocational training, with financial support provided through a combination of reduced-rate unemployment benefits and optional loans. Funded by the national government and municipalities, the programme has an annual budget of approximately €20.1 million.[6]

Another cornerstone of Denmark's workforce development strategy is the 'Arbejdsmarkedsuddannelser' (AMU) system, which focuses on continuous upskilling for both skilled and unskilled workers. This system is particularly effective during economic downturns or instances of structural unemployment, such as factory closures, as it quickly designs targeted training programmes to facilitate transitions into new industries. Developed in close collaboration with trade unions, job centres, and employers, the AMU system ensures that workers acquire skills aligned with evolving labour market demands.[7]

To further guide upskilling efforts, Denmark maintains 'Positive lists' that identify occupations facing labour shortages. Updated biannually, these lists help shape training initiatives by prioritising high-demand roles. For example, recent updates have added positions including hardware developers, business intelligence managers, and electronics mechanics, while removing roles that are becoming obsolete; ironically, the obsolete list includes IT support staff and finance assistants.[8]

At the regional level, Regional Labour Market Councils play a crucial role in coordinating upskilling efforts based on local workforce needs. These councils collaborate with vocational education providers, businesses, and job centres to develop targeted training programmes that address skills shortages in industries undergoing significant transformations, such as digitisation and the green economy.[9]

Denmark has also integrated sustainability into its vocational education system as part of its green transition strategy. The government allocates approximately €13.44 million annually to fund programmes focused on climate adaptation and sustainability skills, ensuring that both unemployed and employed individuals are prepared for emerging roles in the green economy.[10]

Through these initiatives, Denmark takes a proactive approach to workforce displacement, equipping workers with the skills needed to adapt to economic and technological shifts.

By contrast, in emerging economies, public administration often serves as a primary source of employment, particularly in rural areas. Automation in these economies risks creating severe social disruptions. For instance, India's extensive bureaucratic system employs millions in clerical roles. As AI systems increasingly handle administrative tasks, entire communities that rely on government employment may face significant economic instability.

For these reasons, the Indian government is focusing on skilling and livelihood diversification to create sustainable opportunities. India's 2025 budget introduced the Rural Prosperity and Resilience Programme, designed to equip rural youth, women, and small farmers with new skills, particularly in technology-driven fields such as AI. By integrating advanced training methods and fostering entrepreneurship, this initiative aims to reduce rural reliance on agriculture and open pathways to new industries.[11]

Through a combination of employment guarantees, targeted skilling, and entrepreneurial support, India is working to create a more resilient rural workforce, capable of adapting to economic and technological shifts while ensuring social security for vulnerable populations.

Psychological and Social Impacts of Displacement

As we have already pointed out, the loss of administrative roles to automation can have far-reaching psychological and social consequences. Automation diminishes workers' sense of achievement by disconnecting their tasks from meaningful outcomes. A 2024 study found that industrial automation led to lower perceived accomplishment, as workers felt detached from final products. This disconnect often results in a diminished sense of purpose.[12] Similarly, administrative workers who derive identity from their roles experience crises when automation replaces them. A mixed-method study in 2024 revealed that displaced workers had lower self-esteem scores compared to the general population, with many expressing existential uncertainty and feelings of betrayal by their employers.[13]

A 2024 analysis of European workers found that robotisation decreased workplace autonomy and meaningfulness, fostering detachment. Marginalised groups report isolation in reorganised workplaces, often feeling like 'outsiders'. At a broader level, automation has weakened social cohesion in regions dependent on at-risk industries, widening urban–rural divides. Redesigning work by fostering human–machine collaboration, where AI handles repetitive tasks while preserving roles requiring empathy, can help restore workers' sense of purpose.

The psychological impact of automation extends beyond economic loss, reshaping workers' self-perception and social integration. Addressing these challenges requires comprehensive policies that prioritise mental health support and ensure a more inclusive technological transition.

Community-Level Impacts

In regions where government employment forms the backbone of local economies, the displacement of administrative workers can have cascading effects. Reduced income among displaced workers diminishes consumer spending, weakens local businesses, and strains social safety nets. This is particularly evident in rural areas or small towns, where alternative employment opportunities may be scarce.

Governments must consider these broader socio-economic impacts when planning automation initiatives. Without proactive measures, the economic benefits of automation may be overshadowed by the social costs of unemployment and community destabilisation.

Opportunities for Workforce Resilience

Amid the challenges of automation lies an opportunity to reimagine the nature of public administration. Rather than focusing solely on the risks, governments can leverage AI to create a more dynamic and resilient workforce.

As AI takes over routine tasks, administrative roles can evolve to focus on higher-order functions that require human judgement, creativity, and interpersonal skills. For example:

- Citizen engagement: Public servants can dedicate more time to interacting with their clients, addressing complex inquiries, and building trust in government services.
- Policy development: Administrative workers can transition into roles that involve analysing data insights generated by AI systems to inform policy decisions.
- Oversight and ethics: New roles can emerge in monitoring and auditing AI systems to ensure fairness, accountability, and compliance with ethical standards.

A Vision for the Future

The automation of administrative roles presents both a challenge and an opportunity for public administration. While AI systems are increasingly capable of managing structured workflows and rule-based tasks, a new horizon is emerging in which human capabilities can be redirected towards more meaningful public service. By turning vulnerability into resilience, governments have the chance to shape a public-sector workforce that combines technological efficiency with a more human-centred approach to service delivery.

Achieving this shift will require more than technical adaptation. It calls for a fundamental reimagining of administrative work, where displaced employees are able to find renewed purpose through citizen engagement, policy development, and the ethical oversight of the very systems that have replaced their previous roles.

The path forward depends on proactive investment in both digital infrastructure and human capital, with a particular focus on the socio-economic inequalities that risk being deepened by this transition. Success should not be measured by cost savings alone but by our ability to preserve social cohesion, protect vulnerable communities, and build public institutions that use automation to become more responsive, empathetic, and equitable.

As we navigate this pivotal moment in public administration, the true test will be whether we can harness the transformative power of AI while upholding our collective responsibility to those whose livelihoods and identities are tied to the very functions now being redefined.

In the next chapter, we explore the broader implications of AI-driven job transformation, examining how public service work itself is being redefined in the AI era.

Notes

1 Financial Times (2025), Transcript: Martin Wolf talks to David Autor — could AI be a bigger threat to US jobs than China?, www.ft.com/content/4e260abd-2528-4d34-8fa4-a21eabfd6db9 (accessed on 22 April 2025).

2 Tony Blair Institute for Global Change (2024), *The Potential Impact of AI on the Public Sector Workforce: A Companion to the Economic Case for Reimagining the State*, https://institute.global/insights/economic-prosperity/the-potential-impact-of-ai-on-the-public-sector-workforce (accessed on 28 March 2025).
3 Model Evaluation & Threat Research conducts research on, develops, and runs evaluations of frontier AI systems' ability to complete complex tasks without human input.
4 Financial Times (2025), Why hasn't AI taken your job yet?, www.ft.com/content/471b5eba-2a71-4650-a019-e8d4065b78a0 (accessed on 12 April 2025).
5 Kiplinger (2024), U.S. Treasury's AI is catching tax cheats and saving billions, www.kiplinger.com/taxes/treasury-ai-catching-tax-cheats-and-savings-billions (accessed on 30 March 2025).
6 European Employment Policy Observatory (2015), *EEPO Review Spring 2015: Upskilling Unemployed Adults*, https://vbn.aau.dk/files/227968798/Denmark_Review_Upskilling_Mar2015_final.pdf (accessed on 30 March 2025).
7 Electronic Platform for Adult Learning in Europe (2022), The AMU system lets the Danish workforce continuously improve its skills, https://epale.ec.europa.eu/en/blog/amu-system-lets-danish-workforce-continuously-improve-its-skills (accessed on 30 March 2025).
8 Fragomen (2025), Denmark: Positive Lists for graduates, skilled workers updated in January 2025, www.fragomen.com/insights/denmark-positive-lists-for-graduates-skilled-workers-updated-in-january-2025.html (accessed on 30 March 2025)
9 CEDEFOP (No date), The Regional Labour Market Councils (RAR), www.cedefop.europa.eu/en/tools/matching-skills/all-instruments/regional-labour-market-councils-rar (accessed on 30 March 2025).
10 CEDEFOP (2022), Denmark: Green transition in vocational education, www.cedefop.europa.eu/en/news/denmark-green-transition-vocational-education (accessed on 30 March 2025).
11 Business Standard (2025), Budget 2025: Rs 1.88 trn for rural sector, MGNREGS allocation unchanged, www.business-standard.com/budget/news/budget-2025-rs-1-88-trn-for-rural-sector-mgnregs-allocation-unchanged-125020101503_1.html (accessed on 30 March 2025).
12 Vienna University of Economics and Business (2024), Humans vs. machines? Impact of automation on mental health, www.wu.ac.at/en/the-university/news-and-events/news/details-news/detail/humans-vs-machines-impact-of-automation-on-mental-health (accessed on 30 March 2025).
13 M. M. Khan, N. Aslam, and M. Fuzail (2024), Navigating the emotional turmoil: Understanding the psychological impact of robotics-induced job displacement, *Bulletin of Business and Economics*, 13(3).

Chapter 7

Beyond Job Losses

AI's Impact on the Nature of Public Work

As artificial intelligence (AI) continues to reshape public administration, its impact extends well beyond job elimination. In fact, many public-facing administrative staff would argue that current workloads are already unsustainable, and that budget constraints make it unlikely that more staff will be recruited to meet growing demand.

AI is not merely a substitute for human labour in repetitive tasks; it is a transformative force that is redefining the nature of work across the public sector. While much attention has been paid to the displacement of administrative roles, far less has been said about AI's potential to enhance existing positions, create entirely new categories of employment, and redefine the relationship between human workers and intelligent systems.

This chapter explores the evolving nature of public-sector work in the age of AI. It highlights examples of successful upskilling, examines the potential of human–AI collaboration, and outlines strategies for preparing a resilient, adaptive workforce.

Evolving Public-Sector Roles: A Shift in Focus

The integration of AI into public service is leading to a redefinition of traditional administrative roles. As AI systems take over routine tasks such as data entry, compliance checks, and scheduling, public servants will eventually have more time to focus on responsibilities that require creativity, emotional intelligence, complex problem-solving, and, above all, empathy.

DOI: 10.4324/9781003673897-10

From Clerks to Analysts

One notable transformation is the shift from clerical to analytical roles. For example, tax agencies using AI to automate routine audits allow human auditors to concentrate on more complex cases requiring nuanced judgement. In Denmark, the tax administration's use of AI-driven fraud detection systems has enabled staff to focus on interpreting patterns and devising strategies to address systemic tax evasion.

Similarly, in healthcare administration, AI systems handle appointment scheduling and resource allocation, freeing administrators to engage in patient advocacy and system-wide planning. The Cleveland Clinic's Virtual Command Centre exemplifies the use of AI in healthcare administration. Developed in collaboration with Palantir Technologies, this AI-powered platform enhances patient flow, staffing, and operating room scheduling by analysing vast datasets, including historical patterns and real-time information.[1] By forecasting patient demand and detecting potential bottlenecks, the system enables more efficient resource allocation. For example, it ensures that an optimal number of nurses, doctors, and support staff are available when needed. Additionally, it streamlines operating room scheduling, minimising delays and maximising resource efficiency. These improvements have resulted in reduced patient wait times, smoother hospital operations, cost savings, and enhanced overall care delivery.

Transforming Government Service Delivery

In June 2024, Slack's Workforce Lab conducted a global survey of over 10,000 desk workers, revealing a significant gap between executive enthusiasm for AI and its actual adoption among employees. While 96 per cent of executives expressed an urgency to integrate AI into business operations, a sevenfold increase over six months, only 32 per cent of desk workers reported having experimented with AI tools, and a mere 7 per cent considered AI outputs completely trustworthy for work-related tasks.

Among those who have used AI, 81 per cent reported increased productivity, with many also noting higher levels of engagement and satisfaction. However, broader adoption is hindered by concerns about privacy, data security, and the absence of clear usage guidelines. Nearly 40 per cent of surveyed companies have yet to establish formal AI policies.

The survey also highlighted an emerging gender gap in AI usage, particularly among Gen Z workers, where men are 25 per cent more likely to have tried AI tools compared to women. Additionally, workers spend approximately one-third of their day on low-value tasks, and there's a risk that time saved through AI could be redirected towards more administrative work rather than strategic activities.[2]

To address these challenges, the report recommends the *PET plan: Permission, Education, and Training*. Establishing clear AI usage guidelines, providing comprehensive education, and offering training will enhance trust and facilitate greater adoption of AI tools in the workplace.

What we learn from this transformatory time is clear: organisations must actively create environments where employees feel safe to explore and experiment with AI. Just as early digital tools required onboarding and structured support, today's AI demands thoughtful implementation. This means setting up clear guardrails, offering practical guidance, and establishing policies that promote confident, responsible use. The reward for this investment is significant; according to the report, companies that create the right environment gain up to six times more engagement with AI tools.

Yet, the data also shows that 43 per cent of desk workers still haven't used AI in their daily workflows. That's not simply resistance; it reflects a fundamental challenge to AI implementation. It is a complex, evolving technology that remains imperfect and, at times, unreliable. Treating AI solely as a cost-cutting mechanism, rather than a tool to augment human capability, risks undermining both trust and long-term impact.

As AI agents begin to act more autonomously on behalf of users, a key question emerges: how do we build trust in systems that make decisions for us? The answer lies in rapid experimentation, guided by human oversight. However, technical roadblocks persist, as messy data, poor IT integration, and unclear workflows often slow progress. There is also a financial reality: AI is expensive. While much of the current cost is borne by technology providers, sustainable adoption will ultimately require a clear return on investment. Navigating this frontier demands both strategic vision and practical patience.

Box 7.1 – Case Study: Revolutionising Teamwork in the AI Age

A recent Harvard Business School working paper, titled *The Cybernetic Teammate: A Field Experiment on Generative AI Reshaping Teamwork and Expertise*, reveals that the integration of generative AI into teamwork significantly enhances overall performance.

The experiment showed that generative AI significantly boosts team performance. Both individuals and teams using AI outperformed their non-AI counterparts, with performance improvements of 0.37 and 0.39 standard deviations, respectively, compared to just 0.24 for traditional teams without AI. For readers who are unfamiliar with statistics, think of the standard deviation as a way to measure how far performance has moved from the average. The data suggests that AI makes a clear difference, especially when used by teams. AI users also completed tasks faster: individuals saved 16.4 per cent of time and teams saved 12.7 per cent, while producing more comprehensive solutions.[3]

Generative AI also helped level the playing field across different expertise areas. Without AI, commercial experts tended to produce market-focused ideas while technical professionals created more technical solutions. With AI assistance, this division faded as participants generated more balanced proposals spanning both domains. Notably, non-product development employees using AI-created solutions comparable to those from core product development teams, effectively bridging expertise gaps.

The emotional impact was equally significant. AI users reported more positive emotions such as excitement and enthusiasm, while experiencing less anxiety and frustration. These emotional benefits matched or exceeded those in traditional team environments, though interestingly, AI users were less confident about their performance despite objectively better results.

Teams using AI were also more likely to generate breakthrough ideas ranking in the top 10 per cent of all submissions. While individuals with AI also showed improvement in this area, the combination of AI and human collaboration proved especially powerful. Rather than simply copying AI outputs, participants engaged in an iterative process that blended AI suggestions with human expertise.

These findings position generative AI as a *cybernetic teammate* that enhances performance, bridges expertise gaps, and creates more positive work environments. By doing so, AI challenges traditional notions of teamwork. As organisations integrate AI at scale, they may need to reconsider team structures and processes to capitalise on these combined human and AI capabilities, paving the way for more flexible and efficient work configurations.

Emerging Roles in AI-Enhanced Public Work

The rapid advancement of AI has not only transformed existing professions but also created entirely new job categories tailored to the unique challenges and opportunities of this technology. For instance:

- Algorithm Auditors: Responsible for evaluating the fairness, transparency, and accuracy of AI systems.
- Citizen Experience Designers: Focused on ensuring that AI-powered services are accessible and user-friendly.
- Data Stewards: Oversee the ethical collection, storage, and use of government data, ensuring compliance with privacy regulations.
- Digital Librarians: Responsible for managing a national data library, making siloed data accessible across agencies where appropriate.

These roles reflect the growing importance of ethical oversight, user-centred design, and data governance in the public sector.

Human–AI Collaboration: A New Model of Work

The future of public service work lies in collaboration between humans and AI systems. Rather than replacing human workers, AI is increasingly viewed as a tool to augment their capabilities.

Hybrid Workflows

In hybrid workflows, humans and AI systems complement each other's strengths. AI excels at processing large datasets, identifying patterns, and performing routine tasks with consistent accuracy. Humans, meanwhile, bring creativity, empathy, and ethical judgement to the table.

For example, in environmental management, AI systems in South Korea analyse satellite imagery to detect illegal logging or pollution incidents. Human inspectors then investigate flagged issues, engage with stakeholders, and develop remediation strategies. This collaboration ensures that environmental policies are enforced efficiently, thoughtfully, and transparently.

In disaster management, AI models predict natural disasters by analysing weather patterns and historical data. Emergency responders use these predictions to coordinate evacuations and resource allocation, allowing more timely and effective interventions.

AI is transforming the nature of work, particularly in home-working contexts. In 2023 in the UK, around 48 per cent of public-sector employees were engaged in hybrid or fully remote work,[4] compared to 40 per cent in the private sector.[5] AI's integration into workplaces is expected to further revolutionise productivity by automating repetitive tasks and enabling more flexible work arrangements. However, while AI offers opportunities for efficiency, it also raises concerns about data security, equitable access to technology, and the preservation of human-centric roles in tasks requiring empathy or creativity. These developments underscore the need for inclusive policies that address both digital accessibility and the responsible use of AI in reshaping work environments.

Enhancing Decision-Making

AI's ability to provide data-driven insights enhances human decision-making across various domains. In urban planning, AI models simulate the impact of proposed developments on traffic, housing, and the environment. Planners use these insights to design more sustainable and liveable cities.

Upskilling for the AI Era: Building a Resilient Workforce

To maximise the benefits of AI-enhanced work, governments must invest in upskilling their workforce. Training programmes should focus on developing both technical and soft skills, enabling employees to collaborate effectively with AI systems.

Box 7.2 – Case Study: Successful Upskilling Initiatives

Several governments have launched programmes to prepare their workforce for the AI era. Successful initiatives provide valuable lessons:

- The UK government has launched the *Artificial Intelligence Playbook* through the Government Digital Service (GDS) to provide guidance on the safe and effective use of AI in the public sector. Civil Service Learning offers free courses on AI and there is additional training available on Government Campus, a learning platform for UK civil servants.
- Singapore's SkillsFuture initiative offers Singaporeans aged 25 and above with an initial credit of S$500 to invest in skills development, such as training in AI, data analytics, and other digital skills to help public-sector employees transition into new roles. In the 2025 budget, new initiatives have been introduced, including the SkillsFuture Level-UP programme; this is aimed at mid-career individuals and offers enhanced training support, including allowances of up to S$3,000 per month for full-time courses. Grants covering up to 70 per cent of costs are offered to support job redesign and workforce transformation projects.
- Estonia's digital governance training: Estonia has integrated regular digital literacy training into its public-sector workforce development, ensuring that employees remain adept at using and managing AI systems. The e-Governance Academy, founded in 2002, assists public-sector institutions in digital transformation. It offers training, consultancy, and research services and has collaborated internationally to help other countries implement digital solutions. Tallin University of Technology runs a master's programme in e-Governance technologies and services.[6]
- Germany's job transition programmes: Germany's labour market policies emphasise vocational training and career counselling, helping displaced workers find new opportunities in emerging fields.
- Canada's Digital Academy: Offers courses on AI and digital transformation for public servants, fostering a culture of continuous learning and adaptability.

These initiatives demonstrate the importance of proactive workforce development in ensuring that employees can thrive in an AI-enhanced environment.

Challenges in Transitioning to an AI-Enabled Workforce

While the potential of human–AI collaboration is vast, the transition to an AI-enabled workforce is not without challenges.

Overcoming Resistance to Change

Resistance to AI adoption is a common barrier, driven by fears of job displacement, scepticism about the technology's reliability, and sometimes a general fear of technology by older managers. Governments can address these concerns through clear communication, transparency, and inclusive planning processes. For example, Finland's phased rollout of AI systems in welfare administration included extensive employee consultations and training programmes, fostering trust and acceptance. In December 2017, Finland introduced its national AI strategy, Finland's Age of Artificial Intelligence, which aims to position the country as a global leader in AI application. The strategy emphasises training and life-long learning and recognises the challenges that workers face to adapt to evolving job requirements. Finland's strategy involves extensive consultation with employees to address ethical considerations. Finland has made significant strides in digital public services, with 92 per cent of internet users engaging with e-government platforms, significantly surpassing the EU's 65 per cent. The Finnish Centre for Artificial Intelligence projected that effective AI implementation could boost Finland's GDP by EUR 20 billion, translating to an 8 per cent annual increase.[7]

Ensuring Fairness and Inclusivity

Without careful planning, the shift to AI-enhanced work risks exacerbating existing inequalities. Marginalised communities may face greater barriers to accessing training programmes or adapting to new roles. To address this, governments must prioritise equity in workforce development, offering tailored support for disadvantaged groups.

Redefining the Nature of Public Service

AI's integration into public administration is not just about efficiency; it is an opportunity to redefine the relationship between governments and citizens.

In June 2025, the UK government announced that all civil servants would undergo AI training from the autumn, with officials 'tasked with assessing how they can use the technology to streamline their own work wherever possible'. The government said it was part of plans to 'create a civil service that will take more calculated risks', with cabinet secretary Sir Chris Wormald saying he wanted them to consider how it 'needs to evolve and reform'.[8]

Ethical Considerations and Equity

As governments integrate AI into public administration, ethical considerations must guide the process. New legislation, such as the EU AI Act, emphasises the importance of ensuring fairness and inclusivity to maintain public trust and social cohesion.

Addressing Algorithmic Bias: Canadian and UK Models

AI systems are prone to replicating and amplifying biases present in historical data. Governments must implement rigorous testing and auditing processes to identify and mitigate these biases.

Canada's Algorithmic Impact Assessment (AIA) tool provides an interesting example. The AIA is a mandatory risk assessment instrument designed to help federal institutions understand and manage the risks associated with automation decision systems, requiring public agencies to evaluate the potential risks of AI systems before deployment.[9] Before an AI system goes live, public agencies are required to evaluate the potential risks of AI systems, assessing everything from fairness and bias to transparency and accountability.

The AIA tool guides agencies through a series of methodical steps. Initially, departments define the scope and purpose of their AI projects, establish clear objectives, and identify which communities may be affected. This early stage is important to ensure that every digital initiative is anchored in a well-thought-out plan that anticipates both the potential benefits and the inherent risks.

Once the project is scoped, the tool initiates a risk screening process. The screening examines whether an AI system could inadvertently perpetuate existing inequalities or compromise privacy. It compels decision-makers to ask hard questions about the data used, the algorithmic models, and the possibility of unintended consequences. If significant risks are identified, the process then moves to a detailed risk assessment.

During this phase, the tool scrutinises the system's components. It evaluates whether the system's decision-making processes can be clearly explained and if proper measures are in place to safeguard against bias. By requiring agencies to document every step, from initial design to final deployment, the AIA tool ensures that accountability is maintained throughout the lifecycle of the project. This meticulous approach not only minimises potential harm but also builds public trust in government-run AI systems.

Furthermore, the process is iterative. As technology evolves and new risks emerge, periodic reviews and updates are mandated. Stakeholder engagement is a core component, inviting insights from experts, community representatives, and advocacy groups. This collective scrutiny helps refine the system, ensuring that ethical standards are consistently met.

In summary, Canada's AIA tool is more than a procedural requirement; it embodies a commitment to responsible innovation. By mandating thorough risk assessments and continuous oversight, the Canadian government reinforces its commitment to creating digital solutions that are as fair and transparent as they are innovative.

In 2024, the UK introduced the Public Authority Algorithmic and Automated Decision-Making Systems Bill. The bill aims to regulate the deployment of automated and algorithmic tools in the public sector. If enacted, the bill would have three key elements. First, to conduct and publish impact assessments prior to deploying an algorithmic or automated decision-making system, public authorities are required to evaluate the system's fairness and compliance with anti-discrimination laws, including mandatory bias assessments. Second, to maintain algorithmic transparency, records – including the extent of human oversight – must be documented and made publicly available. Third, logging mechanisms are required to automatically generate logs of public authorities' decision-making processes.[10]

Bridging the Digital Divide

Ensuring equitable access to AI-driven services is another foundational priority. Programmes like Kenya's Ajira Digital initiative,[11] which trains young people in digital skills, demonstrate how technology can create opportunities for underserved populations. By combining automation with efforts to close the digital divide, governments can ensure that AI benefits are shared broadly.

A Vision for the Future

The future of public service work lies in collaboration, adaptability, and innovation. AI will not replace public servants; rather, it will empower them to focus on higher-value tasks, deliver improved services, engage more meaningfully with citizens, and address complex societal challenges with greater capacity.

To realise this vision, governments must:

- Invest in workforce development, equipping employees with the training and resources needed to take on new roles and responsibilities.
- Foster collaboration, encouraging human–AI partnerships that combine the unique strengths of both.
- Prioritise ethics, ensuring that AI systems are designed and deployed in ways that uphold public trust and promote fairness.

By embracing these principles, public-sector organisations can build a workforce that is not only prepared for change but also equipped to thrive in the AI era.

The next chapter will examine the broader challenges and opportunities presented by AI in the management of public-sector human resources.

Notes

1 Ensora Health (No date), Using AI to improve healthcare efficiency: Three case studies, https://ensorahealth.com/blog/using-ai-to-improve-healthcare-efficiency-three-case-studies/ (accessed on 30 March 2025).

2 Slack (2024), Despite AI enthusiasm, workforce index reveals workers aren't yet unlocking its benefits, https://slack.com/intl/en-gb/blog/news/the-workforce-index-june-2024?utm_source=chatgpt.com (accessed on 11 April 2025).

3 E. Mollick *et al.* (2025), The cybernetic teammate: A field experiment on generative AI reshaping teamwork and expertise, Harvard Business School Working Paper No. 25-043, https://papers.ssrn.com/sol3/papers.cfm?abstract_id=5188231 (accessed on 12 April 2025).

4 Civil Service World (2023), Hybrid working more common among public servants than in private sector, www.civilserviceworld.com/professions/article/public-sector-hybrid-home-working-more-common-than-private-sector (accessed on 30 March 2025).

5 StandOut CV (2025), Remote working statistics UK, https://standout-cv.com/stats/remote-working-statistics-uk (accessed on 30 March 2025).

6 Estonian Association of Information Technology and Telecommunications (No date), e-Governance training programme, https://itl.ee/en/estonian-ict-cluster/projects/e-governance-training-programme/ (accessed on 30 March 2025).

7 FCAI (No date), Artificial intelligence doesn't exist in a vacuum: We promote AI that benefits society and industry and helps solve the real-life problems of real people, https://fcai.fi/impact (accessed on 30 March 2025).

8 Financial Times (2025), Nvidia chief says UK lacks digital infrastructure as Keir Starmer pledges £1bn for AI, www.ft.com/content/cc04adfb-81b2-477f-b85c-cc042e8f83a8 (accessed on 15 June 2025).

9 Government of Canada (2024), Algorithmic Impact Assessment tool, www.canada.ca/en/government/system/digital-government/digital-government-innovations/responsible-use-ai/algorithmic-impact-assessment.html (accessed on 30 March 2025).

10 UK Parliament (2025), Public Authority Algorithmic and Automated Decision-Making Systems Bill, https://bills.parliament.uk/bills/3760 (accessed on 30 March 2025).

11 Kenya's Ministry of Information, Communication, and Digital Economy (No date), Ajira Digital Program, https://ajiradigital.go.ke/#/index (accessed on 30 March 2025).

Chapter 8

Reinventing Public Service

The AI–HR Revolution

The evolution of artificial intelligence (AI) is creating unprecedented opportunities to transform human resource management in the public sector. Traditional HR functions, once defined by manual processes and rigid structures, are being reimagined through the integration of AI technologies that support more responsive, data-driven, and personalised approaches to talent management.

This transformation elevates HR from a primarily administrative function to a strategic driver of organisational success. By using AI-powered analytics, government HR departments can deliver individualised coaching, training, and career development based on real-time insights into employee performance and skill gaps. This personalisation reflects the tailored experiences people increasingly expect in their daily lives, addressing individual development needs while remaining aligned with the broader goals of public service. As governments compete for talent in high-demand fields such as AI, machine learning, and data science, modernising recruitment processes becomes essential. AI-enhanced selection and onboarding can improve efficiency while upholding the transparency, fairness, and ethical standards that are central to public service. This balanced approach helps public institutions attract and retain critical expertise without compromising the core values of equity and accountability.

However, significant obstacles remain. Public-sector recruitment is often slowed by bureaucratic constraints. Requirements such as mandatory national advertising, even when a suitable local candidate is available, and fixed pay scales

DOI: 10.4324/9781003673897-11

that do not reflect market conditions, make the process less appealing to skilled IT professionals who are in high demand.

Rethinking Government HR: More Digital, More Personal, More Impactful

In the public sector, traditional HR functions have become increasingly outdated amid rapid technological advances, especially in generative AI, combined with evolving work practices, shifting employee expectations, and heightened demands for transparency and accountability. Public agencies that modernise their people management practices are better positioned to deliver effective services, optimise resource allocation, and enhance public trust.

A 2025 McKinsey article, 'A new operating model for people management: More personal, more tech, more human',[1] outlines a vision for transforming people management through a re-engineered operating model that integrates technology, personalisation, and human-centric leadership.

The article emphasises that just as consumers now expect personalised experiences, employees also benefit from tailored approaches that address their individual development needs. AI-enabled tools can help by analysing performance data and identifying skill gaps, supporting more targeted professional growth. This, in turn, allows managers to focus their time on delivering empathetic, people-centred leadership.

As AI reshapes the workforce, the public sector needs to rethink its people management strategies, embracing systems that deliver personalised coaching, targeted training, and tailored career development to meet the evolving needs of employees.

Union membership in the United Kingdom Civil Service and the wider public sector is much higher than in the private sector. An estimated 60 to 65 per cent of civil servants are members of a trade union compared to 13 per cent in the private sector. The trade union's coordinating body, the Trades Union Congress, has actively participated in the evolution of thinking about the application of AI and contributed ideas to the draft AI bill in 2024, the Artificial Intelligence (Regulation and Employment Rights) Bill.[2] The bill's four key provisions are: transparency and explainability, rights to human review, prohibition of harmful AI practices, and the right to disconnect that covers disconnecting from work communications outside agreed working hours.

Traditional bureaucratic hierarchies and rigid, siloed functions are identified as significant obstacles to agility and innovation. The report advocates for a reimagined structure in which dynamic talent marketplaces align employee skills with the evolving needs of every agency. In this framework, workforce planning shifts from static role definitions and infrequent promotions to a proactive, data-driven process that continuously adapts to policy changes and public priorities.

Central to the proposed transformation is a new operating model for the people function, structured around a *strategic triumvirate* of specialised roles. The model redefines the HR function into three distinct areas:

- Strategists, who translate policy and service objectives into actionable people priorities.
- Scientists, who leverage data analytics to design and implement interventions that enhance employee experience and operational efficiency.
- Technologists, who develop and maintain the technological infrastructure necessary to support these functions.

Traditional Centres of Excellence are envisioned to evolve into flexible, cross-functional teams that can be reassembled dynamically as strategic priorities shift, while routine administrative tasks are largely automated through advanced AI and robotic process automation.

This shift has major implications for the public sector, where tight budgets, complex regulations, and changing employee expectations call for a more flexible and data-informed approach to human resources. By adopting this model, public-sector organisations can improve how they attract and keep talented people, make better use of their resources, and deliver higher-quality services to the public. AI and automation can also ease the burden of routine administrative tasks, freeing HR teams to focus on long-term strategies that create lasting public value.

Investing in modern technology is presented as essential to enabling this transformation. The report recommends the development of centralised, cloud-based data platforms that integrate workforce and operational data from multiple sources. These platforms would provide real-time insights to support more informed, evidence-based decision-making. It also calls for replacing outdated and fragmented systems with a modern, AI-enabled digital infrastructure designed to support more personalised employee experiences, from onboarding to ongoing professional development.

New tools such as digital twins (virtual models that use real-time data to show how systems are working) and personal agents (software that acts on a person's behalf) are highlighted as promising ways to deliver continuous, tailored support in both the public and private sectors.

However, adopting these more efficient, modern models requires substantial investment in both people and technology. Many European countries are under serious budget pressure, with rising costs for social services and increasing demands for defence spending. Bridging the funding gap will be a major challenge to swift implementation.

For the public sector, this shift to AI-enabled technology is especially important for overcoming the inefficiencies of legacy systems and delivering more responsive, citizen-focused services. By adopting centralised, cloud-based platforms, governments can break down data silos, improve workforce planning, and make faster, more informed decisions based on real-time data.

The McKinsey article outlines this transformation by grouping organisations into different categories, or *archetypes*, depending on their stage of progress. Those just beginning are encouraged to set a clear vision and test new ideas through pilot projects. Organisations that have already started to benefit from technology should focus on refining their processes through ongoing learning. Meanwhile, more advanced organisations are ready to adopt fully AI-driven models, where data insight plays a central role in strategic decision-making. A common theme across all these groups is the importance of having a long-term vision, building cross-functional teams, and maintaining momentum through continuous experimentation and improvement.

In the public sector, this maturity-based approach is essential for navigating the unique challenges of large-scale transformation, such as regulatory constraints, stakeholder complexity, and budgetary limitations. Government agencies and public institutions can use this framework to assess their current capabilities, prioritise targeted interventions, and gradually scale innovations that enhance workforce efficiency and service delivery.

Despite the focus on technological innovation and automation, the McKinsey article maintains that human qualities such as empathy, judgement, and inspiration remain indispensable. The transformation is not intended to replace human interaction but rather to empower managers to focus on cultivating a supportive, ethical, and engaging work culture that meets the needs of employees. In this reimagined framework, the people function evolves into a strategic partner that effectively balances technological efficiency with the essential values of public accountability and service excellence.

By combining advanced technology with more personalised employee experiences and a flexible, streamlined structure, the proposed model aims to shift HR from an administrative function to a key driver of public service success. The report presents this transformation as both urgent and achievable, offering early adopters a clear advantage in today's increasingly complex and fast-changing public-sector landscape.

The Future of Public Hiring: AI-Driven Selection and Onboarding

Staff turnover in the public sector in the UK and the US runs at a staggering one in eight – that is, 12 per cent of employees leave each year. So, the recruiting process is both costly and time-consuming. AI selection and onboarding in the public sector represent a significant evolution in the management of human resources within government institutions. While private companies have adopted AI-driven hiring solutions that offer greater flexibility, the public sector must navigate stricter regulatory frameworks, union requirements, and ethical considerations. Understanding the key distinctions between these domains highlights the unique challenges and opportunities associated with AI integration.

In corporate environments, AI-driven recruitment tools are increasingly utilised to improve hiring efficiency. Companies leverage AI for résumé screening, candidate assessments, and automated interview scheduling, significantly reducing time-to-hire. These systems prioritise efficiency, cost reduction, and competitive advantage, often allowing for rapid experimentation with new technologies. AI-powered insights help organisations identify high-performing candidates by analysing patterns in skills, experience, and behavioural attributes.

Conversely, AI adoption in government recruitment must align with strict compliance, transparency, and accountability requirements. Unlike private firms, public institutions must ensure that AI-driven processes uphold fairness, mitigate bias, and adhere to legal frameworks such as data protection laws and public procurement guidelines. The integration of AI in the public sector primarily aims to enhance efficiency while maintaining public trust and equitable hiring practices.

One of the primary benefits of AI in public-sector recruitment is enhanced efficiency. Automating repetitive tasks such as document verification and background checks reduces administrative workload. AI streamlines initial candidate evaluations, shortening recruitment timelines and allowing HR professionals to focus on higher-value activities. Another advantage is improved transparency and fairness. Standardised algorithms assist in mitigating unconscious bias by evaluating candidates based on objective criteria. AI-generated data insights help ensure consistency and fairness in decision-making processes. Additionally, AI facilitates customised onboarding experiences tailored to specific roles and departmental needs. Virtual training modules and adaptive learning platforms improve employee engagement and retention.

Exciting new HR software like Metaview.ai uses AI to take notes directly from spoken interviews, automatically identifying the interviewer and candidate. An AI-generated summary suggests questions and automates the write-up of interview notes. The software highlights the questions asked, generates bullet points or prose of responses, and generates interview statistics. The software can play back transcripts and prefill client-designed score cards. Not only does this type of software speed up the recruitment process, but it also improves the process by increasing transparency and providing a permanent record of the process. Should a candidate not be suitable for the current position, the database can flag them for a more suitable position in the future.

Despite these benefits, several challenges must be considered. Public-sector AI deployment must adhere to legal standards concerning data privacy, fairness, and accountability. Governments are subject to heightened scrutiny, requiring transparency in AI decision-making processes. Human oversight and contextual judgement remain essential, as AI can support candidate evaluations, but human intervention is necessary for nuanced decision-making. Experienced HR professionals must interpret AI-generated insights to ensure ethical and practical hiring decisions. Furthermore, bias and algorithmic limitations pose another challenge. Despite efforts to create fair AI models, eliminating bias entirely will always be challenging. Ongoing monitoring and adjustments are necessary to prevent unintended discrimination in hiring practices, and this needs to be combined with a fair appeals process.

Box 8.1 – Case Study: The UK Department for Science, Innovation & Technology's Recruitment Toolkit

The UK Department for Science, Innovation & Technology produced a recruitment toolkit in 2024. The toolkit aims to support employers, HR teams, and tech providers in using AI ethically, fairly, and legally. Figure 8.1 covers five risk themes.

Figure 8.1 Risk themes in the UK Department for Science, Innovation & Technology's recruitment toolkit

Source: Authors' elaboration

The toolkit includes risk identification templates, procurement checklists, various guidance notes and case studies.[3]

As AI technology continues to evolve, public-sector institutions are encouraged to adopt a hybrid model that balances automation with human expertise. This approach ensures that recruitment processes remain efficient while upholding core values of transparency, fairness, and public accountability. Investments in AI should be accompanied by comprehensive training programmes for HR personnel, ensuring they can effectively oversee and interpret AI-driven decisions. Regular assessments of AI systems will be crucial to maintaining ethical standards and optimising their effectiveness. By embracing responsible AI integration, the public sector can modernise their HR functions while safeguarding the principles of equitable hiring and workforce development.

The UK NHS is currently facing a staffing crisis, with approximately 112,000 vacancies across the organisation. While the NHS is often described as *data rich, but not data smart*, there is a growing recognition that more sophisticated data analysis could help address recruitment challenges. Advanced analytics and AI can be leveraged to better understand why employees leave, identify delays in the hiring process, and pinpoint inefficiencies that contribute to prolonged vacancies. For example, recruitment software provider Oleeo reported that its AI-driven platform reduced time-to-hire by 29 per cent at a particular NHS hospital trust with over 6,000 employees.[4]

The integration of AI into public-sector personnel selection and onboarding marks a transformative shift in government human resource management. While automation offers efficiency and data-driven insights, maintaining human oversight and adhering to strict ethical and legal standards remain imperative. A well-balanced approach, leveraging AI while preserving the essential role of human judgement, will enable public-sector institutions to harness the full potential of technology while ensuring fair and transparent hiring practices. The appendix features a sample checklist on how AI can be effectively utilised in human resources.

Future Jobs: How the Public Sector Can Navigate the Search for Specific Candidates

In January 2025, the World Economic Forum published the report *Future of Jobs Report 2025*.[5] The report underscores that AI is emerging as a key driver of labour market transformation, with AI-related roles among the fastest growing in the 2025–2030 period. It identifies several key AI-related roles that are central to driving future workforce transformation.

AI and machine learning specialists play a critical role in shaping intelligent systems by designing, implementing, and optimising machine learning and deep learning models. Their work involves developing sophisticated algorithms capable of analysing vast datasets, automating decision-making processes, and driving innovation across various products and services.

Big data specialists play a crucial role in managing and processing vast amounts of structured and unstructured data that power AI systems. They are responsible for building and maintaining data architecture, pipelines, and storage solutions, ensuring that high-quality data is readily available for analysis and decision-making.

Software and applications developers are at the forefront of creating AI-driven solutions that enhance user experiences and improve operational efficiency. They design, build, and refine software applications that integrate AI, enabling smarter automation, predictive capabilities, and personalised interactions. Their work involves coding, testing, and optimising software to ensure seamless performance and adaptability in an ever-evolving digital landscape.

AI and machine learning specialists are expected to see significant job growth as AI and information processing technologies continue to evolve. The report suggests that these roles are among the fastest growing, with net employment growth potentially exceeding 75 per cent between 2025 and 2030. This indicates that, relative to current employment levels, the demand for AI and machine learning specialists could more than double in the coming years. Existing rigid pay grades will exacerbate the challenge the public sector faces in competing for these high-demand employees. The common solution of resorting to hiring consultants avoids the pay-grade challenges but, of course, greatly increases costs.

Similarly, jobs for software and applications developers are expected to see substantial expansion, aligning with the broader trend of integrating AI into software platforms. The projected growth rates for these roles exceed 50 per cent a year, highlighting the increasing demand for developers who can embed intelligent automation, predictive analytics, and AI-driven functionalities into modern software applications.

This reality underscores a critical challenge for the public sector.[6] Without an updated HR strategy that aligns with the evolving job market, it will be extremely challenging to recruit and retain these professionals. Traditional hiring models, rigid structures, and slow adaptation to new workforce expectations put government institutions at risk of falling behind. To remain competitive and continue delivering effective public services, the public sector must embrace a more agile approach to talent acquisition. Without urgent reform, it risks being left without the expertise necessary to navigate an increasingly AI-driven world.

Conclusion

The integration of AI into government human resources marks more than a technological shift; it signals the beginning of a new era. As public institutions stand at this critical juncture, they face a clear choice: embrace AI-driven transformation or risk falling behind in the competition for specialised talent.

The future of public service excellence depends on a fundamental reimagining of how governments attract, develop, and support their workforce. This transformation requires moving beyond outdated bureaucratic structures towards dynamic, data-informed systems that can adapt to rapidly changing demands. A strategic alliance between HR professionals, data scientists, and technologists must lead this transition, turning policy goals into measurable outcomes and using analytics to improve both employee experience and organisational effectiveness.

Government agencies that succeed will move beyond traditional constraints, creating environments where AI handles routine tasks and public servants focus on work that is complex, creative, and impactful.

As demand for skills in AI, machine learning, and data science continues to rise, governments without modern HR capabilities will struggle to recruit and retain the talent they need. The public sector must respond with urgency and vision, adopting innovation while safeguarding the human judgement, ethical oversight, and empathy that underpin good governance.

By committing to this AI-enabled future, governments can unlock not only operational efficiencies but also a renewed capacity to serve the public with responsiveness, purpose, and integrity. The time for incremental change is over. The era of intelligent public-sector HR has arrived, and those who lead will shape its legacy.

Notes

1 McKinsey & Company (2025), A new operating model for people management: More personal, more tech, more human, www.mckinsey.com/capabilities/people-and-organisational-performance/our-insights/a-new-operating-model-for-people-management-more-personal-more-tech-more-human (accessed on 1 March 2025).

2 Trades Union Congress (2024), Artificial Intelligence (Regulation and Employment Rights) Bill, www.tuc.org.uk/research-analysis/reports/artificial-intelligence-regulation-and-employment-rights-bill (accessed on 28 March 2025).

3 UK Department for Science, Innovation & Technology (2024), Responsible AI in recruitment, www.gov.uk/government/publications/responsible-ai-in-recruitment-guide/responsible-ai-in-recruitment (accessed on 28 March 2025).

4 Oleeo (No date), University Hospitals Birmingham NHS Foundation Trust, www.oleeo.com/resources/university-hospitals-birmingham-nhs-trust/ (accessed on 20 May 2025).

5 World Economic Forum (2025), *Future of Jobs Report 2025*, https://reports.weforum.org/docs/WEF_Future_of_Jobs_Report_2025.pdf (accessed on 2 March 2025).

6 According to Eurostat, approximately 32 million individuals are employed in public service across the European Union. In comparison, data from the US Federal Reserve Bank indicates that around 23 million people are employed in public-sector roles in the United States.

Chapter 9

How Agentic AI Can Influence the Public Sector

What Is Agentic AI?

Agentic AI is a form of artificial intelligence (AI) that enables systems to operate autonomously, making decisions and executing actions with minimal human intervention.[1] It combines technologies such as machine learning, natural language processing, and large language models to create intelligent agents capable of interpreting context, setting goals, and adapting their behaviour in real time to achieve specific objectives.

This form of AI is defined by four key attributes: autonomy, decision-making ability, adaptability, and integration with other advanced technologies. Agentic systems function independently, requiring limited human oversight to complete tasks. They can analyse complex scenarios, evaluate multiple options, and determine optimal courses of action based on predefined objectives. These systems also learn continuously from experience, adjusting their strategies as conditions change, which allows them to manage complex, multi-step workflows over time.

Unlike traditional generative AI, which is often limited to content creation, agentic AI builds upon those outputs and applies them towards achieving particular goals. For example, in a customer service setting, agentic AI does more than generate replies to inquiries. It can prioritise support tickets, direct issues to the correct departments, and follow up with customers automatically, thereby improving both efficiency and user satisfaction. An example checklist for setting up agentic AI systems can be found in the appendix.

DOI: 10.4324/9781003673897-12

The Impact of Agentic AI in the Public Sector

Agentic AI is set to revolutionise the public sector by improving efficiency and reducing costs, enabling more informed decision-making, enhancing citizen services, and strengthening security and fraud detection. It also plays a crucial role in streamlining various government functions, ensuring smoother operations across departments. However, because of the greater decision-making autonomy, it is even more important to consider public support and trust, as well as address potential challenges and ethical considerations associated with its implementation.

Agentic AI can automate repetitive and time-consuming tasks in government administration, resulting in significant efficiency gains and cost reductions. For example, it can autonomously process applications for benefits or licences, handle routine inquiries through AI-powered chatbots and virtual assistants, and streamline administrative workflows to minimise bureaucratic bottlenecks. These advancements have the potential to save governments billions annually by optimising resource allocation and reducing operational costs.

By leveraging vast amounts of data, agentic AI can improve policy formulation and administrative decision-making. It analyses patterns, trends, and correlations to generate data-driven insights, helping guide decisions on resource allocation, public health initiatives, and urban planning. Additionally, it enhances the ability to predict and respond to crises more effectively, for example during pandemics. In public healthcare, agentic AI can build on generative AI by not only generating patient treatment recommendations but also autonomously scheduling follow-ups, optimising resource allocation, and ensuring compliance with medical guidelines, enhancing its ability to solve real-world healthcare challenges.

Agentic AI has the potential to greatly enhance the citizen experience when engaging with government services. It can provide instant information and assist individuals in navigating complex procedures, personalising services to meet specific needs and preferences. In the United States the U.S. Bureau of Labor Statistics estimates that 32 per cent of salaried workers do not work regular Monday to Friday daytime schedules. This reflects changes in the labour market with increasing 24-hour service, and the increase in flexible hours and remote working. These changes in work patterns have important implications for the delivery of public services. AI-driven systems offer an important benefit, offering round-the-clock availability for routine inquiries and basic services.

Government agencies can leverage agentic AI to strengthen security measures and identify fraudulent activities. By recognising anomalies and potential threats in real time – detecting fraud in tax filings, benefit claims, and procurement processes – and safeguarding sensitive information more effectively, agentic AI enhances overall security and integrity in public administration.

Several tax agencies around the world are using agentic AI to detect fraud. According to a *New York Times* article the Inland Revenue Service (IRS) is deploying new AI tools to better detect patterns of tax evasion. These AI tools are designed to spot complex structures and flag suspicious patterns, especially in entities that have been difficult to audit because of their complexity. The IRS is also reported to be using AI technology to examine crypto asset tracing using natural language processing.[2] The United Kingdom's HM Revenue and Customs (HMRC) utilises AI systems such as the "Connect" platform and large language models to detect VAT evasion and other tax discrepancies, successfully recovering billions in unpaid taxes.[3] In Australia, the Taxation Office employs advanced AI models, including gradient-boosting algorithms, to combat fraud and identify unpaid taxes, preventing billions in fraudulent claims while achieving an 85 per cent accuracy rate in detecting high-risk cases. Italy's tax authority leverages the Ve.Ra. algorithm (for further details, see Chapter 2: 'AI's Potential: Transforming Public Service Delivery') to compare financial data and uncover discrepancies in tax returns, identifying over one million high-risk cases within a single year. In Poland, the tax authority uses the STIR model to analyse taxpayer datasets for VAT fraud, significantly reducing the country's VAT gap over time.[4] Similarly, India's Business Intelligence and Fraud Analyst (BIFA) system employs agentic AI tools to detect fraudulent registrations and falsified income tax deductions.[5]

In the cultural heritage sector, AI can improve access to cultural data and streamline research processes, for example the Italian Ministry of Cultural Heritage's AI agent, Alphy. The use of Alphy is explored in greater detail later in the chapter.

Recent research by Salesforce.com indicated remarkably strong public support for AI integration in government services, with 90 per cent of respondents to a survey saying they would use an AI agent to engage with their government.[6] This presents an opportunity for governments to rebuild public trust by improving service delivery and response times.

In conclusion, agentic AI is expected to revolutionise the public sector in the near future, unlocking unparalleled opportunities for increased efficiency, better services, and data-driven governance. However, its successful implementation will require thoughtful planning, a focus on ethical issues, and efforts to preserve public trust.

How Can Governments Balance the Use of Agentic AI with Human Oversight?

Because of the potential increased autonomy of agentic AI, governments need to carefully balance its deployment with human oversight, implementing several key strategies to do so effectively.

Governments should establish a comprehensive AI governance framework that sets out clear policies and objectives for the use of AI, specifying acceptable applications, risk thresholds, and performance metrics. This framework should include integrated oversight structures, such as AI ethics committees or dedicated AI officers, to ensure proper monitoring and compliance with governance policies. In addition, robust risk management processes should be put in place to assess the technical, operational, and reputational risks associated with AI systems. A sample checklist to support initial assessment is provided in the appendix.

To maintain human control over AI systems, it is essential to implement adjustable autonomy, allowing the level of AI independence to vary according to the context, task complexity, and risk. Real-time monitoring systems should be introduced to continuously track AI status and decision-making, ensuring transparency and accountability. Incorporating feedback loops will also enable AI systems to integrate human input, enhancing both performance and reliability. Ideally, the use of AI will free up personnel to handle appeals, ensuring that individuals have clear and accessible processes to challenge machine-generated decisions, particularly in borderline or complex cases.

Governments must take a proactive and principled approach to addressing the ethical challenges posed by AI. Promoting transparency in decision-making processes is vital, not only to demystify how AI systems operate but also to uphold public trust. Maintaining detailed audit trails allows for meaningful accountability and the ability to trace decisions back through the system. Regular, independent audits should be embedded into the governance cycle to uncover and correct systemic biases before they cause harm. Just as importantly, the roles and boundaries of AI agents must be clearly defined, with explicit parameters for transparency and oversight. Establishing these safeguards is essential to ensuring that AI is deployed in a way that is fair, explainable, and aligned with democratic values.

To address the impact on the workforce, it is vital to provide training that equips people in charge of human oversight with sufficient AI literacy, expertise, and authority. AI is transforming workforce training, making learning more efficient, personalised, and engaging. By enhancing AI literacy, adapting to individual learning needs, and streamlining content development, AI is reshaping how employees gain and apply new skills.

One of AI's more self-reinforcing contributions is its ability to improve AI literacy. As businesses increasingly rely on AI-driven processes, employees must develop the knowledge to understand, manage, and oversee these systems. Platforms like agentacademy.ai provide specialised, role-based training to equip professionals with the necessary skills to work alongside AI effectively.[7]

Beyond foundational knowledge, AI is also redefining how employees learn through personalised experiences. AI-driven tools analyse individual learning styles, career goals, and skill gaps to create customised training paths. These systems ensure that employees receive content tailored to their specific roles, helping them develop relevant expertise. AI-powered recommendation engines further enhance this process by suggesting learning resources at the right moment, making training more effective and aligned with real-world applications.

The automation of content creation is another area where AI is making a profound impact. Generative AI significantly reduces the time and cost associated with developing training materials. By analysing existing content, AI can identify gaps, refine learning materials, and ensure training programmes remain up to date with industry trends. Customisable chatbots like Google NotebookLM, which has the capacity to instantly build lifelike audio overviews, can assist in this process by enhancing content quality and adapting it based on employee feedback.

Real-time support is another advantage AI brings to workforce training. Knowledge bots and AI-driven assistants provide immediate answers to employee queries, reducing downtime and increasing confidence in day-to-day tasks. Walmart, for example, uses AI-powered chatbots to guide employees during their shifts, offering instant assistance when needed.[8]

AI-driven tutoring systems act as virtual mentors, offering real-time feedback and personalised coaching. AI-powered chatbots streamline onboarding by delivering bite-sized training content and tracking employee progress, easing the burden on HR teams while improving retention rates.

AI is also revolutionising skill mapping and workforce planning. Advanced AI models assess employee competencies against industry trends, helping organisations identify skill gaps and implement targeted reskilling initiatives. Meanwhile, immersive technologies such as augmented reality (AR) and virtual reality (VR), powered by AI, create realistic simulations for hands-on training in high-risk or complex environments.

In addition to training employees, AI enhances knowledge management within organisations. By analysing historical data, AI-driven chatbots help maintain consistency across training programmes and provide insights to refine future learning strategies.

As AI evolves, its role in workforce training will expand rapidly. By integrating AI into learning and development initiatives, the public sector can prepare employees for an increasingly automated world, ensuring their skills and thinking are agile, knowledgeable, and ready for the changing future of work.

Governments should develop clear legal frameworks to address challenges related to agentic AI, including data privacy, liability, and ethical considerations. They must also enforce compliance with industry regulations and standards through regular audits and certifications.

By adopting these measures, governments can leverage the benefits of agentic AI while maintaining essential human oversight and control.

The Main Challenges to Implementing Agentic AI in Government Agencies

The implementation of agentic AI in government agencies faces several key challenges. A significant issue is the skills and expertise gap, as many agencies report a shortage of the necessary technical capabilities. Additionally, attracting and retaining staff with specialised expertise, particularly in data science, remains a major obstacle. Financial constraints also pose a challenge, as many agencies are hindered by tight budgets, which make it difficult to afford the costs associated with AI infrastructure, talent acquisition, and system maintenance. In the March 2025 Public Accounts Committee report, the UK government explicitly warned about the severe lack of digital and AI skills within the public sector. They stated that around half of the roles advertised in digital services went unfilled in 2024, and 70 per cent of government departments reported difficulty recruiting and retaining staff with AI skills. In an attempt to address the skills shortages, the UK government launched a 12-week AI accelerator programme aimed at improving machine learning engineering skills.

Ethical and governance concerns are central to the debate over agentic AI. The autonomous nature of AI systems raises questions about accountability, especially when AI makes independent decisions. Moreover, as we have highlighted earlier, concerns about bias in AI algorithms could perpetuate existing inequalities, and the lack of clear governance frameworks further complicates ethical AI use. One well-documented example is the use of the COMPAS risk assessment tool in the US criminal justice system. COMPAS was designed to predict a defendant's likelihood of reoffending and help guide sentencing decisions. However, studies, most notably by ProPublica, revealed that the algorithm often assigned higher risk scores to black defendants compared to white defendants, even when controlling for factors such as prior criminal activity.[9] This bias raised serious concerns about fairness and contributed to disproportionate impacts on minority communities, thereby influencing public trust in the justice system.

On the technical side, outdated legacy systems and data quality issues present serious obstacles to AI adoption, and the opacity of AI decision-making processes makes it difficult to understand or address potential errors.

Privacy and security risks are also major concerns. There are growing fears about the misuse of user data by AI systems, as well as new vulnerabilities in critical infrastructure that could arise as AI becomes more integrated. For example, the Department of Government Efficiency (DOGE) in the United States raised concerns when it accessed sensitive federal databases, including those of the IRS and the Social Security Administration. Critics warned that this data could be misused to train private AI systems, such as Elon Musk's xAI, potentially resulting in serious privacy violations and granting private entities extraordinary influence over societal outcomes. As AI systems gain greater autonomy, cybersecurity risks are also likely to intensify.[10]

In terms of workforce implications, there are concerns about job displacement resulting from automation, as well as resistance from public-sector unions. Significant investments in upskilling will be essential to ensure that employees can work effectively alongside AI systems.

Finally, the legal and regulatory landscape remains poorly equipped to handle the widespread deployment of agentic AI. In the public sector, potential legal challenges arise from fragmented regulations, complex governance requirements, and persistent concerns around transparency, accountability, and data security. Navigating compliance with overlapping frameworks, such as the EU's AI Act and the General Data Protection Regulation (GDPR), adds further complexity. At the same time, unclear rules around liability, and a shortage of relevant skills within public institutions, present additional obstacles. To ensure AI is used ethically and responsibly, governments must pursue standardised regulations, strengthen oversight mechanisms, and modernise legal frameworks. Evolving these structures is essential, not only to enable innovation but also to prevent misuse and protect citizens' rights.

In conclusion, while agentic AI offers great potential for government agencies, overcoming these challenges is an important part of successful implementation. It will require thoughtful planning, investment in skills and infrastructure, the development of robust ethical frameworks, and ongoing collaboration between policymakers, technologists, and public-sector employees.

Box 9.1 – Case Study: Italian Ministry of Cultural Heritage's AI Agent, Alphy

Italy's Alphy is a conversational agent created to simplify and streamline access to bibliographic information on the Alphabetica portal.[11] As an experimental service, it allows users to perform both direct and advanced searches. Developed through a collaboration between I.PaC and ICCU, it is supported by the Central Institute for the Digitisation of Cultural Heritage, Digital Library.

The next-generation conversational agent has been upgraded with significant new features, including an advanced thematic search that enables users to automatically filter out irrelevant keywords and apply search filters from the outset. Additionally, users can create and save search templates for quicker information retrieval in future conversations. These enhancements make content access faster and more intuitive, ensuring a direct pathway to the information users need.

Generative AI is a fundamental component of the service, playing a vital role in understanding users' search needs. By leveraging advanced natural language analysis and semantic disambiguation, Alphy precisely interprets queries, delivering relevant search pathways within the Alphabetica portal. The integration of generative AI in the Alphy conversational agent represents a significant initial step, showcasing the advantages of advanced content processing services within a research platform dedicated to cultural heritage.

A Vision for the Future: Agentic AI in Public Service

In envisioning the future of public service, agentic AI stands out as a transformative force with the potential to enhance operational efficiency, stimulate innovation, and deepen citizen engagement. By harnessing the capabilities of agentic AI, government agencies can streamline processes, enable more accurate data-driven decision-making, and deliver personalised, responsive services. This technology can optimise resource allocation, improve transparency, and strengthen overall service delivery, thereby supporting a more effective and modern model of governance.

As we have repeatedly emphasised, realising this potential demands a sustained commitment to ethical principles, transparency, and the building of public trust. Policymakers, technologists, and community stakeholders must work together to confront the complex challenges surrounding the implementation of agentic AI. These include addressing risks related to privacy, security, and algorithmic bias while also ensuring that the benefits of this technology are equitably distributed across all segments of society.

Looking ahead, the integration of agentic AI in public services must be guided by principles of equity and inclusivity. With thoughtful planning, robust governance, and continued dialogue among stakeholders, agentic AI could profoundly reshape public service delivery. This would foster a model of government that is more responsive, accountable, and citizen focused. By embracing this innovation with responsibility and foresight, public institutions can both modernise their capabilities and reaffirm their commitment to serving the public good in an increasingly complex world.

Notes

1 IBM (2025), What is agentic AI?, www.ibm.com/think/topics/agentic-ai (accessed on 2 March 2025).

2 New York Times (2023), I.R.S. deploys artificial intelligence to catch tax evasion, www.nytimes.com/2023/09/08/us/politics/irs-deploys-artificial-intelligence-to-target-rich-partnerships.html (accessed on 30 March 2025).

3 K. O. Ariyibi *et al.* (2024), Leveraging artificial intelligence for enhanced tax fraud detection in modern fiscal systems, *GSC Advanced Research and Reviews*, 21(2), 129–137.

4 PwC (No date), Role of AI in transforming how tax authorities work, www.pwc.com/lv/en/about/services/IT-services/related-articles/Role-of-AI-in-transforming-how-tax-authorities-work.html (accessed on 30 March 2025).

5 Innovate Tax (2025), 5 ways AI is set to revolutionise the tax industry, https://innovatetax.com/blog/ai-revolutionising-tax/ (accessed on 30 March 2025).

6 Salesforce (2025), Salesforce Research: 90% of constituents ready for AI agents in public service, www.salesforce.com/news/stories/agentic-ai-government-statistics-davos/?bc=OTH (accessed on 7 February 2025).

7 Digital Workforce (2025), Digital Workforce launches agentacademy.ai to accelerate enterprise AI literacy and upskilling, https://digitalworkforce.com/rpa-news/digital-workforce-launches-agentacademy-ai-to-accelerate-enterprise-ai-literacy-and-upskilling/ (accessed on 31 March 2025).

8 Udutu (2025), The AI revolution: Chatbots and microlearning transform employee training, www.udutu.com/role-of-chatbots-and-microlearning-in-training/ (accessed on 31 March 2025).

9 ProPublica (2016), Machine bias, www.propublica.org/article/machine-bias-risk-assessments-in-criminal-sentencing (accessed on 31 March 2025).
10 The Conversation (2025), DOGE threat: How government data would give an AI company extraordinary power, https://theconversation.com/doge-threat-how-government-data-would-give-an-ai-company-extraordinary-power-250907 (accessed on 31 March 2025).
11 Italian Ministry of Culture – Digital Library, 'Alphy 1.7. 0 – Nuove integrazioni per l'Agente conversazionale di Alphabetica' (2024), https://ipac.cultura.gov.it/2024/05/17/alphy-1-7-0/ (accessed on 11 February 2025).

Part III

Overcoming Challenges and Unlocking Opportunities

Chapter 10

Engaging Stakeholders

Realising the Promise of AI in Public Service

> There is nothing more difficult to take in hand, more perilous in conduct, or more uncertain in its success, than to take the lead in the introduction of a new order of things. Because the innovator has for enemies all those who have done well under the old conditions, and lukewarm defenders in those who may do well under the new.
>
> Niccolo Machiavelli, *The Prince*, 1532

As Machiavelli astutely observed five centuries ago, few people welcome change, particularly when it threatens established interests. Organisations and individuals have countless ways to resist reform, ranging from passive non-cooperation and foot-dragging to more overt forms of defiance, such as leaks, whistleblowing, lobbying, strikes, or even outright sabotage. One recent example comes from a major American law firm, where internal user logs reportedly revealed that senior partners had deliberately undermined an artificial intelligence (AI) initiative because its efficiency drastically reduced billable hours.

The transformative potential of AI in public administration is enormous. It promises not just increased efficiency but improved decision-making and services that are more responsive to the needs of citizens. However, the road to adoption is anything but smooth. Governments must navigate a complex landscape of technical limitations, institutional inertia, political sensitivities, and ethical dilemmas. If left unaddressed, these barriers can prevent even the most promising AI applications from delivering real impact.

DOI: 10.4324/9781003673897-14

This chapter examines the principal obstacles to AI integration in the public sector, from outdated legacy systems and workforce resistance to deep-rooted cultural challenges and governance concerns. It also offers practical strategies for managing these risks, including the importance of transparency, contingency planning, and building organisational readiness for change. The goal is not simply to deploy AI but to ensure it serves the public interest and strengthens trust in government.

The Challenge of Legacy Systems

One of the most significant barriers to AI adoption in government is the prevalence of legacy systems, including outdated software, hardware, and processes that are poorly suited to modern technological advancements. As noted in the UK Public Accounts Committee report referenced in Chapter 9, legacy IT systems and poor data quality remain major challenges. The report stated that, of the 72 highest-risk legacy systems prioritised in the 2022–2024 roadmap, 21 still lacked remediation funding. It also found that problems with data quality and data sharing are persistent and long-standing.[1]

Examples of Legacy System Failures

The IRS office in Austin, Texas, serves as a striking example. According to a *Wall Street Journal* report in 2024, employees were still reliant on a single fax machine to process critical tax documentation and used a shelving system for filing paper records designed in the 1960s.[2] These inefficiencies hinder service delivery and exacerbate delays during peak periods, such as tax filing season or during pandemic relief efforts. It is self-evident that applying AI to a paper-based system is impossible.

Similarly, Thames Water, the UK's largest water company, struggled for years with Lotus Notes, a software system from the late 1980s. The outdated platform created inefficiencies in data sharing and workflow management, delaying responses to customer complaints and infrastructure maintenance. Transitioning to a modern digital system required significant investment and caused operational disruptions, underscoring the high cost of neglecting infrastructure updates.

Not so many years ago, a California water utility was still storing its IBM punched cards. The IBM system was introduced in the 1960s and was phased out in the mid-1980s. Each card held about 80 bytes of data. As an amusing comparison, a modern smartphone has the capacity to hold the data equivalent of more than 12 billion punch cards.

Pathways to Modernisation

Governments can overcome the challenges posed by legacy systems through strategic investments and phased modernisation. Successful examples include:

- Estonia's X-Road platform: This secure data exchange infrastructure enables seamless communication between government agencies, eliminating redundancies and creating a foundation for advanced AI applications.
- Singapore's Smart Nation initiative: By integrating AI across sectors like urban planning, transportation, and healthcare, Singapore has replaced fragmented systems with a cohesive digital ecosystem.

Incremental approaches, such as using middleware solutions to bridge legacy systems with new AI tools, can ease the transition and reduce service disruptions.

Data Management: The Foundation of AI Success

Data quality and governance are critical to the success of AI systems. Fragmented, inconsistent, or incomplete datasets can compromise the accuracy of AI predictions and decisions.

Integral to the implementation of AI is the establishment of government standards for data collection, storage, and sharing to ensure interoperability and reliability. Estonia's approach to standardising data protocols through its X-Road platform demonstrates how structured governance can enable secure and efficient data exchange.

As we have highlighted earlier, historical biases embedded in datasets can perpetuate systemic inequalities in AI-driven decisions. Governments must audit datasets for fairness and diversity, ensuring that AI systems are trained on representative data. The UK's Centre for Data Ethics and Innovation (CDEI) is a UK government expert body, now part of the Department for Science, Innovation and Technology, that plays a central role in guiding the ethical use of data and AI. It was established in 2018 as part of the UK's broader AI strategy. The CDEI's mission is to help the UK navigate the ethical challenges of new data-driven technologies and bridge the gap between innovation and regulation. Its key focus areas include developing frameworks to ensure AI systems are trustworthy and transparent, as well as determining how to identify bias and ensure fairness.

The United States has a number of organisations that cover similar work to the UK's CDEI, including the Office of Science and Technology, the National Institute of Standards and Technology, the National AI advisory committee, and the Federal Trade Commission, which investigates algorithmic bias and data misuse.

Cybersecurity in the AI Era

The rise of AI is reshaping the landscape of cybersecurity, introducing both unprecedented capabilities and new vulnerabilities. As AI becomes more integrated into digital systems, it is being used by both defenders and attackers, revolutionising how threats are identified, analysed, and executed. While AI empowers security teams with real-time threat detection and automated response, it also enables cybercriminals to launch more targeted, adaptive, and deceptive attacks. In this evolving race, understanding the dual-use nature of AI is essential to developing effective strategies for securing digital infrastructure in an increasingly risky environment.

The global cost of cybercrime is projected to reach $10.5 trillion annually in 2025, up from $3 trillion in 2015.[3] This enormous figure, based on an extrapolation of historical data, includes estimates such as operational disruptions, theft of IP, and reputational damage, so the number should be treated with caution. However, there is no disagreement that the threat from cybercrime is serious and increasing. The cyber-threat landscape continues to intensify, with 72 per cent of organisations reporting a rise in cyber risks, with ransomware attacks remaining one of the most pressing concerns.[4] This evolution has led 40 per cent of security professionals to anticipate that AI will worsen ransomware threats in 2025.[5] In the UK, the prevalence of ransomware attacks doubled between 2024 and 2025, now impacting approximately 1 per cent of all businesses.

Cybersecurity incidents are occurring at a staggering rate, with an average of 2,200 major incidents reported daily around the world. In the UK alone, businesses faced 8.58 million cybercrimes over the past year, with phishing being the most widespread form of attack, affecting 93 per cent of those targeted.[6] A well-publicised attack on the UK retailer Marks & Spencer in 2025 is estimated to have cost the firm £300 million in lost profits.

Evolving cybersecurity threats are increasingly powered by AI, enabling more advanced, targeted, and elusive attacks. Techniques like AI-generated phishing and social engineering exploit personal data to craft highly convincing messages that are harder to detect. Deepfake technology allows for realistic impersonations in scams and fraud. Launched in mid-2025, Google's new Veo3 is an AI video generator that can create staggeringly realistic videos with audio from text prompts. The software can be rented for just a few dollars a month. To bypass traditional defences, adversarial attacks manipulate input data to mislead AI systems. Similarly, automated malware and ransomware leverage AI to adapt in real time, evade detection, and exploit vulnerabilities more effectively.

AI systems themselves face threats such as data poisoning and model manipulation,[7] where compromised training data or altered parameters result in malicious behaviour. Proprietary model theft exposes algorithms to misuse or replication, while privacy attacks, including model inversion[8] and membership inference,[9] can extract confidential data.

These risks underscore AI's dual-use nature in cybersecurity. Mitigating risks requires secure data pipelines, continuous threat monitoring, and investment in AI-specific security frameworks to defend against increasingly intelligent adversaries.

On the opposite side, AI-powered tools are transforming cybersecurity by enabling real-time threat detection, automated response, and predictive defence strategies. By processing large data volumes instantly, AI systems can detect anomalies and identify both known and unknown security flaws (called zero-day threats) more effectively than traditional methods. Automating tasks like log analysis, vulnerability scanning, and incident response also reduces manual workload, allowing security teams to focus on high-priority issues.

Incorporating threat intelligence and historical data, AI enhances risk management by anticipating attack patterns and prioritising vulnerabilities based on potential impact. Implementing AI in cybersecurity requires scalable infrastructure, efficient data integration, and continuous model training to maintain performance and resilience against evolving threats.

The integration of exposure management data into threat detection,[10] investigation, and response is expected to surge dramatically, with projections indicating that by 2026, over 60 per cent of these capabilities will rely on such data, up from less than 5 per cent today.[11]

In the AI era, cybersecurity stands at a pivotal crossroads: AI is both a powerful tool and a formidable threat. While malicious actors use AI to create sophisticated, evasive attacks, defenders harness AI's capabilities for faster detection, automated responses, and predictive insights. As threats grow more complex and intelligent, safeguarding digital systems requires robust AI-specific security measures, proactive threat management, and a commitment to continuously evolving defensive strategies. The future of cybersecurity will depend on how effectively we balance AI's risks with its immense potential to protect.

Overcoming Resistance to AI Adoption

Resistance to AI adoption often stems from institutional inertia, employee apprehension, and public scepticism. Addressing these concerns requires transparent communication, stakeholder engagement, and a commitment to inclusivity.

Building Stakeholder Trust

To gain employee buy-in, governments must emphasise that AI is a tool designed to enhance, not replace, human roles. For example, Finland introduced AI-driven processing for unemployment benefits, accompanied by an extensive training programme for staff. The initiative demonstrated how AI could streamline routine administrative tasks, enabling employees to concentrate on more complex and sensitive cases. This approach fostered trust and acceptance by showing that technology could support, rather than undermine, professional judgement and public service values.

Engaging the Public

Public scepticism, often fuelled by fears of surveillance or algorithmic bias, must be addressed through proactive communication. New Zealand's Ministry for Children provides a model by openly explaining its predictive analytics system for child welfare and conducting independent audits to ensure fairness and transparency. Such efforts build public confidence in AI initiatives.[12]

Navigating AI Funding Challenges

The integration of AI into government operations holds immense transformative potential, but it also introduces notable funding challenges. Without sufficient and strategically allocated resources, AI initiatives risk stagnation or outright failure. To succeed, governments must adopt a forward-looking approach that secures dedicated funding, addresses implementation barriers, and ensures coordinated efforts across departments.

In the United Kingdom, many public bodies are facing such severe funding constraints that expecting major investment in IT upgrades or new AI initiatives is simply unrealistic. County councils, which deliver essential social services from adult care to child protection, are under acute financial strain. Alarmingly, 26 out of 38 have warned they are at risk of issuing a Section 114 notice – a formal declaration that a council can no longer balance its books. When a Section 114 notice is issued, all non-essential spending must stop, signalling a crisis not just in finance but in the very capacity of local government to function.

In Canada, municipalities face mounting financial pressure that directly affects their ability to invest in digital infrastructure and AI adoption. For example, the Federation of Canadian Municipalities (FCM) has reported that local governments are responsible for nearly 60 per cent of public infrastructure yet receive only 10 cents of every tax dollar. As a result, cities like Toronto and Montreal have had to delay or scale back modernisation efforts, including upgrades to data platforms and implementation of AI-based service tools for traffic management and predictive maintenance. The lack of sustainable, long-term funding has been cited as a key barrier to innovation and digital transformation across Canadian municipalities.

AI implementation comes with high upfront costs, although the payback through efficiency gains should be significant. Infrastructure, talent acquisition, and ongoing maintenance require significant investment, which can be especially burdensome for smaller agencies or those operating with limited budgets. Additionally, governments struggle to attract and retain AI-skilled professionals due to fierce competition with the private sector and a limited talent pool. These skills shortages can force agencies to rely on costly external contractors or consultants.

To address these challenges, several strategic solutions should be considered. Establishing dedicated, ring-fenced budgets for AI projects ensures that funding is not diverted to other areas. This could include staged funding models where smaller initial investments support prototypes, allowing successful projects to scale with additional resources. Adopting a priority-based budgeting approach can further ensure that resources align with strategic goals, directing funds towards high-impact initiatives like AI-driven public service enhancements.[13]

Collaborations with private-sector partners can also alleviate financial pressure while bringing in valuable expertise. Public–private partnerships enable shared investment in innovation and access to cutting-edge knowledge. Centralised leadership plays a crucial role in coordinating these efforts; appointing a dedicated minister or senior official to oversee AI transformation can promote cohesive strategies across departments. Examples from Spain and the UAE, where roles such as the Secretary of State for Digitalisation and the Minister of State for Artificial Intelligence have been established, demonstrate a commitment to strong leadership in driving digital agendas.

Investment in talent development is equally important. Governments need to build internal capacity by offering competitive salaries, training programmes, and career growth opportunities to attract and retain tech-savvy professionals. Moreover, specific funding should be allocated to modernise legacy systems through cloud migration and modular infrastructure upgrades, providing scalable solutions that reduce long-term costs.

A clear and actionable implementation roadmap is essential to ensure that investments are used effectively. Each agency should develop detailed implementation plans with defined timelines and measurable goals. Beginning with pilot projects can help test the feasibility of AI solutions and refine approaches before broader deployment. Impact should be measured using robust evaluation frameworks, while collaboration across departments should be encouraged to optimise resource use and share data effectively. Transparency and accountability, through regular progress reporting, will help maintain public trust and demonstrate the value of taxpayer investment.

There are already successful and inspiring examples: Estonia's digital transformation showcases effective AI integration through strategic resource allocation and partnerships with local tech firms. In the UK, an agile funding model inspired by startup practices has enabled rapid prototyping and scaling of AI projects. The UAE's appointment of a Minister of State for Artificial Intelligence, as mentioned earlier, has been instrumental in streamlining its digital transformation and fostering global cooperation.

Overcoming the funding challenges of AI adoption in government requires a comprehensive strategy that combines dedicated financing, initial pump-priming funding, visionary leadership, cross-agency coordination, and strong collaboration with the private sector. With careful planning and effective execution, governments are well positioned to harness the full potential of AI, leading to more efficient, responsive, and citizen-focused public services.

Ethical and Governance Concerns

AI in public administration raises profound ethical questions, from algorithmic transparency to accountability for automated decisions.

Algorithmic Accountability

Governments must establish clear frameworks for algorithmic accountability. This includes defining who is responsible for managing the correction of errors and providing strong and easily accessible mechanisms for appeals. Canada's Algorithmic Impact Assessment Tool (AIA) offers a structured approach to evaluating the ethical risks of AI systems before deployment (see Chapter 7 for further details). The AIA's purpose is to assess and mitigate the risks associated with automated decision systems before they are deployed. It uses an interactive online questionnaire to evaluate the type of decision, its impact on individuals or communities, the data sources involved, and the levels of human oversight and mitigation measures in place. From these inputs an impact-level score from 1 (low) to 4 (high) is produced. Level 4 impact projects require a formal review, continuous monitoring, public disclosures, and ministerial oversight. The Canadian project is notable because it is a mandatory algorithmic risk assessment from a national government and this pioneering project is helping shape EU, UK, and OECD programmes.

Transparency and Inclusivity

As we have stressed, transparency is essential to maintaining public trust. Governments should disclose how AI systems make decisions and involve citizens in the oversight process. Participatory governance models, such as citizen advisory boards, can provide valuable input on AI implementations and ensure inclusivity.

Addressing the Challenge of AI Hallucinations

AI hallucinations pose a significant challenge to the development and use of AI systems. These occur when AI models generate outputs, whether text, images, or other data, that seem reasonable but are false or nonsensical. Unlike human mistakes, which are often due to misunderstanding or lack of knowledge, AI hallucinations stem from the inherent nature of generative models. For instance, large language models (LLMs) predict the next word or phrase based on statistical probabilities rather than understanding the context or verifying the truth. This can lead to confident but incorrect information, including fabricated historical facts, false legal references, or defamatory claims. The impact of these errors can be severe, ranging from reputational damage to ethical concerns and even safety risks in critical fields like healthcare or autonomous systems. Tackling this issue requires enhanced training data, better model designs, and ongoing human oversight to reduce misinformation and maintain trust in AI technologies.

The Importance of Contingency Planning

AI systems, like other complex technologies, can malfunction or produce harmful outcomes. Governments must develop robust contingency plans, including regulatory oversight and crisis response strategies, to manage disruptions, protect public safety, and preserve trust.

Learning from Failures

We have already highlighted the UK Post Office Horizon scandal and the long public trial of Post Office managers, senior executives, and many high-profile politicians. There are other similar cases that provide a salutary warning of the damage caused by the irresponsible implementation of new IT systems.

The UK's A-level grading controversy of 2020 highlights the risks of overreliance on AI without adequate safeguards. Due to the COVID-19 pandemic, traditional A-level exams were cancelled in 2020. An algorithm used to assign grades disproportionately penalised students from underprivileged schools, leading to public outrage and the abandonment of the system. Teachers submitted predicted grades together with a rank order of students within each subject. The UK government's exam regulator adjusted these predictions based on each school's historical performance, prior attainment of students, and national statistical norms. In theory, this was a reasonable basis for assessing grades during a challenging health crisis. About 40 per cent of grades were lowered.[14] However, the lack of transparency, poor public communication, and the omission of an adequate appeal process resulted in a public backlash and nationwide protests. The absence of a robust contingency plan exacerbated the crisis. Within days of the results being released, the UK government scrapped the algorithm and grades were reissued based on teachers' predictions. The debacle highlights the risk that poorly designed implementation and a lack of transparency undermine public confidence in algorithmic decision-making. Clearly, human oversight matters.

The Dutch childcare benefits scandal, known as the *toeslagenaffaire*, was a significant political and social crisis in the Netherlands. Approximately 35,000 parents were wrongly accused of welfare fraud by the Dutch Tax and Customs Administration (Belastingdienst), forcing them to repay their childcare allowances.[15] These repayments often amounted to tens of thousands of euros, pushing many families into severe financial hardship.

Parents were falsely labelled as fraudsters due to administrative errors and discriminatory practices, with many affected individuals coming from ethnic minority backgrounds or holding dual nationalities. The scandal also involved AI algorithms that flagged welfare recipients as high risk based on biased indicators such as nationality. These systems disproportionately targeted non-Dutch residents, leading to racial profiling and systemic discrimination. As a result, families not only faced extreme financial burdens but also lost access to other forms of assistance and, in some cases, even custody of their children. Some individuals were blacklisted by banks and other institutions, further deepening their struggles.

The political fallout was severe. In January 2021, Prime Minister Mark Rutte's third cabinet collectively resigned as the scandal came to light, just months before the general elections. Several government officials, including State Secretary for Finance Menno Snel and former Minister of Social Affairs Lodewijk Asscher, resigned or faced criticism for their roles. While criminal investigations were initially ruled out due to sovereign immunity, affected parents filed complaints against government officials, including Prime Minister Rutte himself.

Multiple investigations exposed systemic failures. A parliamentary inquiry titled *Unprecedented Injustice* (Ongekend Onrecht) criticised the Tax Administration's discriminatory practices and lack of transparency, highlighting severe violations of the rule of law.[16] The Dutch Data Protection Authority's audit revealed questionable data governance practices, including the use of blacklists and nationality-based filtering to identify supposed fraudsters.[17] Amnesty International condemned the algorithmic systems used in the process, describing them as 'xenophobic machines' that perpetuated racial discrimination.[18]

In response to public outrage, the government announced compensation plans in May 2021, pledging to reimburse affected families and cover private debts incurred due to wrongful accusations. The scandal also intensified calls for stricter regulation of algorithmic governance, as it underscored the dangers of unregulated AI systems in public administration.

Beyond its immediate impact, the *toeslagenaffaire* exposed deep institutional biases within Dutch governance structures and raised concerns about the ethical use of AI in public administration. It serves as a cautionary tale for other nations employing algorithmic decision-making, highlighting the risks of exacerbating inequality through automated governance systems.

The Robodebt case in Australia is considered one of the most significant public administration failures in the country's history. It involved an unlawful automated debt recovery scheme implemented by the Australian government between 2016 and 2019. The system was designed to detect overpayments of welfare benefits by comparing income data from the Australian Taxation Office (ATO) with Centrelink records. However, it relied on a flawed income-averaging method that frequently resulted in inaccurate debt calculations. Welfare recipients were required to disprove these debts, reversing the burden of proof and placing them in a precarious position.

The scheme wrongly raised over 794,000 debts against approximately 526,000 individuals, many of whom belonged to vulnerable populations. In total, the government unlawfully claimed an estimated A$1.7 billion. Legal challenges soon followed, with Federal Court rulings in 2019, for example in *Amato vs The Commonwealth*, confirming that the income-averaging method was unlawful. A class action led by Gordon Legal resulted in a settlement where the government was forced to repay A$751 million in unlawfully collected debts and provide A$112 million in compensation to affected individuals.[19]

Beyond the legal ramifications, Robodebt had a devastating human impact. Many individuals, struggling to repay debts they did not owe, were forced into financial hardship, taking out loans or selling assets to meet government demands. The psychological toll was severe, with stress and stigma leading to mental health crises, including suicides directly linked to the scheme. Victims reported experiencing anxiety, depression, and a profound sense of criminalisation due to the government's aggressive debt recovery tactics.

In response to the widespread harm caused, a Royal Commission was launched in October 2022 and concluded in July 2023. Its findings were damning, describing Robodebt as a 'crude and cruel' scheme with extensive negative consequences.[20] The report labelled it a 'gross betrayal' of citizens and set forth 57 recommendations to prevent similar failures in the future.[21]

The Australian government acted swiftly to implement significant reforms. Stronger oversight mechanisms for public service agencies were introduced, giving the Ombudsman enhanced powers to investigate systemic issues. A new Administrative Review Tribunal (ART) was established to ensure greater transparency in administrative decisions. Legislative changes aimed at rebuilding public trust included protections for whistleblowers and stricter codes of conduct for ministers. By November 2024, most of the Royal Commission's recommendations had been implemented or were in progress, with reforms designed to prevent future abuses of government power.[22]

The Robodebt scandal has left a lasting impact on Australia's political and social landscape, exposing deep failures in governance and accountability. It underscored the need for fair treatment of welfare recipients and stronger safeguards for vulnerable populations. While public trust in government institutions was significantly damaged, ongoing reforms seek to restore confidence. The case serves as a stark warning about the risks of unchecked automation in public administration, the necessity of maintaining rigorous legal and ethical standards, and the need for a robust system of appeal.

Public Attitudes and Security Concerns Around AI in UK

A recent survey from the Alan Turing Institute and the Ada Lovelace Institute captures the diverse perspectives of the UK public regarding AI, highlighting how individuals perceive AI's role in society, its potential benefits, and concerns surrounding its development and use. Additionally, the report explores the public's awareness and perception of various AI applications, their experiences of harm, and their expectations concerning governance, regulation, and the role of AI in decision-making.

With 72 per cent of the UK population stating that laws and regulations would increase their comfort with AI amid rising public concerns, some of the report's key findings reveal that public awareness of different AI uses varies widely. For example, awareness is high of driverless cars, with 93 per cent of respondents familiar with their use, while only 18 per cent are aware of AI's role in benefits assessments. Additionally, half of the UK public feels they are not represented in decision-making around AI. Furthermore, two-thirds of the public have experienced AI-related harms, with false information, financial fraud, and deepfakes being the most common. Ethnic minorities express more concern about the use of facial recognition in policing compared to the general population.

The Turing report also draws attention to the fact that the UK's AI research sector faces growing security risks from espionage, data theft, and covert collaborations. It identifies gaps in research security awareness, a lack of incentives for compliance, and difficulties in assessing risks – particularly in international partnerships. The report calls for urgent collaboration between government and academia, recommending stricter guidelines, better funding for research security, and mandatory training for researchers.

Just as resistance to AI adoption is often rooted in institutional inertia, apprehension, and scepticism, the report suggests that balancing open research with national security requires proactive, transparent measures. It advocates for embedding strong security protocols within the existing open research framework, such as conducting pre-publication risk assessments and setting up oversight bodies similar to ethics committees to manage dual-use risks from the start. Mandatory security training and clearer government guidance further ensure that open academic practices remain secure without hindering innovation. This integrated approach redefines security not as a barrier but as a critical element of high-quality research that protects and sustains UK innovation.[23]

Proactive Strategies

Governments can mitigate risks associated with AI by implementing robust safeguards that enhance reliability and accountability. Stress-testing AI systems through simulated scenarios helps identify vulnerabilities and refine algorithms before full deployment, ensuring they perform effectively in real-world conditions. Combining AI with human oversight in hybrid systems provides an additional layer of accountability, allowing human judgement to correct potential errors and biases. Establishing clear accountability frameworks further strengthens trust by defining roles and responsibilities for managing AI failures while ensuring there are redress mechanisms for affected citizens. By integrating these strategies at the systems design stage, governments can create a more resilient AI-driven public service.

Stimulating Progress: Strategies for Accelerating AI Adoption

Despite the challenges, governments can harness the potential of AI in public service by adopting a strategic approach that balances innovation with responsibility.

Investing in modern data infrastructure and establishing clear governance protocols will create a solid foundation for AI implementation, ensuring data quality and security. Equally important is upskilling the workforce, equipping employees with the knowledge and tools needed to collaborate effectively with AI systems. Promoting interoperability through open standards will enable seamless integration across various government platforms, fostering efficiency and accessibility. Encouraging collaboration between government agencies, academia, and the private sector can further accelerate AI adoption by facilitating knowledge exchange and resource sharing. Finally, running small-scale trials of AI applications allows governments to identify challenges early, refine best practices, and scale successful initiatives nationwide. By taking these steps, governments can navigate the complexities of AI adoption while delivering more effective and equitable public services. Promoting public trust and democratic values must remain core priorities.

A Vision for Resilient Public Services

Overcoming the obstacles to AI adoption requires a comprehensive and coordinated strategy that tackles technical, institutional, and ethical challenges directly. It is not merely a question of acquiring new technologies. Governments must confront budgetary constraints, update or integrate outdated systems, foster a mindset open to innovation, establish robust data governance, and ensure that ethical standards guide all AI deployments.

Unlocking AI's transformative potential while protecting democratic values and human dignity is a careful balancing act. The success of AI in public service will not be determined by technological capability alone but by the wisdom and integrity with which it is applied to make governance more responsive, efficient, and fair.

As the following chapters illustrate through global case studies, the successful integration of AI is not simply a technical feat. It reflects collaborative leadership, thoughtful planning, and a shared commitment to the public good.

Notes

1 UK Parliament (2025), Uphill struggle ahead for Govt's use of AI as PAC report reveals the scale of the challenge, https://committees.parliament.uk/committee/127/public-accounts-committee/news/206078/uphill-struggle-ahead-for-govts-use-of-ai-as-pac-report-reveals-the-scale-of-the-challenge/ (accessed on 30 April 2025).

2 The Wall Street Journal (2024), Dumbphones and fax machines are the new boss flex, www.wsj.com/lifestyle/careers/low-tech-executives-security-focus-a495f9e7 (accessed on 1 April 2025).

3 Bluetree (No date), Exploring the explosive growth of the cybersecurity market, https://bluetree.digital/cybersecurity-market-growth/ (accessed on 20 May 2025).

4 World Economic Forum (2025), *Global Cybersecurity Outlook 2025*, www.weforum.org/publications/global-cybersecurity-outlook-2025/digest/ (accessed on 20 May 2025).

5 Forbes (2025), Key cybersecurity challenges in 2025 – trends and observations, www.forbes.com/sites/chuckbrooks/2025/04/05/key-cybersecurity-challenges-in-2025-trends-and-observations/ (accessed on 20 May 2025).
6 Government of the UK – Cyber security breaches survey 2025, www.gov.uk/government/statistics/cyber-security-breaches-survey-2025/cyber-security-breaches-survey-2025 (accessed on 20 May 2025).
7 Model manipulation involves deliberately altering a machine learning model's internal parameters, activations, or structure to change its behaviour, outputs, or capabilities. This can serve various purposes, such as enhancing performance, updating information, enabling or disabling specific functions, or – when done with malicious intent – exploiting vulnerabilities or circumventing safety measures.
8 Model inversion is a security and privacy risk in machine learning in which an attacker uses the outputs of a trained model to deduce details about its training data, model parameters, or sensitive attributes of individuals represented in the dataset.
9 Membership inference is a privacy attack targeting machine learning models, where an adversary seeks to identify whether a particular data point was part of the model's training dataset. This type of attack takes advantage of the tendency of models to respond differently to data they were trained on (members) compared to data they have not seen before (non-members).
10 Exposure management data encompasses the full range of information gathered, integrated, and analysed as part of an organisation's cybersecurity exposure management efforts. It offers insight into the organisation's digital assets, their vulnerabilities, and the related risks, allowing security teams to proactively detect, evaluate, prioritise, and address potential threats across the entire attack surface.
11 Segura (2025), 32 cybersecurity stats you can't ignore in 2025, https://segura.security/post/cybersecurity-stats-you-cant-ignore (accessed on 20 May 2025).
12 OECD (2024), New Zealand's Integrated data Infrastructure: Using data to identify need and improve the well-being of children and youth, www.oecd.org/en/publications/new-zealand-s-integrated-data-infrastructure-using-data-to-identify-need-and-improve-the-well-being-of-children-and-youth-en.html (accessed on 3 January 2025).
13 A ring-fenced budget refers to funding that is set aside exclusively for a specific purpose and cannot be redirected to other activities or unrelated expenses. This approach ensures that the allocated resources are preserved for their intended use, offering protection against reallocation or misuse. In government and project management, ring-fencing supports sustained focus on priority initiatives – like AI implementation or infrastructure upgrades – by shielding them from competing financial pressures.
14 The London School of Economics and Political Science (2020), "F**k the algorithm"?: What the world can learn from the UK's A-level grading fiasco', https://blogs.lse.ac.uk/impactofsocialsciences/2020/08/26/fk-the-algorithm-what-the-world-can-learn-from-the-uks-a-level-grading-fiasco/ (accessed on 1 April 2025).
15 J. Arts and M. van den Berg (2024), What the Dutch benefits scandal and policy's focus on "fraud" can teach us about the endurance of empire, *Critical Social Policy*, 45(1),177–187.
16 House of Representatives of the States General (2020), *Unprecedented Injustice*, www.houseofrepresentatives.nl/sites/default/files/atoms/files/verslag_pok_definitief-en-gb.docx.pdf (accessed on 1 April 2025).
17 TaxAdmin.AI (No date), The toeslagenaffaire (The Dutch childcare allowance scandal) https://taxadmin.ai/taxadminai-toeslagenaffaire/ (accessed on 1 April 2025).

18 Amnesty International (2021), Dutch childcare benefit scandal an urgent wake-up call to ban racist algorithms, www.amnesty.org/en/latest/news/2021/10/xenophobic-machines-dutch-child-benefit-scandal/ (accessed on 1 April 2025).
19 The University of Sydney Law School (2023), Unravelling Robodebt: Legal failures, impact on vulnerable communities and future reforms, www.sydney.edu.au/law/news-and-events/news/2023/12/13/unraveling-robodebt-legal-failures-impacts.html (accessed on 1 April 2025).
20 BBC (2023), Robodebt: Illegal Australian welfare hunt drove people to despair, www.bbc.com/news/world-australia-66130105 (accessed on 1 April 2025).
21 State Government of Victoria (2025), Learning from the failures of Robodebt – building a fairer, client-centred social security system, www.legalaid.vic.gov.au/learning-from-the-failures-of-robodebt (accessed on 1 April 2025).
22 Australia Department of the Prime Minister and Cabinet (2024), Update on Robodebt royal commission reforms, https://ministers.pmc.gov.au/gallagher/2024/update-robodebt-royal-commission-reforms (accessed on 1 April 2025).
23 The Alan Turing Institute – Centre for Emerging Technology and Security (2025), *Securing the UK's AI Research Ecosystem*, https://cetas.turing.ac.uk/sites/default/files/2025-03/cetas_research_report_-_securing_the_uks_ai_research_ecosystem_2.pdf (accessed on 9 April 2025).

Chapter 11

Mastering Data for AI in the Public Sector

Strategies, Challenges, and Transformative Potential

In the rapidly evolving landscape of digital governance, data has become the most critical strategic asset in the public sector. As governments around the world adopt artificial intelligence (AI) to transform service delivery and decision-making, a fundamental truth has become clear: data is not a mere byproduct of administrative processes. It is the indispensable foundation on which all AI initiatives must be built.

As Nitin Seth, former Chief Digital Officer at Fidelity Investments, remarked:

> Data is the fuel that powers AI, and organisations have failed to devote the necessary attention and resources to build data as a strategic asset. And if there is a single reason why AI has not delivered the promised value, it is the myopic view of data. For the longest time, organisations have treated data as an afterthought.[1]

Moving towards a more data-driven public sector requires confronting a central tension: the need to make data accessible for AI analysis while safeguarding individual privacy. This dilemma is often referred to as the privacy paradox, our readiness to surrender personal information to platforms like Google and Facebook in return for convenience, without fully understanding the implications. Generational differences compound the issue; younger cohorts such as Gen Z and Millennials tend to be more willing to exchange personal data for personalised experiences.

DOI: 10.4324/9781003673897-15

The truth, however uncomfortable, is that meaningful data privacy has already eroded. Most of us, knowingly or not, have forfeited it. When we use credit cards or mobile phones, drive connected electric vehicles, or simply browse the internet, our data is being collected, processed, and traded. Alerts from credit card companies or software such as Microsoft Defender are daily reminders that our personal details are already circulating on the dark web.

The EU's General Data Protection Regulation (GDPR), widely criticised as an expensive failure, was founded on a well-intentioned but misguided attempt to control privacy. Unfortunately, we must now accept that meaningful data privacy is largely a thing of the past.

Ironically, while governments express concern over data privacy, they often pursue policies that reduce it. In the UK, Companies House allows open public access to the records of every company, including financials and directors' names, addresses, and dates of birth. There are around six million CCTV cameras operating across the country, monitoring citizens with little public outcry. These examples illustrate the contradictions in the current approach: while privacy remains a rhetorical priority, it is routinely undermined in practice.

Nevertheless, political and public sentiment still demands that the paradox be addressed, especially when AI systems are designed to operate on sensitive personal or social data. Ensuring public trust remains essential. In the appendix, we include a Data for AI Readiness Checklist to assist policymakers in preparing for the integration of data-driven technologies in a responsible and transparent manner.

The Data-First Paradigm Shift

We have already entered the data-first world, a revolution where data does not just facilitate but fuels transformation across all fronts. Effective impact now depends on the differentiation created by maximising the value realised from data, especially as the AI age draws upon us.

For public-sector organisations, this fundamental change in approach requires a thorough re-evaluation of how data is collected, managed, and used. Unlike private enterprises, which are primarily driven by profit maximisation, government agencies must deliver efficient and personalised services while maintaining public support through clear, measurable improvements in a transparent and accountable manner. Although often more symbolic than real, the protection of privacy and, to some extent, civil liberties remains essential. Equally important is the promotion of equity and inclusivity. However, we must acknowledge the trade-offs between privacy and practicality, a debate that has largely been stifled by the rigid application of GDPR regulations. At the heart of this evolving data landscape is the need to maintain public trust, which remains a critical and perceptual responsibility for government institutions.

The transition to a data-first approach requires public-sector leaders to reconceptualise data not as a secondary byproduct of administrative processes but as a valuable strategic asset. This reconceptualisation necessitates systematic changes across structural frameworks, technological infrastructures, workforce capabilities, and institutional cultures. Traditional governance models, often marked by departmental silos and fragmented information management, must and inevitably will evolve towards more integrated and holistic approaches that enable the secure flow of data across institutional boundaries.

Moreover, the unique position of government agencies as both providers and regulators of services introduces additional complexities. As they develop more sophisticated data capabilities, the public sector must develop clear rules to ensure data is used responsibly and transparently. This dual role demands exceptional clarity in policy development and implementation, with public agencies serving as models of responsible data stewardship even as they pursue innovative applications.

The economic and social implications of this paradigm shift extend far beyond operational efficiencies. By effectively harnessing data through AI, the public sector can fundamentally transform its relationship with citizens, moving from reactive service provision to proactive anticipation of needs. This transformation, however, requires navigating significant cultural and political challenges, including addressing public concerns about surveillance, algorithmic decision-making, and the appropriate boundaries of state information gathering and utilisation.

The Critical Components of Data Infrastructure

In today's data-driven era, building a robust data infrastructure is not just a technological imperative but a strategic cornerstone of the public sector. Faced with the challenges of legacy systems, diverse data sources, and stringent security and compliance requirements, these organisations must weave together efficient data pipelines, harmonise disparate datasets, and uphold high standards of data quality. This intricate framework not only enables the effective use of AI to derive actionable insights but also reinforces governance structures that secure and sustain trust in public data.

Data Pipelines

Robust data pipelines form the backbone of effective data infrastructure, ensuring that information flows seamlessly from collection to decision-making. These pipelines must overcome challenges such as legacy systems with limited interoperability and the requirement to maintain robust security. They serve as vital channels that not only transport data securely but also maintain data integrity and usefulness.

Automation plays a key role here, streamlining processes that would otherwise become bottlenecks, while clear data management policies define ownership, access, and quality standards.

Data Harmonisation

Public entities often face fragmented data from legacy systems. Data harmonisation, aligning formats and structures, enables better analysis and decision-making. Achieving this requires technical precision and careful coordination across departments. Incremental integration, focused on high-impact areas, helps navigate legal, regulatory, and organisational hurdles.

According to a BBC report from April 2023, UK police forces were operating with outdated IT systems, with significant variation between different forces. Case management software was often obsolete and non-interoperable, leading to repeated failures in information transfer. One widely cited example of the problems caused by outdated data systems was the Home Office's destruction of the paper-based Windrush records. The failure to digitise this information in a modern format contributed directly to the wrongful detention of many citizens.

Another example of these data challenges was the outdated computers used by Border Force. Staff were using decades-old machines and unstable software that frequently crashed, delaying the processing of passengers and cargo. Until a few years ago, at Heathrow, Britain's busiest airport, immigration officers were still handed strips of paper each morning listing the names of passengers they were to monitor.

In the United States, the Social Security Administration's legacy systems were still using the almost forgotten programming language COBOL, written over 45 years ago. The results of this outdated software were systems outages, slow response times, and a shortage of software engineers familiar with this old software.

According to the UK's National Audit Office (NAO), total UK government IT spending in 2023 was £19 billion; alarmingly, more than half was spent on maintaining outdated legacy systems. The NAO noted that at least a third of the UK's critical IT systems are at least 20 years old, ancient by IT standards. (NAO. *The Government Digital and Data Roadmap* 2023).[2]

To put this in perspective, UK government IT spending represents about 1.6 per cent of total government expenditure; in contrast, large business IT spending ranges from 3 to 6 per cent, and is significantly higher, 7 to 10 per cent, in the banking and financial sectors. When considering the scale of the old legacy problems in government the difference is even greater.

These examples highlight one of the challenging areas facing AI implementation.

Data Quality

Maintaining high-quality data is both a technical challenge and an ethical imperative, particularly in the public domain where decisions may affect millions of people. Accuracy, completeness, timeliness, and consistency are the cornerstones of trustworthy data, yet issues like human error, outdated records, and inconsistent collection practices can undermine these standards. Systematic approaches, ranging from cross-referencing authoritative sources to employing statistical validations, are critical. For AI applications, ensuring that data is representative and free from bias is as important as the technological measures in place, demanding an integrated approach that blends automated checks with a culture of quality stewardship.

Data for AI

When it comes to preparing data for AI, the requirements extend well beyond traditional data management. AI systems demand large, diverse, and well-labelled datasets to tackle tasks that vary in complexity. Effective AI data strategies involve not only gathering and curating data but also employing innovative techniques such as data augmentation and rigorous documentation practices. Collaboration between subject matter experts and data scientists is crucial to ensure that the data is both feature-rich and reflective of real-world diversity.

Data Governance

Effective data governance is the foundation of modern data infrastructure, ensuring that data is available, usable, and secure. In today's AI-driven environment, governance frameworks must evolve to clearly define roles, from data owners to custodians, and incorporate both technical safeguards, such as encryption, and procedural measures, such as approval workflows. These frameworks must balance innovation with privacy by setting standards for data quality, ensuring accuracy, completeness and reliability, and for metadata, ensuring that data assets are properly documented and catalogued. Regulatory compliance must also be upheld through alignment with legal requirements. By embedding governance into daily operations and fostering ethical oversight, public-sector organisations can strengthen citizen trust and promote the responsible use of data.

As Nitin Seth observed, 'Poor data governance and quality are proving to be among the most critical challenges to truly realising value from data and artificial intelligence capabilities.'[3] Overcoming these challenges necessitates an integrated approach that combines technological solutions, organisational processes, and cultural transformation. Automated monitoring tools enable continuous quality assessment, while data stewardship programmes clarify accountability across teams and roles.

Most importantly, fostering a culture that prioritises data quality, where all stakeholders recognise its significance and their role in maintaining it, lays the groundwork for sustainable improvements in AI-driven decision-making.

The Role of AI and Machine Learning in Improving Data Quality

The relationship between data and AI is profoundly symbiotic: high-quality data is essential for effective AI, and AI, in turn, offers powerful tools to enhance data quality.

Data Cleaning and Processing

AI algorithms are revolutionising how data is cleaned and processed by automating the detection and correction of issues such as duplicates and missing values. These methods can standardise formats, identify errors, and reconcile conflicting information, all while reducing reliance on labour-intensive manual processes. Yet, even as AI streamlines these tasks, human oversight remains critical for managing more complex or sensitive cases.

Anomaly Detection

Machine learning techniques excel at identifying anomalies, those subtle deviations from normal patterns that might indicate data errors. By analysing temporal trends and spotting statistical outliers, these models can flag inconsistencies that might otherwise go unnoticed, enabling swift responses to potential issues while fine-tuning sensitivity to avoid false alarms. Of course, this level of sophistication requires solid data.

Data Validation

AI-driven validation extends beyond simple format checks by continuously assessing data against established business rules and historical patterns. This dynamic process ensures that logical relationships within the data remain intact and that new information is consistently benchmarked against trusted standards, thereby safeguarding the reliability of data used in decision-making.

In situations where data is scarce or imbalanced, AI can generate synthetic data that mirrors the statistical properties of real datasets. Techniques such as Synthetic Minority Over-sampling (SMOTE) or more advanced generative models help enrich existing data, ensuring that AI systems are trained on comprehensive and representative datasets.[4] This approach not only mitigates bias but also prepares models to handle diverse real-world scenarios. For example, in credit card fraud detection, where fraudulent transactions are vastly outnumbered by legitimate ones, synthetic data plays a crucial role. Techniques such as SMOTE or other generative models can create realistic synthetic fraud cases, enriching the dataset and enabling AI systems to better recognise rare but critical patterns. This approach enhances model performance, reduces bias, and ensures more reliable detection in real-world applications.

Natural Language Processing

Unstructured text, from policy documents to citizen feedback, holds valuable insights that are often locked away in raw form. Natural language processing transforms this information into structured data by identifying key entities, standardising terminology, and even gauging sentiment. This process not only unlocks hidden value but also integrates seamlessly with structured data to support more robust AI applications.

Automated Data Governance

Finally, AI is increasingly being used to automate governance functions, monitoring compliance in real time and documenting data lineage with minimal human intervention. By intelligently classifying data by sensitivity and adapting access controls dynamically, these systems bolster security and ensure that governance frameworks are both efficient and resilient. Despite these technological advances, human judgement remains indispensable in navigating complex governance challenges and upholding ethical standards.

Public-Sector Data Governance Essentials

In an era where technology impacts every facet of public service, data governance has emerged as a cornerstone of effective government operations. As AI becomes increasingly integrated into public services, the traditional models of managing data must evolve to meet new challenges and opportunities.

Defining Data Governance in the AI Era

Modern AI governance is all about making decisions clear and traceable. It means tracking the flow, from where it started to how it's changed, so users can see how data shapes AI's choices. Explainable AI tools are at the heart of this effort: they break down complex machine learning results into understandable insights, building trust and accountability.[5] This isn't just about ticking legal boxes like GDPR; it's about showing users that data is handled responsibly and ethically. As regulations tighten and public scrutiny grows, governance has become a team effort, bringing together lawyers, ethicists, and community voices to craft policies that balance cutting-edge innovation with moral responsibility. This collaborative approach ensures AI systems don't just follow the rules but also respect society's values, setting the stage for trustworthy technology designed with people in mind.

Ethical data practices now require obtaining proper consent (although this is usually a meaningless click in a box where the user has no real alternative and is obviously designed by hyper-sensitive legal teams, trying to comply with poorly drafted legislation rather than protecting users), respecting data ownership, and applying guidelines that prevent discriminatory practices.

Transparency is vital. Citizens, or more likely their representatives – such as lobby groups, the press, legal or political representatives, unions, or ombudsmen – must at least be able to understand how an AI system made a decision. Explaining the data and algorithms behind these decisions builds trust, as stakeholders gain insight into the reasoning that guides public service delivery.

While few citizens will seek or even grasp the technical intricacies of AI decision-making, the potential impact of opaque systems on public trust cannot be ignored. For many civil servants and elected officials, the greater concern lies not in the mechanics of algorithms but in the political fallout from mistakes, especially those that spark media scrutiny. In risk-averse governmental cultures, where innovation is often overshadowed by the fear of failure, this creates a significant barrier to embracing AI. Building trust, therefore, requires more than technical explainability; it demands a shift towards environments where responsible experimentation is encouraged and where transparency serves to protect both public interest and institutional integrity.

Equally important is the establishment of accountability mechanisms. Through auditing and reviewing algorithms, it becomes possible to address errors or biases, ensuring that AI systems remain responsible and their impacts justifiable.

Managing the full lifecycle of AI, from development and deployment to ongoing monitoring, is clearly complex and often paradoxically challenging. Thus, continuous oversight improves the likelihood that AI tools adapt to changing data landscapes and evolving public needs.

Finally, measuring and openly communicating the quality of both data and AI outcomes provides stakeholders with clear, objective indicators of system performance, reinforcing trust in public initiatives.

Building Interoperable Data Ecosystems

The potential of all this rich data in the public sector is hampered by historically siloed systems and the legacy issues we have discussed. Modern governance is fundamentally reliant on interoperability – the capability of disparate government IT systems to work together – and this is made possible by standardised data exchange protocols. These protocols, which define how data is structured, formatted, and transmitted, are crucial for enabling seamless communication and collaboration across agencies, thereby maximising efficiency in operations.

This effort relies heavily on a unified metadata framework and shared data dictionaries across the entire organisation. A unified metadata framework provides a central system for managing metadata or, to put it simply, information that describes and gives context to other data. This consistent approach to defining, organising, and applying metadata is crucial for enhancing data integration, ensuring proper data governance, and improving overall data usability. Furthermore, a shared data dictionary serves as a centralised repository containing key details about datasets, such as object names, data types, data sizes, data relationships, and data usage rules.

Such consistent definitions and classifications are vital for enabling different stakeholders to interpret and utilise data effectively, thus supporting more robust analysis and decision-making.

It is perhaps helpful to give a practical example of why this metadata framework issue is important. Imagine the UK NHS wants to use AI to improve patient care by coordinating how someone moves between different healthcare providers, for example from their GP to hospital surgery and then to community care. AI could be incredibly helpful in tracking the patient's progress, watching for adverse treatment reactions, scheduling appointments, and allocating resources. If data is not unified – for example, a date format in one database is recorded as DD/MM/YYYY and in another DD/MM/YY, and the community nurse writes Jan 20th, 1955 – it is harder for AI to keep track of the dates and errors can occur. Establishing technical standards and legal frameworks for systems integration is equally crucial. These measures promote best practices while ensuring that sensitive information remains protected through clear guidelines for data sharing

Striking a balance will be challenging. While enhanced interoperability can drive innovation and efficiency, it must not come at the cost of compromising citizen privacy or diluting accountability in data management, but perhaps a greater challenge is the cost of moving to efficient interoperability.

Implementing Continuous Data Quality Assurance

Moving away from sporadic assessments, the public sector needs a vision that incorporates continuous data quality assurance to maintain high standards. Real-time monitoring through dashboards and analytics tools enables immediate detection of issues like inconsistency or inaccuracy.

Automated validation processes, often powered by machine learning, help ensure that new data adheres to established standards right from the point of collection, reducing the chance of error.

Routine audits provide another layer of assurance, systematically reviewing data practices and uncovering hidden issues that could affect overall data integrity.

Feedback loops, which gather insights from various stakeholders, are instrumental in driving ongoing improvement, while clearly defined escalation paths ensure that any quality concerns are addressed promptly and effectively.

By embedding quality controls throughout the data lifecycle, public-sector organisations not only optimise their operations but also enhance the reliability of the services they deliver.

Strategic Implementation Frameworks for AI Adoption

Implementing AI in the public sector requires more than just new technology; it calls for a clear, phased strategy that guides the journey from initial exploration to full-scale transformation. This section outlines the strategic frameworks that enable public institutions to methodically adopt AI, balancing innovation with ethical considerations and risk management. By charting a path from foundational capabilities to pilot projects and scalable initiatives, these frameworks ensure that AI is deployed responsibly, effectively, and in a way that most importantly enhances public service delivery.

Phase-Based Deployment Methodology

Adopting data-driven AI is a journey best managed in distinct phases.[6] In the *Foundation Phase*, the focus is on building robust data governance, technological infrastructure, and quality frameworks, laying the groundwork for future AI initiatives.

During the *Exploration Phase*, pilot projects are launched to test high-value use cases. These experiments allow agencies to learn from real-world applications and refine their strategies based on initial outcomes.

The *Expansion Phase* involves scaling successful pilots and broadening the range of AI applications while simultaneously managing change through staff training and improved data practices.

In the *Transformation Phase*, AI reshapes core operations and service delivery, with teams reimagining workflows to boost efficiency and responsiveness.

Finally, the *Institutionalisation Phase* embeds AI into the organisational culture, ensuring that data-driven decision-making becomes a routine part of public-sector operations.

Ethical Considerations and Risk Mitigation

As public entities deploy AI, it is essential, as we have repeatedly stressed, to address bias and ensure transparency as integral parts of the process. A robust framework for bias assessment enables organisations to systematically evaluate datasets and mitigate risks before they influence decision-making.

Diverse testing scenarios ensure that AI models perform equitably across various demographic groups, while open documentation about model limitations fosters trust and accountability. Anticipating problems, or perceived problems, before they happen is always challenging, so building in readily accessible feedback systems can head off issues before they get out of hand.

Regular audits and clearly defined response protocols for identified biases are critical. These practices not only improve model fairness but also affirm the commitment of public institutions to the sensitive application of AI.

Like the provision of all government services, the use of AI must be seen as a constantly evolving set of tools that are continually tested, modified, tested and modified.

Transformative Applications and Measurable Outcomes

Data-driven AI is revolutionising public service delivery by enabling predictive models that anticipate citizen needs. By analysing trends and historical data, governments can prepare for challenges, such as surges in demand for social services or shifts in public health needs, before they escalate.

Personalised interactions powered by AI allow for more tailored services, while proactive intervention systems help address issues early, helping to prevent larger crises. Dynamic resource allocation and the creation of integrated service ecosystems mean that public agencies can work together more effectively, providing seamless, citizen-centric services that build trust and satisfaction.

Quantifying Public Value Creation

The success of data and AI investments is ultimately measured by their tangible impact on citizens' lives. Improved outcomes in health, education, and safety demonstrate how AI can directly enhance quality of life. If carefully thought through and implemented, AI should lead not only to greatly improved services but to higher levels of job satisfaction for those providing public services as they see the benefits to their target clients.

Equitable access to services is clearly important,[7] as data-driven platforms can be designed to address the needs of all citizens, including marginalised communities. However, in many areas, access is far from equitable. For instance, many students from low-income households lack access to the necessary devices or high-speed internet, creating a *homework gap* that limits their ability to fully participate in digital learning. In healthcare, marginalised groups such as ethnic minorities and low-income individuals often face barriers – for example, fewer nearby healthcare facilities or higher out-of-pocket costs – making it harder for them to receive care. Additionally, many rural areas suffer from inadequate infrastructure, including mobile data and internet access. These disparities highlight how unequal access to services can perpetuate social and economic divides, especially for marginalised communities.

Safeguarding Citizen Privacy in the Age of AI: Strategies for Ethical Data Use in the Public Sector

As AI becomes integral to public services, and cybercrime proliferates, protecting personal data is increasingly important.

Differential privacy techniques, a mathematical framework that allows data analysis and sharing while safeguarding the privacy of individuals whose data is part of the dataset,[8] offer one promising solution, allowing organisations to extract useful insights from data while preserving individual anonymity.

Federated learning, a decentralised machine learning approach where multiple devices or entities collaboratively train a shared model without transferring their raw data to a central server, represents another innovative approach. In federated learning, AI models are trained across decentralised data sources, ensuring sensitive information remains on local systems rather than in a central repository. A well-known real-world use of federated learning is in Google's Gboard keyboard app. In this case, the model learns directly from users' typing behaviour on their own smartphones, without ever transferring raw text data to a central server. Instead, only anonymised model updates, such as adjustments to learned patterns, are sent back and combined with updates from millions of other devices. This decentralised approach enables the global model to improve over time while keeping personal data securely on users' devices.

Encryption methods further secure personal data by enabling computations on encrypted datasets, thereby preventing unauthorised access even during AI processing.

Data minimisation and purpose limitation strategies reduce the risk of data breaches by ensuring that only necessary information is collected and used strictly for its intended purpose.

Together, these strategies create a resilient framework for ethical AI, balancing the transformative benefits of technology with a clear commitment to citizen privacy.

By prioritising privacy alongside innovation, public-sector entities can create a future where AI serves as a tool for positive change, enriching the lives of citizens while safeguarding their rights. Its deployment comes with complex risks that must be handled with caution. One major concern is privacy violations, including data breaches, where AI systems require large datasets that often contain sensitive personal information, such as health records or tax data. This makes these systems attractive targets for cyberattacks, which can result in widespread exposure of citizen data and a loss of public trust. There has, in recent years, been a significant growth in remote working. The UK Office of National Statistics (ONS) estimated that 28 per cent of UK adults were hybrid working in the autumn of 2024,[9] and this trend is creating new privacy challenges and vulnerabilities. Employees frequently use personal devices and unsecured networks, heightening the risk of data breaches and cyberattacks. The overlap of personal and professional environments also makes it harder to comply with data protection regulations, such as GDPR, as sensitive data may be improperly handled or exposed. Additionally, AI can unintentionally reveal personally identifiable information or infer sensitive attributes, such as health conditions or financial status, from unrelated data, leading to privacy violations. Unauthorised use of personal data is also a risk, especially if AI systems use it without proper consent, raising ethical concerns. This commitment to privacy-preserving AI will be important as the public sector navigates the complex landscape of data ethics, citizen expectations, and technological advancement in the years to come. However, the balance between realistic levels of privacy versus the pressures to improve government service delivery will be an ongoing political challenge.

Call for Global Cooperation on Data Privacy Standards

In an interconnected world where data frequently crosses borders, global standards for data privacy are complex. Such standards protect citizens from potential abuses in a borderless digital landscape, ensuring that personal information is handled responsibly regardless of where it is processed. The different attitudes to the use of data in the United States and Europe have been exposed through high-profile cases brought in the European courts against American big tech. Unified data privacy norms facilitate international collaboration on global challenges, be it public health, climate change, or economic development, by easing the flow of critical data across jurisdictions.

Simplifying compliance for multi-jurisdictional operations also benefits both public and private partners, aligning expectations and fostering trust. For instance, the Common Reporting Standard (CRS), developed by the OECD in 2014,[10] facilitates the automatic exchange of private financial information between tax authorities across jurisdictions. Its primary goal is to combat tax evasion and ensure fiscal transparency. Over 100 jurisdictions, including all EU member states, have adopted the CRS, embedding it into their legal frameworks through measures such as Council Directive 2014/107/EU. This system mandates financial institutions to collect detailed information about their customers' tax residency and report it annually to relevant tax authorities, who then share the data with other jurisdictions. The scope of information exchanged under CRS is extensive, including personal identifiers such as names, addresses, Taxpayer Identification Numbers (TINs), account balances, and details about dividends or interest earned. While privacy safeguards are in place to ensure compliance with domestic and international data protection laws, the sheer scale of this automatic exchange highlights how deeply integrated global data-sharing systems have become.

As data flows become increasingly transnational, the urgency of establishing global standards for data privacy intensifies. Public-sector organisations play a pivotal role in this effort, advocating for frameworks that protect citizens, facilitate legitimate data sharing, reduce compliance complexities, establish common expectations for private partners, and build public trust. By embracing this responsibility, public-sector leaders can help create a secure and equitable digital environment that not only safeguards individual rights but also harnesses the power of data to address the shared challenges facing humanity. This dual focus on privacy and progress is essential for navigating the complexities of our interconnected world and ensuring a better future for all. Ultimately, establishing and adhering to global data privacy standards not only safeguards individual rights but also reinforces public confidence in the institutions that depend on data-driven insights.

Conclusion

As we enter a period of significant change, the mastery of data for AI represents not just a technological advancement but a fundamental reimagining of the public sector's relationship with its citizens. This transformation promises a future where government can anticipate needs rather than merely respond, where resources are allocated dynamically to where they are most needed, and where services become personalised while remaining fair and accessible to all.

Yet this powerful vision brings equally powerful responsibilities. It demands robust data governance, interoperability across systems, a clear respect for privacy, ethical use, and strong international cooperation on data standards. These are not optional extras but essential foundations for building public trust.

Public institutions that rise to this challenge, by using data to improve outcomes while maintaining high standards of stewardship and accountability, will not only improve their operations but also strengthen the democratic contract: to serve all citizens with equity, efficiency, and respect.

The way forward calls for leadership that blends technical understanding with clarity. Only by combining these qualities can governments unlock the full potential of data-driven AI while preserving the values that underpin public service.

Notes

1 N. Seth (2024), *Winning in the Digital Age*, Haryana: Penguin Random House India.
2 National Audit Office (2023), *The Government Digital and Data Roadmap 2023*, London.
3 N. Seth (2024), *Winning in the Digital Age*, Haryana: Penguin Random House India.
4 The synthetic minority over-sampling technique is a preprocessing technique used to address a class imbalance in a dataset.
5 IBM (2025), What is explainable AI?, www.ibm.com/think/topics/explainable-ai (accessed on 29 March 2025).
6 REI Systems (2025), AI in government: A strategic framework for digital transformation, www.reisystems.com/ai-in-government-a-strategic-framework-for-digital-transformation/ (accessed on 25 February 2025).
7 Equitable access means ensuring fair and just distribution of resources and services so that everyone – regardless of race, gender, income, or geography – has an equal opportunity to benefit. It goes beyond treating everyone the same, focusing instead on removing systemic barriers and tailoring solutions to meet the needs of underserved communities.
8 It does this by adding specially calibrated noise to data queries or computations, ensuring that the inclusion or exclusion of any one individual's information does not notably impact the results.
9 UK Office for National Statistics (2024), Who are the hybrid workers?, www.ons.gov.uk/employmentandlabourmarket/peopleinwork/employmentandemployeetypes/articles/whoarethehybridworkers/2024-11-11 (accessed on 29 March 2025).
10 OECD (2017), *Standard for Automatic Exchange of Financial Account Information in Tax Matters*, Second Edition, OECD Publishing, Paris.

Chapter 12

Case Studies

AI in Action in the Public Sector

Artificial intelligence (AI) is already reshaping the public sector, offering innovative solutions across a wide range of functions. From simplifying administrative procedures to tackling complex social challenges, AI holds transformative potential for public service delivery. Yet its implementation has not been without setbacks. This chapter presents global case studies that illustrate both effective and flawed deployments, examining the lessons they provide for the design and management of future AI initiatives in government.

Exemplars of Success: Realising AI's Promise

Estonia: The Digital Governance Leader

Estonia is frequently celebrated as a pioneer in digital governance. Through its e-Estonia initiative, the country has seamlessly integrated AI into public administration, enhancing efficiency and transparency.

Estonia's X-Road platform serves as the foundation of the country's digital society, enabling secure and efficient data exchange between public and private-sector organisations. Developed by the Information System Authority (RIA) and launched in 2001, X-Road is a distributed data exchange layer that allows different information systems to interoperate without relying on a centralised database.

DOI: 10.4324/9781003673897-16

Box 12.1 – Summary of Estonia's X-Road Project

Estonia's X-Road is a groundbreaking data exchange platform that underpins the country's digital society, enabling secure, decentralised communication between public and private-sector systems. Launched in 2001 and now open source, X-Road allows organisations to share data directly through a peer-to-peer network, ensuring scalability, cybersecurity, and interoperability. It supports over 3,000 e-services and connects more than 450 organisations, with cross-border functionality demonstrated in collaborations like the one with Finland. Its distributed architecture eliminates single points of failure, while digital signatures, encryption, and logging ensure data integrity and confidentiality. X-Road powers key e-government services such as e-Tax, e-Voting, and digital prescriptions, and its adoption by more than 20 countries has inspired similar systems globally.

In recent years, X-Road has begun integrating AI in alignment with Estonia's Kratt AI strategy, aiming to enhance public services while safeguarding transparency and trust. This includes an AI model training platform that leverages X-Road's data infrastructure for applications like document classification and automation, all within EU data protection guidelines. Tools for text analysis and anonymisation have been developed for sectors like the judiciary, while virtual assistants such as Bürokratt offer citizens personalised, AI-driven services. This fusion of secure data exchange and ethical AI not only improves efficiency and service delivery but also positions Estonia as a global leader in digital governance, providing a model for nations seeking to responsibly incorporate AI into public administration.

In 2016, its source code was released under the MIT License,[1] making it open source and allowing other countries to adopt and adapt the platform. Written in Java, X-Road is maintained by the Nordic Institute for Interoperability Solutions (NIIS), a collaboration between Estonia, Finland, and Iceland.

X-Road features a distributed, peer-to-peer architecture, allowing organisations to exchange data directly without a single point of failure. This structure enhances both scalability and cybersecurity. All data sent through the system is digitally signed and encrypted, while incoming data is authenticated and logged to ensure confidentiality and integrity.

Designed for interoperability, X-Road seamlessly integrates diverse systems, supporting more than 3,000 e-services within Estonia and connecting over 450 organisations.[2] The platform also enables cross-border data exchange, as demonstrated by the 2018 federation between Estonia and Finland, which allows services such as taxation, mobility, and health insurance registration to function across borders.

The impact of X-Road on Estonia has been transformative. It powers essential e-government services like the e-Tax Board, e-Voting, e-School, and digital prescriptions. By adhering to the *ask-once-only* principle, it reduces redundancy and simplifies citizen interactions with the state. This real-time data sharing significantly improves efficiency in public service delivery and lowers operational costs thanks to its decentralised design.

Globally, X-Road has been adopted by over 20 countries, including Finland, Iceland, Namibia, Brazil, and Cambodia. Its influence has spurred the development of similar platforms such as UXP[3] and PlanetCross,[4] while NIIS continues to expand the technology's global reach and capabilities.[5]

Estonia's X-Road platform is undergoing a significant evolution as it begins to integrate AI, reinforcing its role as a secure and interoperable data exchange system. This development is closely aligned with the country's broader Kratt AI strategy, which focuses on enhancing public services through the responsible use of AI technologies.

One of the key advancements is the creation of an AI model training platform, which enables government agencies to build and deploy AI models tailored to specific domains. This platform is designed to work in harmony with X-Road, allowing agencies to leverage their existing data for purposes such as classification and automation while adhering to EU data protection standards. AI models can now automatically route communications or identify sensitive information within documents, improving both efficiency and accuracy.

Central to this transformation is the Kratt AI initiative, which includes the development of an open-source repository of AI tools accessible to both public institutions and private entities.[6] These tools cover functions like text analysis and document anonymisation, which are particularly useful in fields such as the judiciary, where identifying and removing personal data from court decisions is important. The strategy underscores the ethical use of AI, using X-Road's secure infrastructure to guarantee data integrity and safeguard privacy in all AI-driven applications.

Another practical application of this integration is *Bürokratt*, an AI-powered virtual assistant that connects to X-Road to deliver personalised digital services to citizens.[7] It enhances user experience by enabling context-aware interactions for tasks such as filing taxes, seeking healthcare information, or applying for social benefits, simplifying access to essential public services.

The incorporation of AI into X-Road brings several advantages. It boosts efficiency by automating routine administrative tasks, reduces the burden on public servants, and enhances decision-making processes. Citizens benefit from faster and more tailored service delivery, and the system's design allows it to scale across numerous government entities while maintaining high standards of performance and regulatory compliance.

Looking ahead, Estonia is poised to further strengthen its position as a global leader in digital governance by merging X-Road's robust data exchange infrastructure with new AI capabilities. This integrated approach serves as a blueprint for other nations aiming to responsibly incorporate AI into public administration.

Singapore: AI in Urban Planning and Transportation

Singapore's Smart Nation initiative exemplifies how AI can transform urban management. The Urban Redevelopment Authority uses AI to analyse transportation patterns, land use, and population density to optimise city planning. For example, predictive algorithms suggest optimal locations for housing projects that minimise commute times while preserving green spaces.

In public transportation, AI-powered systems adjust bus and train schedules in real time based on passenger flow. This reduces congestion, shortens waiting times, and improves overall commuter satisfaction. By integrating AI with the Internet of Things (IoT) devices, Singapore has created a responsive and sustainable urban infrastructure.

Rwanda: Leveraging AI for Healthcare Equity

Rwanda has effectively employed AI to address healthcare disparities in underserved regions. Through a partnership with private technology companies, the government deployed AI-powered diagnostic tools for conditions such as malaria and tuberculosis. Mobile health clinics equipped with these tools deliver rapid and accurate diagnoses in rural areas, where access to healthcare is limited.

These initiatives have significantly reduced diagnostic turnaround times and improved treatment outcomes. By focusing on equity and leveraging AI to fill gaps in healthcare delivery, Rwanda has demonstrated how developing nations can harness advanced technology to address local challenges.

The UAE's Journey Towards Automated Lawmaking

The United Arab Emirates has become the first country to systematically employ AI in drafting, reviewing, and amending legislation. This move is part of the UAE's broader strategy to improve governmental efficiency and establish itself as a global leader in AI integration.[8]

The UAE has launched a dedicated cabinet unit, the Regulatory Intelligence Office, to lead the integration of AI into the legislative process. In collaboration with federal and local bodies, this office is coordinating the deployment of AI systems to modernise how laws are created, reviewed, and updated.

By leveraging a vast database of existing legislation, court rulings, and government services, the AI platform is designed to deliver proactive legal recommendations, significantly accelerating the drafting process and improving accuracy. Government estimates suggest that this transformation could cut legislative processing time by up to 70 per cent and reduce costs by 50 per cent while contributing to a projected 35 per cent increase in the national GDP by 2030.

The system not only supports the creation of new laws but also ensures ongoing legal adaptation by continuously proposing updates to existing regulations. While concerns remain around the reliability of AI outputs, potential biases in training data, and the opacity of AI decision-making, the UAE's centralised governance structure enables swift experimentation and implementation. Through this initiative, the UAE is demonstrating how governments can harness AI to drive institutional innovation and reshape the future of public administration.[9]

However, the approach is not without challenges. Experts have raised concerns about the reliability of AI outputs and the potential for bias, which can arise from the data used to train these systems.[10] There are also questions about whether AI can fully grasp the nuanced interpretation of legal language and intent. Furthermore, the often-opaque nature of AI decision-making processes may hinder transparency and accountability in legislative matters.[11]

Despite these challenges, the UAE's centralised governance structure enables swift adoption of AI technologies, allowing the country to move quickly from concept to implementation. This agility places the UAE at the forefront of AI integration in government and positions it as a compelling example for other nations seeking to modernise their public sectors through technological innovation.

AI Use in Visa Processing Around the World

AI is becoming an integral part of visa processing systems globally, transforming how governments manage immigration applications. This innovation seeks to improve efficiency, strengthen security, and streamline decision-making in the visa application process. AI is being used for:

- Document verification and fraud detection: Submitted documents are analysed for authenticity verification using techniques like pattern recognition and digital watermark verification to detect inconsistencies across multiple documents from the same applicant. It also cross-references documents against databases of known genuine and fraudulent documents.
- Biometric processing: Advanced facial recognition compares application photos with passport photos and previous visa applications to detect deepfakes and manipulated photos. It also performs fingerprint matching to help prevent multiple applications under different identities and voice recognition for remote interviews.
- Risk assessment and security screening: AI models assess security risks by analysing travel history patterns, financial transactions, social media presence, known associations, previous immigration violations. These systems

cross-reference data against international security databases and estimate overstay risks based on historical data patterns.
- Application processing and prioritisation: AI tools automatically categorise applications based on visa type and completeness, prioritise time-sensitive applications (like medical emergencies), check eligibility criteria against submitted documentation, identify similar successful/rejected cases to assist decision-making, request additional documentation when needed, and predict application volumes, adjusting staffing accordingly.

It's important to note that in most countries, AI systems are used as support tools rather than decision-makers. Human immigration officers typically retain final authority over visa decisions.

Several countries have begun incorporating AI into their visa processing systems in various ways.

- The United States Customs and Border Protection uses AI for advance passenger screening, facial recognition at airports, predictive analytics for visa overstay risk, and pattern recognition for fraud detection. Three key applications are: Traveler Verification using facial biometric matching to confirm passenger identity, Cargo Screening to identify potential threats, and Situational Awareness to enhance border threats.
- Canada's use of AI has been notably transparent. Since 2021, they've used AI to help process temporary resident visas, looking for straightforward applications that meet all requirements. The system doesn't make final decisions but helps sort applications to speed up processing. Canadian officials have published information about their AI framework and its role in immigration decisions.[12]
- The Brazilian government is planning to utilise AI to analyse residence permit applications for employment, aiming to reduce bureaucracy and speed up processing times.
- The EU is scheduled to launch its much-delayed ETIAS (European Travel Information Authorisation System) by mid-2025. This AI-driven system will pre-register visa-exempt visitors travelling to the Schengen area and assess security or irregular migratory risks before arrival at the border.
- The UK has implemented an AI-driven system to screen visa applications and identify potential security risks. This system analyses application data and cross-references it with various databases to flag applications that may need additional scrutiny.
- The United Arab Emirates has implemented an iris scanner that uses AI to confirm identity, allowing travellers to move quickly through passport control while maintaining security precautions.
- India has implemented AI tools to help verify documents and detect potential fraud in visa applications, though the final decisions remain with human officers.

- China uses AI in their visa processing centres to verify applicants' identities through facial recognition and document authentication. Their system also helps detect fraudulent applications by analysing patterns in submitted documents.

As these examples illustrate, the benefits of AI in visa processing are increased efficiency, enhanced security, improved accuracy, and the cost savings from automation.

The implementation of AI in the visa processes carries several challenges: privacy concerns regarding data collection and storage, potential bias in AI decision-making systems, the need for human oversight and appeal processes, cybersecurity risks, and training requirements for immigration staff. The integration of this type of technology necessitates robust digital infrastructure and specialised expertise, potentially leading to disparities due to uneven access across and within different regions.

At the same time, AI's ability to support real-time translation, speech recognition, and multilingual communication presents a major opportunity to enhance the accessibility of immigration services. This is particularly important in linguistically diverse regions, such as Europe, where more than ten languages are spoken by over 1 per cent of the population, and the United States, where significant communities speak languages like Tagalog, Arabic, Korean, and Chinese.

The emerging trends in visa processing are linked to the development of multilingual AI systems to process applications in various languages, the implementation of explainable AI to provide reasoning for recommendations, the development of standardised international protocols for AI in immigration, and the integration with smart border systems and e-gates.

Modernising Healthcare with the Help of AI

The UK's NHS AI Rollout

The National Health Service (NHS) in the United Kingdom is one of the largest employers in the world, with over 1.5 million staff, surpassed only by the U.S. Department of Defense, the Chinese military, and Walmart. In recent years and still at an early stage of development, the NHS has been weaving AI into the fabric of its operations, with the goal of enhancing patient care, improving administrative efficiency, and advancing preventive medicine.

One of the NHS's most ambitious undertakings is the EDITH trial, Early Detection using Information Technology in Health. This large-scale initiative spans 30 testing sites and involves 700,000 women patients across England. Focused on revolutionising breast cancer screening, the trial explores whether AI can support or even replace the current system, where two radiologists are required to review each mammogram. By allowing a single radiologist to work in tandem with AI, the hope is to address diagnostic bottlenecks and workforce shortages. Though still in its early stages, the trial holds significant promise for reshaping diagnostic practices. Backing this ambition is a £21 million investment aimed at deploying AI to detect a range of conditions, from cancer to strokes and heart disease, faster and more accurately.[13]

Beyond diagnostics, AI is also being harnessed for patient risk stratification. In the Cheshire and Merseyside region, hospitals are piloting systems that combine more than 200 million patient records to generate risk scores.[14] These scores help identify individuals most likely to experience adverse health outcomes, allowing for more efficient prioritisation on hospital waiting lists.

The NHS is also embracing AI to tackle the growing burden of administrative tasks. AI-powered medical note-taking tools, supported by tech giants like Microsoft and Amazon, now assist doctors by transcribing and summarising clinical interactions.[15] This shift is designed to give clinicians more time to focus on patients rather than paperwork.

Virtual wards represent another innovative approach. These systems enable patients to receive hospital-level care from the comfort of their own homes. AI continuously monitors vital signs and detects early warning signs of deterioration, reducing unnecessary hospital admissions and improving long-term outcomes.[16]

Mental health services are also evolving with the help of AI. One notable example is Shout, a 24/7 text-based support platform that uses AI to analyse messages and guide timely responses. Since its launch in 2019 by a royal charity, the service has handled over three million conversations, becoming a vital resource for mental healthcare in the UK.[17]

Looking ahead, the NHS is exploring the role of AI in genomics and preventive medicine. By partnering with companies like Genomics, the health service aims to develop predictive tools for conditions such as heart disease and diabetes, potentially allowing for earlier interventions and personalised care.[18]

However, the journey towards AI integration hasn't been without setbacks. Efforts to optimise hospital resources and predict patient demand through AI have encountered several roadblocks. Incompatible legacy systems, a lack of comprehensive staff training, and minimal stakeholder engagement led to operational disruptions and public frustration. Implementation has also been hampered by the increasing number of NHS administrators who work from home. Budget overruns compounded these issues, attracting criticism from both policymakers and the public. These challenges underscore the need for gradual implementation, robust training programmes, and careful alignment between technological tools and the NHS's operational realities.

Despite the hurdles, the NHS's exploration of AI marks a significant step towards modernising healthcare delivery, balancing innovation with the complex demands of a national health system.

Box 12.2 – Case Study: AI and the Transformation of NHS Patient Care in the UK

Despite the cases mentioned above, the UK's National Health Service (NHS) is facing mounting pressure due to chronic inefficiencies in patient navigation. Every day, people seeking care encounter confusion and delays, whether it's being directed to the wrong service, waiting for hours in overwhelmed Accident & Emergency (A&E) departments, or struggling to access General Practitioner (GP) appointments. These issues don't just inconvenience patients; they can have severe consequences, including an estimated 300 deaths each week due to delays in emergency care, according to the Royal College of Emergency Medicine.[19]

At the core of the problem lies fragmented and outdated systems, where most managers are operating in crisis mode. There is little time to engage in the process of updating systems and dealing with the complexities of solution design, testing, feedback, and implementation of new AI initiatives.

For patients, the experience of interacting with the NHS can be exasperating. This is not a reflection of the dedicated staff but the result of a service that is overwhelmed by demand. Patients often don't know where to turn, whether to contact NHS 111,[20] book a GP appointment, or visit A&E. These services frequently overlap, offering inconsistent advice and assessments. Many of the triage systems in place are inflexible, relying heavily on receptionists or call centre scripts that can't adapt to the complexity of real-life situations. Digital integration is limited, and patient records remain siloed across different parts of the system. As demand for care continues to outpace supply, GP practices are increasingly forced to switch off triage tools altogether, worsening the bottlenecks.

In this environment, AI presents a powerful opportunity to change course. In numerous countries, AI-driven platforms have already begun to reshape patient navigation. Tools developed by companies like Ada, Abi Health, Infermedica, and Visiba are helping patients assess symptoms and make informed decisions about their care, guiding them to the most appropriate services and reducing unnecessary visits. These solutions provide personalised, scalable support that not only improves the patient experience but also alleviates pressure on health systems.

In the UK, the Tony Blair Institute for Global Change (TBI) has proposed making such technology universally available through an AI Navigation Assistant for every citizen. This digital assistant would deliver consistent, high-quality triage, ensuring patients are guided to the right place at the right time. More than just a referral tool, it would also connect users with emerging digital healthcare options such as Sleepio for insomnia, Flok for physiotherapy, or DERM for skin conditions, helping to bridge the gap between traditional and digital care.

The potential impact of this innovation is far-reaching. A significant number of GP and A&E visits could be avoided by enabling patients to self-assess, self-refer, or manage minor conditions independently. Estimates suggest that 29 million GP appointments and nearly 40 per cent of A&E attendances are unnecessary, and AI tools could help reduce these figures dramatically. With fewer patients clogging up critical services, healthcare professionals would be able to dedicate more time to complex cases, improving both efficiency and care quality.

Beyond freeing up clinical capacity, AI navigation could also deliver substantial cost savings. The TBI estimates annual productivity gains of £340 million among non-clinical staff in GP practices and NHS 111. Given the projected cost of implementation, between £10 million and £100 million, the return on investment would be significant. Over time, AI could serve as the foundation for a fully digital-first healthcare experience, enabling patients to manage more of their care remotely using digital therapeutics, remote monitoring tools, and virtual consultations.[21]

AI offers more than just a technological upgrade; it represents a shift towards a smarter, more sustainable NHS. By streamlining navigation, reducing unnecessary pressure on services, and empowering patients to take greater control of their health, AI has the potential to redefine how care is delivered across the UK. Embracing this opportunity is not only a matter of improving efficiency but a vital step towards securing the future of the health service.

The AI Revolution in Medical Imaging

In the United States, the FDA has approved more than 700 AI algorithms to support physicians, with radiology leading the way, representing 76 per cent of all clinical AI clearances.[22] However, adoption remains low, with only 2 per cent of radiology practices integrating these tools.[23] This hesitancy stems from limited real-world validation and a lack of clarity around how the technology works. In a 2020 consultation, the FDA rejected proposals to allow AI systems to function without human oversight.[24]

In contrast, Europe has embraced a more forward-thinking approach. In 2022, regulators approved Oxipit's ChestLink software, the first fully autonomous AI system for analysing X-rays and generating reports.[25] Oxipit is now seeking FDA approval in the US, aiming to revolutionise radiology workflows by automating routine imaging tasks and freeing radiologists to focus on more complex cases.

AI's potential in medical imaging is especially evident in cancer detection, where it could help close critical gaps. Radiologists, for instance, miss around 20 per cent of breast cancers during routine mammograms. Swedish studies have shown that combining AI with a single radiologist boosts cancer detection by 20 per cent, compared to two radiologists working independently. The MASAI trial further demonstrated that AI-assisted breast screening can increase detection rates by up to 29 per cent, catching invasive cancers earlier while also reducing false positives.[26]

AI holds immense promise for transforming radiology, with growing evidence of its impact on diagnostic accuracy and efficiency. However, widespread adoption remains slow, especially in the US, due to scepticism and regulatory caution. Bridging this gap will be essential to fully realise AI's potential in improving patient care.

Lessons from Failures: Pitfalls of AI Implementation

Predictive Policing in the United States

Several American cities, including Chicago and Los Angeles, piloted predictive policing systems that used AI to identify crime hotspots. These systems analysed historical crime data to predict where future crimes might occur, enabling law enforcement to allocate resources more efficiently. However, systemic biases in the training data led to disproportionate targeting of minority neighbourhoods.

The programmes faced widespread criticism for perpetuating racial profiling and eroding community trust. In Los Angeles, public backlash and evidence of discriminatory outcomes led to the termination of the programme. This case underscores the need for careful oversight and community engagement in deploying AI, particularly in sensitive areas like law enforcement.

Kenya's Huduma Namba Biometric ID System

Kenya's Huduma Namba initiative aimed to centralise citizen identification through a biometric ID system powered by AI. Despite its ambitious goals, the project was marred by technical failures, data privacy concerns, and inadequate safeguards against misuse.

Civil society raised alarms about the potential for surveillance and data exploitation. Additionally, operational setbacks and lack of transparency eroded public trust. This initiative highlights the risks of deploying large-scale AI systems without clear privacy protections and robust accountability mechanisms.

AI Faces Interoperability Challenges at the United States Department of Health and Human Services (HHS)

In recent interviews and discussions regarding the Department of Government Efficiency's (DOGE) mission to modernise federal operations, DOGE officials have highlighted the significant data and technology challenges facing government agencies. A prime example comes from DOGE's latest report, which reveals that the Department of Health and Human Services (HHS) currently operates more than 700 distinct IT systems, most of which lack interoperability and are managed by 27 different chief information officers.[27] With an annual IT budget surpassing $5 billion, HHS represents the single largest federal investment in IT infrastructure.[28] To tackle these long-standing inefficiencies, the department has launched three major initiatives aimed at enhancing system interoperability and streamlining information exchange.

One of these is the Fast Healthcare Interoperability Resources (FHIR) standard, developed by Health Level Seven International (HL7), which facilitates the electronic exchange of healthcare data using modern web technologies to promote seamless communication between disparate health platforms.[29] Another is the eHealth Exchange, formerly the Nationwide Health Information Network (NwHIN), which provides a standardised framework for sharing healthcare data securely across federal agencies, healthcare providers, and other stakeholders.[30] Additionally, the Centers for Disease Control and Prevention (CDC) leads the Public Health Information Network (PHIN), an initiative focused on enhancing data integration and interoperability within public health agencies to support key functions such as surveillance, analysis, and emergency response.[31]

Despite these promising efforts, the integration of AI within government remains constrained by several fundamental challenges. Effective AI implementation depends on three critical components: high-quality data, adequate computing power, and strong leadership with a commitment to execution. As we have already mentioned, government agencies frequently struggle with fragmented, outdated data and siloed systems, which significantly hinder AI adoption. Questions also remain as to whether these agencies possess the necessary computational capacity to support complex algorithms and large-scale data analysis.

Furthermore, leadership must juggle the imperative of embracing AI's transformative potential with competing operational priorities. This includes securing sufficient funding, aligning organisational goals, and navigating bureaucratic inertia. The significant costs of improving data quality, upgrading infrastructure, and fostering a culture of innovation only add to the complexity. These issues highlight the formidable challenge of driving digital transformation within large government entities, where systemic inefficiencies often stand in the way of technological progress.

Multilateral and Regional Collaboration: The Role of Global Partnerships

The European Union's Unified Approach

The European Union (EU) has established itself as a leader in ethical AI governance through initiatives like the AI Act, which sets standards for transparency, accountability, and risk management across member states. The EU's collaborative approach ensures that innovations in one country can be seamlessly integrated across the region.

The AI4EU Platform connects policymakers, researchers, and developers to share resources and best practices. This initiative has accelerated AI adoption while maintaining a strong focus on ethical principles and citizen trust.

UNICEF's AI for Children Initiative

UNICEF's AI for Children project provides a framework for developing AI systems that prioritise the rights and well-being of children. By partnering with governments and private organisations, UNICEF has influenced policies that address unique ethical considerations, such as protecting children's data privacy and ensuring equitable access to technology.

Africa's Continental AI Strategy

The African Union's AI strategy focuses on capacity building, data sovereignty, and equitable development. Initiatives like the African Virtual University's AI training programmes aim to develop local expertise, ensuring that AI adoption benefits all member nations. This regional collaboration reflects a commitment to leveraging technology for inclusive growth.

Key Takeaways: Charting the Path Forward

The successes of Estonia, Singapore, the United Kingdom, and Rwanda highlight the transformative potential of AI when implemented thoughtfully. These initiatives demonstrate the importance of robust infrastructure, transparent governance, and alignment with citizen needs. Conversely, failures in predictive policing, healthcare, and biometric ID systems reveal the dangers of deploying AI without addressing bias, engaging stakeholders, or establishing safeguards.

International and regional partnerships are essential to driving responsible AI adoption. In a world where no single country can tackle AI's challenges alone, collaboration across borders allows governments to share expertise, align regulations, and build trust in emerging technologies. By exchanging knowledge on ethics, governance, and technical innovation, countries can learn from one another's successes and mistakes. Joint efforts help reduce costs, avoid duplication, and create shared solutions to issues like bias, privacy, and security, laying the groundwork for safer, fairer AI systems that serve the public good globally.

To ensure long-term success, governments must take a proactive and layered approach to building AI resilience. This means conducting regular audits to evaluate system performance, fairness, and compliance, helping identify issues before they escalate. Contingency plans are equally vital; clear protocols, backup systems, and recovery procedures can minimise harm when systems fail or are compromised. Ongoing public engagement is just as important. By involving citizens and stakeholders throughout the AI lifecycle, governments can ensure that technologies reflect real needs and societal values. Embedding these practices into governance frameworks not only reduces risk but also strengthens public trust and supports the responsible growth of AI.

A Vision for the Future

The case studies in this chapter highlight both the promise and the risks of applying AI to public service. They demonstrate the importance of adopting a measured approach, one that welcomes innovation while remaining alert to potential pitfalls and unintended outcomes.

As we look ahead, the next chapter will examine the wider implications of these changes, offering a perspective on what the future of public service may look like in an AI-enabled world.

Notes

1 The MIT License is a permissive open-source software licence originating from the Massachusetts Institute of Technology in the late 1980s. It is widely regarded for its simplicity, brevity, and flexibility, making it one of the most popular licences in the open-source community.

2 GovInsider (2024), Estonia's X-Road: Data exchange in the world's most digital society, https://govinsider.asia/intl-en/article/estonias-x-road-data-exchange-in-the-worlds-most-digital-society (accessed on 30 March 2025).

3 Cybernetica's UXP is a secure peer-to-peer data exchange platform that plays a vital role in e-governance, business, and healthcare. It features a decentralised architecture, allowing systems to communicate directly without relying on a central server. UXP has been adopted by various governments, including Estonia and Ukraine, and is also used across sectors such as finance and healthcare. For organisations with limited infrastructure, the 'Managed UXP' offers a cloud-based solution that delivers interoperability as a service.

4 PlanetCross, developed by the Japanese–Estonian startup Planetway, is a secure data collaboration platform adapted from Estonia's X-Road system for private-sector use in Japan. It enables efficient, scalable data exchange across relational databases with minimal system changes, using Transport Layer Security encryption, digital signatures, and robust traceability tools. Supporting both cloud and on-premise deployment, it features a user-friendly interface and an Relational Database Adapter for easy integration. PlanetCross is used in sectors like energy, healthcare, and insurance and has earned international awards for innovation and impact.

5 E-Estonia (No date), X-Road – interoperability services, https://e-estonia.com/solutions/interoperability-services/x-road/ (accessed on 30 March 2025).

6 Invest in Estonia (2019), Estonia is creating a free-to-use source code repository for its AI-based solutions, https://investinestonia.com/estonia-is-creating-a-source-code-repository-of-ai-based-solutions/ (accessed on 30 March 2025.

7 Rootcode (No date), Building an AI model training platform for the Government of Estonia, https://rootcode.io/portfolio/government-of-estonia (accessed on 30 March 2025).
8 Malaymail (2025), UAE becomes first country to use AI for law drafting, review, www.malaymail.com/news/world/2025/04/25/uae-becomes-first-country-to-use-ai-for-law-drafting-review/174461 (accessed on 20 May 2025).
9 The Tribune Express (2025), UAE becomes first country to use AI to write laws, https://tribune.com.pk/story/2542164/uae-becomes-first-country-to-use-ai-to-write-laws (accessed on 20 May 2025).
10 Financial Times (2025), UAE set to use AI to write laws in world first, www.ft.com/content/9019cd51-2b55-4175-81a6-eafcf28609c3 (accessed on 20 May 2025).
11 The Indian Express (2025), AI to reboot UAE's skyscraping tech ambitions, away from fossil fuels, https://indianexpress.com/article/business/ai-to-reboot-uaes-skyscraping-tech-ambitions-away-from-fossil-fuels-9969406/ (accessed on 20 May 2025).
12 Government Canada (2023), CIMM – Question Period note – Use of AI in decision-making at IRCC – November 29, 2022, www.canada.ca/en/immigration-refugees-citizenship/corporate/transparency/committees/cimm-nov-29-2022/question-period-note-use-ai-decision-making-ircc.html (accessed on 3 January 2025).
13 Government of the UK (2023), £21 million to roll out artificial intelligence across the NHS, www.gov.uk/government/news/21-million-to-roll-out-artificial-intelligence-across-the-nhs (accessed on 12 April 2025).
14 The Times (2025), App spots patients at risk and moves them up the NHS waiting list, www.thetimes.com/uk/healthcare/article/nhs-waiting-list-pilot-ai-patient-risk-score-mw2v0pc76 (accessed on 12 April 2025).
15 Financial Times (2025), Healthcare turns to AI for medical note-taking 'scribes', www.ft.com/content/5c356658-6db4-47c1-940b-b2e3cf3a51f3 (accessed on 12 April 2025).
16 NHS SBS (2023), Emerging remote patient monitoring solutions, www.sbs.nhs.uk/news/emerging-remote-patient-monitoring-solutions-made-easier-to-procure-for-the-nhs-and-social-care-sector/ (accessed on 12 April 2025).
17 Digitalhealth (2019), 24/7 text messaging services launched to support those in crisis, www.digitalhealth.net/2019/05/shout-text-messaging-service-support-crisis/ (accessed on 12 April 2025).
18 Government of the UK (2022), Genome UK: 2022 to 2025 implementation plan for England, www.gov.uk/government/publications/genome-uk-2022-to-2025-implementation-plan-for-england/genome-uk-2022-to-2025-implementation-plan-for-england. (accessed on 12 April 2025).
19 Tony Blair Institute for Global Change (2025), *Preparing the NHS for the AI Era: Why Smarter Triage and Navigation Mean Better Health Care*, https://institute.global/insights/public-services/preparing-the-nhs-for-the-ai-era-why-smarter-triage-and-navigation-mean-better-health-care (accessed on 12 April 2025).
20 NHS 111 is a free, non-emergency medical helpline available in England, Scotland, and Wales. It provides 24/7 access to healthcare advice and services for urgent but non-life-threatening medical concerns. The service can be accessed by calling 111 or, in England, through the NHS 111 online platform.
21 Tony Blair Institute for Global Change (2025), *Preparing the NHS for the AI Era: Why Smarter Triage and Navigation Mean Better Health Care*, https://institute.global/insights/public-services/preparing-the-nhs-for-the-ai-era-why-smarter-triage-and-navigation-mean-better-health-care (accessed on 12 April 2025.

22 HealthImaging (2023), FDA has now cleared 700 AI healthcare algorithms, more than 76% in radiology, https://healthimaging.com/topics/artificial-intelligence/fda-has-now-cleared-700-ai-healthcare-algorithms-more-76-radiology (accessed on 12 April 2025)
23 Lexology (2023), Where does AI radiology's use in clinical practice stand today? What is its future?, www.lexology.com/library/detail.aspx?g=c75d9aa1-6093-4aed-b0f8-628ba330677b (accessed on 12 April 2025).
24 HIMSS (2019), Proposed regulatory framework for modifications to artificial intelligence/machine learning, www.himss.org/news/proposed-regulatory-framework-modifications-artificial-intelligencemachine-learning (accessed on 12 April 2025).
25 The Imaging Wire (2022), Autonomous AI milestone, https://theimagingwire.com/2022/03/30/autonomous-ai-milestone/ (accessed on 12 April 2025).
26 Emjreviews (2025), AI boosts cancer detection in Swedish mammography trial, www.emjreviews.com/radiology/news/ai-boosts-cancer-detection-in-swedish-mammography-trial/ (accessed on 12 April 2025).
27 Medpagetoday (2025), Musk, DOGE created New HHS org chart, www.medpagetoday.com/special-reports/features/114915 (accessed on 12 April 2025).
28 U.S. Department of Health and Human Services (2015), Federal Information Technology Acquisition Reform Act – HHS Implementation Plan, www.hhs.gov/sites/default/files/hhs-fitara-implementation-plan.pdf (accessed on 12 April 2025).
29 eCQUI (2025), FHIR – Fast Healthcare Interoperability Resources, https://ecqi.healthit.gov/fhir?qt-tabs_fhir=about (accessed on 12 April 2025).
30 Assistant Secretary for Technology Policy (2025), The eHealth Exchange, www.healthit.gov/faq/what-ehealth-exchange (accessed on 12 April 2025).
31 CDC (No date), About PHIN tools and resources, www.cdc.gov/phin/php/index.html (accessed on 12 April 2025).

Chapter 13

The Future of Public Service

A Vision for an AI-Enabled Workforce

The rise of artificial intelligence (AI) represents more than a technological shift; it signals a fundamental transformation in how governments function, engage with citizens, and deliver essential services. As AI assumes a greater role in public administration, the nature of public service work must evolve to meet new demands and expectations.

This chapter examines the future of public service, focusing on how adaptive governance models can be shaped by AI, the strategies required to preserve public trust, and the development of ethical frameworks capable of guiding decision-making in an increasingly complex technological environment.

Adaptive Governance Models: Dynamic and Data-Driven Policymaking

Traditional governance models often rely on rigid structures and fixed cycles, making it challenging to respond swiftly to evolving societal needs. AI offers a transformative opportunity to create dynamic governance, an approach that uses real-time data to inform and continuously adapt policies as circumstances change.

Reimagining Routine Operations

Between 2022 and 2023, UK government agencies handled a staggering 40 million remote interactions with the public, including 30 million phone calls with an

DOI: 10.4324/9781003673897-17

average duration of 8 minutes, 4.5 million emails, and 5 million webchats. These numbers reflect activity across major central government contact centres, and the total volume increases significantly when local authorities are included. HMRC alone received a staggering 18 million inquiries, by far the largest share.[1] Many of these interactions are time-consuming, frustrating, and costly for both citizens and government employees, yet they could be managed far more efficiently with AI.

AI-driven tools, such as chatbots and virtual assistants, have already demonstrated their ability to streamline public services. By automating routine tasks, such as answering frequently asked questions or guiding users through online forms, AI can drastically reduce wait times, minimise errors, and enhance citizen satisfaction through faster, more accurate responses.

The potential of AI to revolutionise administrative processes is vast. Beyond managing inquiries, AI can automate data processing, document management, and scheduling, allowing employees to focus on higher-value tasks. This extends to the interpretation of complex regulations, where AI can support civil servants in navigating lengthy and detailed policy documents. In the UK, for instance, the Department for Work and Pensions' Benefits Handbook spans over 2,000 pages, outlining rules for determining payments for recipients. AI tools with contextual awareness can quickly scan and analyse these rules, helping officials identify relevant guidance, particularly in complex or exceptional cases, thereby enhancing both accuracy and efficiency in decision-making.

Moreover, AI-powered analytics can uncover patterns in citizen interactions, providing agencies with valuable insights to improve service delivery and optimise resource allocation during peak demand periods. The integration of AI in public services goes beyond mere efficiency; it signals a shift towards a more responsive and inclusive form of governance. With natural language processing (NLP) capabilities, AI can offer multilingual support, breaking down barriers for diverse populations. Furthermore, AI-driven automation facilitates smoother cross-departmental collaboration by enabling real-time data sharing, eliminating the need for manual interventions.

As governments increasingly turn to AI to enhance public service delivery, NLP models like BERT are emerging as key enablers of more responsive, informed, and citizen-centred engagement. BERT, or less snappily, Bidirectional Encoder Representations from Transformers,[2] brings a transformative edge to NLP. Why is this important? By analysing text in both directions, considering words that come before and after something in a sentence, BERT captures the full context of language, enabling a more nuanced understanding of meaning and intent. This capability is particularly valuable in public service environments, where client inquiries often reflect complex personal situations, often with emotional undertones. Through advanced NLP techniques, BERT can detect subtle cues such as frustration or dissatisfaction, allowing agencies to respond with greater empathy and precision. Furthermore, the availability of pre-trained BERT models for applications like sentiment analysis, clinical documentation, and toxic language detection accelerates the deployment of AI-driven solutions. BERT's next-sentence prediction functionality also enhances the system's ability to follow conversational flow, supporting more natural and effective engagement. In this way, BERT strengthens the foundation for responsive, human-centred public services and, inevitably, customer satisfaction.

These innovations empower governments to rethink how routine administrative operations are managed, enabling them to deliver faster, more accessible, and transparent services. In doing so, they can build greater public trust while addressing the ever-changing needs of citizens.

Box 13.1 – Case Study: Humphrey Suite Tools

The integration of AI tools like the UK's Humphrey is revolutionising public administration by automating routine tasks and complex workflows.[3] Incidentally, the name Humphrey adds a touch of British humour as it is named after the fictional senior civil servant in the popular TV show *Yes Minister*. Developed by the Department for Science, Innovation and Technology and launched in 2025, Humphrey helps civil servants focus on strategic priorities by streamlining tasks like summarising public consultation responses, providing instant access to parliamentary documents, and offering rapid legal analysis.

The key tools in the Humphrey Suite include:

Table 13.1 Humphrey Suite tools

Tool	*Description*
Consult	Analyses and summarises large volumes of public consultation responses, significantly reducing the time and cost associated with manual analysis.
Parallax	Provides civil servants with quick access to relevant parliamentary debates and policy documents.
Minute	Automates the transcription and summarisation of meetings, freeing up staff time for more strategic tasks.
Redbox	Assists in summarising policies and preparing briefings for government officials.
Lex	Offers legal analysis tools to support decision-making processes within the civil service.

Source: Authors' elaboration

These tools not only enhance efficiency but also improve interdepartmental collaboration by enabling seamless data sharing. For example, the system quickly summarises feedback or finds legislative information, reducing decision-making delays.

The Netherlands employs AI to manage flood risks. By integrating data from weather forecasts, soil moisture sensors, and historical flooding patterns, AI systems dynamically update flood defences and emergency response strategies. This adaptability has significantly reduced the economic and human costs of natural disasters.

The Netherlands, renowned for its innovative water management strategies, has increasingly turned to AI to address the persistent threat of flooding. Situated largely below sea level, the country faces unique and ongoing challenges from rising sea levels, heavy rainfall, and river overflows. To mitigate these risks, Dutch authorities have implemented advanced AI-driven systems that integrate a wide array of data sources, including real-time weather forecasts, soil moisture sensors, river flow rates, and historical flooding records.

These AI systems continuously analyse incoming data to predict potential flood events. By leveraging machine learning algorithms, the systems can identify subtle patterns and correlations that might elude traditional forecasting methods. This allows for dynamic, real-time adjustments to flood defence mechanisms such as storm surge barriers, sluices, and dikes. For example, if the AI system detects an increased risk of flooding in a particular region, it can automatically trigger the closure of floodgates or the activation of pumps to redirect water flow.

Moreover, AI enhances emergency response strategies by providing authorities with up-to-date risk assessments and actionable recommendations. Emergency services can use these insights to deploy resources more efficiently, issue timely evacuation warnings, and coordinate relief efforts. The adaptability and predictive power of AI have greatly improved the Netherlands' resilience to flooding, resulting in a significant reduction in both economic losses and the human toll associated with natural disasters.

By harnessing the capabilities of AI, the Netherlands sets a global standard for proactive and intelligent flood risk management, ensuring the safety and sustainability of its communities in the face of climate change.

Maintaining Public Trust in AI-Driven Systems

To reiterate a point we have highlighted earlier, one of the challenges behind AI adoption is the opacity of complex algorithms. To address this, governments must be cognisant of demands by interested agencies to understand what is going on behind automated decision-making, ensuring that AI decisions are understandable to both officials and the public.

In New York City, the Algorithmic Accountability Task Force mandates that agencies disclose how AI systems operate and their role in decision-making processes. Similarly, Finland's public chatbot system provides clear explanations for its responses, helping citizens understand the logic behind AI-driven recommendations.

Public trust grows when citizens or groups that represent them are involved in shaping AI systems. Participatory models, such as citizen advisory boards, can provide valuable input on AI deployment. For example, Estonia's e-governance model includes dashboards where citizens can track how their data is used, fostering transparency and accountability.

Governments must actively educate the public about AI's capabilities and limitations. Canada's AI for the Common Good initiative offers workshops and online resources that demystify AI, addressing misconceptions and building confidence in its use.

From Prohibition to Permission in Algorithmic Decision-Making

An increasingly common use of AI and algorithmic tools is making significant decisions about workers, ranging from hiring to evaluating performance. A recent OECD survey of over 6,000 mid-level managers across France, Germany, Italy, Japan, Spain, and the US found that algorithmic management, once associated mainly with gig platforms like Uber, is now widely used. Adoption rates vary, with 90 per cent of managers in the US reporting use, compared to 40 per cent in Japan. Despite this widespread adoption, many managers expressed discomfort: while 60 per cent believed the tools enhanced their decision-making, nearly two-thirds also reported at least one concern. The top worries included a lack of accountability when things go wrong, opaque decision-making processes, and insufficient safeguards for workers' physical and mental well-being.[4]

In the UK, these concerns are playing out in legislative debates, particularly around the Data (Use & Access) Bill currently moving through Parliament. Trade unions have voiced alarm over a proposed change that would shift the legal framework from a general prohibition on automated decision-making (with some exceptions) to a general presumption of permission, provided certain safeguards are in place. These include the right to challenge a decision, demand an explanation, and request human review.[5] This marks a critical shift in mindset, from assuming automation is the exception to viewing it as the norm, constrained only by specific protections.

Evolving Ethical Frameworks for AI in Public Service

Ethical considerations must keep pace with technological advancements to ensure that AI systems align with societal values and public service principles.

To navigate the complex and evolving ethical landscape of AI, governments could establish dedicated ethics committees perhaps reporting to an ombudsman or regulatory body. Comprising ethicists, technologists, and community representatives, these committees would help ensure that AI systems reflect public values and societal priorities. Their key responsibilities may include evaluating AI deployments, developing ethical guidelines, monitoring system performance, engaging with a diverse range of stakeholders, and publishing transparent findings and recommendations. As this book aims to show, many countries are actively participating in the debate over AI regulation. By sharing insights and examples of best practice, governments can more effectively manage the challenges of AI implementation.

A multidisciplinary approach is essential for these committees to grasp both the technical intricacies and broader social impacts of AI. This diversity of expertise enables rigorous oversight, fosters accountability, and helps build public trust in the responsible use of AI technologies. However, the challenge remains of balancing regulation with progress and innovation.

Redefining Public Service Work: The Human–AI Partnership

It is worth emphasising that the integration of AI into public service does not signal the replacement of human workers but rather a shift in their roles. AI can handle repetitive, data-intensive tasks, freeing public servants to focus on responsibilities that require human judgement, creativity, and empathy.

In hybrid workflows, humans and AI systems complement each other's strengths. For example, in healthcare, AI can analyse patient data to identify disease trends, while human administrators coordinate responses and ensure that resources reach underserved communities. This collaboration maximises efficiency while preserving the human touch.

The rise of AI will create new roles in public service, including:

- AI trainers: Professionals responsible for refining AI models to reflect changing policy priorities.
- Algorithm auditors: Specialists tasked with evaluating AI systems for fairness, transparency, and compliance with ethical standards.
- Citizens experience designers: Experts dedicated to ensuring that AI-powered services are accessible and user-friendly.

A Vision for the Future: AI-Enabled Public Service

As AI reshapes public service, the future workforce will be characterised by adaptability, creativity, and a commitment to public values. Governments that embrace this transformation will create institutions that are more efficient, equitable, and responsive.

Imagine a world where:

- AI-driven systems provide real-time insights, enabling policymakers to respond swiftly to emerging challenges.
- Citizens interact with government through intuitive platforms that streamline service delivery and amplify their voices in decision-making.
- Ethical AI systems ensure equitable access to resources, eliminating barriers for underserved populations.

Conclusion: Shaping the Future Together

The integration of AI into public service presents an opportunity to fundamentally reimagine governance for the digital age. By embracing innovation while confronting its challenges with foresight and responsibility, governments can build a smarter, more responsive, and more humane public sector that serves all citizens fairly and effectively. As Chapter 15 will explore, the path to realising this vision depends on collective action and sustained commitment to the public good.

Notes

1 Government of the UK (2023), *HMRC Monthly Performance Report: September 2023*, www.gov.uk/government/publications/hmrc-monthly-performance-report-september-2023/hmrc-monthly-performance-report-september-2023 (accessed on 28 March 2025).

2 J. Devlin *et al.* (2019), BERT: Pre-training of deep bidirectional transformers for language understanding, *Proceedings of the 2019 Conference of the North American Chapter of the Association for Computational Linguistics: Human Language Technologies*, Volume 1, 4171–4186, Association for Computational Linguistics, https://aclanthology.org/N19-1423.pdf (accessed on 16 April 2025).

3 Government of the UK (2025), Shake up of tech and AI usage across NHS and other public services to deliver plan for change, www.gov.uk/government/news/shake-up-of-tech-and-ai-usage-across-nhs-and-other-public-services-to-deliver-plan-for-change (accessed on 28 March 2025).

4 OECD (2025), *Algorithmic Management in the Workplace: New Evidence from an OECD Employer Survey*, OECD Publishing, Paris.

5 Financial Times (2025), What can workers do if they're fired by AI?, www.ft.com/content/6ca668c6-60a8-4215-857b-491e74f9599a (accessed on 16 April 2025).

Chapter 14

The AI Empire State

How New York City Is Redefining AI Technology's Future

The emergence of New York City as a centre for applied artificial intelligence (AI) is not merely a story of technological progress; it marks a significant shift in the landscape of urban innovation. What sets New York apart is its dual vision: harnessing the transformative power of AI while ensuring its benefits are distributed equitably among the city's 8.5 million residents.[1]

This chapter explores New York City's leadership in shaping the future of AI, examining how its approach blends public policy, private-sector engagement, and academic collaboration. It presents the city's strategy as a model for how global urban centres can adopt AI in ways that genuinely serve all citizens, placing New York at the forefront of a technological transformation with long-lasting implications.

Empire State of AI: NYC as the Epicentre of Applied AI Innovation

New York City is leading a transformation driven by AI, creating a fertile ground for AI integration across sectors such as finance, healthcare, media, and real estate.[2] AI is no longer theoretical; it is actively enhancing services, streamlining operations, and driving innovation. The city's strategic vision started in 2023 with the launch of the New York City Artificial Intelligence Action Plan. The intention was to position New York as a global leader in AI.

DOI: 10.4324/9781003673897-18

The City's vision is supported by a $2 trillion economy, a concentration of Fortune 500 companies, a growing pool of over 40,000 AI-skilled professionals, and significant investments bolstered by startups that have raised $200 billion in venture capital over the past decade.

The New York City Economic Development Corporation (NYCEDC) is central to this transformative journey. Since its inception in 1991, NYCEDC has worked to strengthen business confidence, diversify economic sectors, and build sustainable infrastructure. Recognising AI as a transformative force, NYCEDC says that it is dedicated to establishing New York as a leader in the field to drive economic growth, ensuring that the benefits of this technological revolution extend to all residents.

The 2023 New York City Artificial Intelligence Action Plan

On 16 October 2023, New York City Mayor Eric Adams and Chief Technology Officer Matthew Fraser unveiled the New York City Artificial Intelligence Action Plan, a pioneering initiative aimed at positioning the city as a leader in the responsible use of AI.[3]

New York's plan addresses core challenges, including the need for strong oversight mechanisms to mitigate risks such as bias, privacy violations, and cybersecurity threats, alongside the establishment of clear policies and guidelines across agencies. Operational implementation is supported by streamlined procurement and project management strategies. These include central directories of approved AI tools, clear role definitions, and structured evaluation processes to reduce redundancies and promote efficient adoption across city departments.[4]

The plan recognises the importance of capacity building. It outlines efforts to assess workforce readiness, identify skill gaps, and deliver targeted training across technical and non-technical staff to ensure a resilient, AI-literate public sector. This includes the creation of a culture of continuous learning to keep pace with the rapid evolution of AI technologies.

The NYC AI team stresses the importance of broad stakeholder engagement. Drawing input from over 50 city employees across 18 agencies, as well as academic, industry, and civil society, the plan underscores the importance of diverse perspectives in shaping AI policy. Initiatives include public listening sessions and a dedicated AI website, designed to educate and involve residents in decision-making processes.

The creation of a City AI Steering Committee and the development of standardised frameworks aim to ensure accountability and consistency in the deployment of AI tools.

Finally, the plan's iterative design ensures long-term relevance. With built-in mechanisms for regular review, progress tracking, and policy updates, the plan positions itself as a living framework, capable of evolving with technological change.

Action Plan Progress in 2024

On 16 October 2024, the NYC Office of Technology and Innovation released the *New York City AI Action Plan Annual Progress Report.*

The rollout of New York City's AI initiatives in 2024 was marked by structured innovation and evolving oversight. Foundational documents, such as the *AI Principles & Definitions* and the *Generative AI Preliminary Use Guidance*, set the stage for citywide alignment on practical standards for AI use. A newly formed AI Steering Committee, comprised of representatives from 16 agencies, convened quarterly to discuss implementation challenges, best practices, and emerging risks. In parallel, an advisory network of academic, industry, and civic experts provide external guidance to strengthen policy development.

Transparency and public input were central to the city's approach. Information about AI tools was shared via NYC Open Data,[5] and public listening sessions invited residents to express concerns and expectations. These sessions underscored a public desire for AI that is both useful and trustworthy.

Despite early achievements, the city encountered several operational challenges. One previously completed action related to AI procurement was re-evaluated and reclassified, highlighting the need for flexible governance structures and iterative policy refinement.[6]

The NYC experience points to the complexities of deploying AI in a dynamic urban environment and the necessity for strong cross-sector coordination combined with adaptive frameworks.

NYC's AI Advantage: Powering Economic Growth and Technological Innovation

In January 2025, NYCEDC published the report *New York City's Artificial Intelligence Advantage: Driving Economic Growth and Technological Transformation.*

New York City's ambition to lead in AI stems from its unique position at the intersection of legacy industries and a dynamic, rapidly evolving tech ecosystem. The city envisions AI not merely as a tool for automation but as a powerful engine for economic transformation, one that sparks innovation, opens new markets, and redefines daily life. Unlocking this potential will require coordinated efforts across government, industry, academia, and civil society to ensure that the benefits of AI are substantial and inclusive.

The position of New York City in the AI landscape is bolstered by a vibrant entrepreneurial culture and unparalleled access to financial capital and academic expertise. With over 2,000 AI startups and more than 1,200 active venture capital firms, the city fosters a climate of continuous innovation and rapid investment. Leading academic institutions such as New York University, Columbia, Cornell Tech, and the City University of New York drive advanced research and supply a steady flow of skilled professionals and opportunities for collaboration. This combination of startup energy, academic excellence, and investor confidence accelerates the development of real-world AI applications. The presence of major global tech companies further amplifies this momentum, enabling a collaborative environment where ideas and solutions move quickly from concept to market.

The integration of AI into everyday operations is expected to drive significant job creation across sectors, with estimates indicating up to 200,000 net new jobs in the New York metropolitan area by 2030. This shift is expected to extend beyond technical fields, introducing emerging roles such as prompt engineers, AI ethics specialists, and compliance officers. This anticipated shift in the job market is supported by surveys and studies conducted among NYC executives, who overwhelmingly believe that the overall impact of AI on society will be positive despite the inevitable changes in the nature of some jobs. However, adapting to this evolving employment landscape will require targeted education, specialised training, and robust workforce development initiatives. Without these combined elements, disparities in access to new opportunities may intensify, particularly among populations lacking exposure to AI-related skills and resources.

AI development in New York City is driven by continued investment from both the public and private sectors, supported by strategic infrastructure planning and cohesive policy efforts. Key initiatives include large-scale funding for technology infrastructure, research institutions, and academic programmes such as Empire AI and NY Creates focused on expanding computational capacity. Specialised investment vehicles such as the NYC Catalyst Fund and the Greenlight Innovation Fund support startups building scalable AI solutions. However, the effectiveness of these investments depends on robust governance frameworks, such as those shaped by the AI Advisory Council in partnership with Tech NYC.

There are also initiatives such as the NYC Startup Internship Programme and partnerships with institutions including the City University of New York to bridge academic learning with industry skills requirements. These efforts offer short-term training and professional development courses to upskill both new graduates and mid-career professionals. These efforts are positioning New York City as the global epicentre of applied AI, establishing its strategic approach as a model for cities worldwide.

Box 14.1 – Case Study: Advancing Public Services Delivery Across New York City

The New York City Economic Development Corporation (NYCEDC) report highlights several tangible examples illustrating how AI is being integrated across New York City to improve public services.

In the green economy, AI is being deployed to promote sustainability and environmental resilience. At the Brooklyn Army Terminal, the NYCEDC facilitated the installation of the Conservation Lab, an AI-powered smart water monitoring system which identifies leaks and supports more efficient water use. Additionally, AI technologies are being used to optimise power distribution within green energy grids and to strengthen environmental forecasting capabilities, helping to reduce the risks associated with natural disasters.

In the education sector, NYCEDC has introduced the AI Policy Lab to embed AI education into New York City's public-school curriculum, with the goal of equipping students with foundational knowledge of generative AI technologies. Complementing this effort, pilot programmes in public libraries across the city are delivering AI literacy training for librarians, enabling them to guide and educate the public on the use and implications of AI tools and applications.

In the area of social services, the Decoded Futures programme facilitates collaboration between New York City-based tech companies and non-profit organisations to enhance service delivery through AI technologies, focusing on improving organisational capacity and streamlining operations. Additionally, the Robin Hood Foundation's AI Poverty Challenge provides funding for innovative AI-driven solutions that target poverty reduction through initiatives in workforce development, education, and financial empowerment.

In the area of public-sector efficiency, the Office of Technology and Innovation has significantly increased the deployment of algorithmic tools across city agencies, growing from 16 to 46 tools over a four-year period. These tools are applied in a wide range of areas, including public health, child welfare, education, emergency response, and environmental protection, with the goal of enhancing service delivery and operational performance.

Programmes supporting the implementation of AI include the NYC AI Nexus, a $3 million initiative that encourages collaboration between start-ups and local businesses to drive applied AI adoption across sectors such as healthcare, finance, and real estate. The Founder Fellowship is another key programme that helps underrepresented tech founders by providing them with resources and tailored networks to enhance their use of AI.[7]

These initiatives demonstrate how New York City is leveraging AI to foster economic development and enhance public services across various sectors.

Shaping the Future: How the Public Sector Is Driving Ethical and Effective AI Adoption

In New York City, the public sector is taking a proactive role in shaping the future of AI by uniting policy innovation, capacity building, and cross-sector collaboration to promote ethical and responsible adoption.

NYC efforts are reinforced by strategic investments in workforce development, offering targeted training and skills assessments that empower public employees to effectively manage, implement, and innovate with AI technologies, ultimately enhancing service delivery.

Collaboration is at the heart of the city's approach. By partnering with academic institutions, industry experts, and community organisations, New York is building dynamic advisory networks that foster the exchange of best practices and provide critical insights into emerging AI trends. In parallel, the city is implementing standardised procurement processes and creating centralised AI tool directories to streamline adoption and eliminate administrative redundancies.

New York's Vision: Pioneering the Future of Urban AI

New York City's approach to AI represents a new paradigm for urban innovation, one that balances technological advancement with a clear focus on the well-being of its residents.

This strategy, grounded in the governance principles of the AI Action Plan and supported by substantial economic investment and cross-sector collaboration, aims to ensure that technological transformation enhances rather than disrupts urban life.

New York is showing how cities can use AI to tackle complex challenges while fostering inclusive growth. The continued evolution of this ecosystem, backed by public–private partnerships and a commitment to measured, responsible implementation, places the city at the forefront of applied AI. It stands not only as a centre for innovation but also as a model of responsible progress that improves public services, expands economic opportunities, and enhances quality of life.

By embedding AI across government functions, traditional industries, and new technology sectors, New York is creating a comprehensive framework that other global cities can study, adapt, and build upon.

Notes

1 The Official Website of the City of New York (2025), Mayor Adams celebrates two consecutive years of population growth in New York City, www.nyc.gov/office-of-the-mayor/news/140-25/mayor-adams-celebrates-two-consecutive-years-population-growth-new-york-city (accessed on 30 March 2025).

2 New York City Economic Development Corporation (no date), AI in NYC, https://edc.nyc/ai-nyc (accessed on 22 February 2025).
3 The Official Website of the City of New York (2023), Mayor Adams releases first-of-its-kind plan for responsible artificial intelligence use in NYC government, www.nyc.gov/office-of-the-mayor/news/777-23/mayor-adams-releases-first-of-its-kind-plan-responsible-artificial-intelligence-use-nyc#/0 (accessed on 22 February 2025).
4 The Official Website of the City of New York (2023), *The New York City Artificial Intelligence Action Plan*, www.nyc.gov/assets/oti/downloads/pdf/reports/artificial-intelligence-action-plan.pdf (accessed on 22 February 2025).
5 NYC Open Data is an online platform that provides public access to a vast repository of data generated by New York City agencies and organisations.
6 NYC Office of Technology and Innovation (2024), *New York City AI Action Plan Annual Progress Report*, www.nyc.gov/assets/oti/downloads/pdf/reports/ai-action-plan-progress-report-2024.pdf (accessed on 23 February 2025).
7 New York City Economic Development Corporation (2025), *NYC's Artificial Intelligence Advantage: Driving Economic Growth and Technological Transformation*, https://edc.nyc/sites/default/files/2025-01/NYCEDC-NYC-AI-Advantage-2025-Report.pdf (accessed on 22 February 2025).

Part IV

Shaping the Future of Governance

Chapter 15

Closing Thoughts

A Call to Action for Rapid Deployment of AI

As the age of artificial intelligence (AI) begins to transform public services, the decisions we make today will shape not only the future of government operations but also the fabric of our societies. The integration of AI into public administration is more than a technological upgrade; it represents a pivotal opportunity to redefine the relationship between governments and the people they serve. This final chapter reflects on the key themes explored throughout this book, identifies the global trends shaping the future of AI in public service, and offers a practical blueprint for governments seeking to navigate this transformative journey with foresight, responsibility, and purpose.

A Stronger Call to Action: Overcoming Real-World Challenges to AI Deployment

AI's deployment in the public sector holds enormous potential, but it also presents significant risks that must be carefully managed. If left unchecked, AI systems could exacerbate inequality, erode trust in public institutions, and prioritise efficiency at the expense of equity. The integration of AI into public services offers immense promise, yet it brings real-world challenges. While fairness and transparency remain crucial, the most pressing obstacles are securing adequate funding to deal with legacy IT problems, cultivating strong leadership, and crafting actionable plans with clear budgets and

DOI: 10.4324/9781003673897-20

timelines. Governments must dedicate financial resources specifically for AI initiatives, ensuring they are insulated from competing fiscal pressures. Equally vital is leadership: appointing AI 'champions' within agencies can provide the vision, accountability, and momentum needed to drive AI adoption and overcome resistance to change.

To successfully implement AI, governments must also define measurable objectives tied to tangible outcomes. Key performance indicators, such as faster service delivery, reduced backlogs and waiting times, or cost savings, should directly align with the public's expectations and track the effectiveness of AI systems. Ensuring public trust requires evidence-based delivery mechanisms, with each phase of an AI project demonstrating tangible benefits. Whether through pilot programmes or large-scale deployments, public services must clearly show how AI improves outcomes, as demonstrated by Estonia's successful use of AI in sectors like healthcare, transportation, and public administration.

A comprehensive, long-term roadmap is an essential foundation for AI's sustainable and ongoing integration into public services. Governments need to develop phased strategies, from piloting technologies to scaling successful projects and embedding them within core functions. Workforce development is another priority, as public-sector employees must be equipped with the necessary skills to work with AI tools and adapt to evolving workflows. Collaboration with private-sector innovators and academic institutions will further enhance these efforts, offering access to cutting-edge technologies and expertise.

By addressing these practical challenges, governments can navigate the risks of AI deployment and unlock its potential, enhancing efficiency, reducing costs, and ultimately improving outcomes for citizens over the long term.

Prioritising Ethical Principles

Ethics is a key element in the action plan for AI integration in public service. Governments must ask critical questions before deploying AI systems:

- Does this system uphold fairness and equality across all demographics?
- Are decisions explainable and transparent to the citizens they impact?
- How will AI address systemic inequities rather than reinforce them?

Frameworks like Canada's Algorithmic Impact Assessment Tool provide a roadmap for governments to evaluate the ethical implications of AI systems and ensure they align with public values.

Fostering Inclusivity

AI's benefits must be accessible to all citizens, including marginalised and underserved populations. Governments must actively involve these communities in the design and implementation of AI systems. For example, public consultations, citizen advisory boards, and participatory governance platforms can ensure that diverse perspectives shape AI deployment.

Building Public Trust

Transparency is the cornerstone of public trust in AI systems. Governments must openly communicate how AI technologies are used, what safeguards are in place, and how citizens can hold these systems accountable. Initiatives like Estonia's data transparency dashboards demonstrate how proactive communication can enhance trust and engagement.

Global and Regional Trends Shaping AI in Governance

AI adoption in public services is being driven by global technological advancements, which are currently funded largely by big tech. However, these private companies will eventually seek a return on their investment and how that will unfold remains uncertain. Understanding these trends is essential for developing effective long-term strategies.

Technological Convergence

The convergence of AI with other technologies, such as blockchain, Internet of Things (IoT), and 5G networks, is revolutionising public service delivery. For instance, South Korea's smart cities leverage AI and IoT to optimise energy use, transportation, and public safety. These integrated systems exemplify the potential of technology to enhance urban living but also underscore the need for robust cybersecurity measures.

Addressing the Digital Divide

While advanced economies lead in AI adoption, many developing nations face significant barriers, including limited infrastructure and digital literacy. Initiatives like Kenya's Ajira Digital Programme, which trains citizens in digital skills, highlight the importance of bridging the digital divide to ensure equitable access to AI-enhanced services. Even in advanced countries, access can be challenging. In the UK, Ofcom, the telecommunications regulator, reports that 38 per cent of UK premises are still not covered by 5G.

Accessibility across multiple platforms is crucial for promoting inclusivity and ensuring equitable access to digital resources. While much focus has been placed on personal devices like computers and smartphones, public access points, such as post offices, schools, and libraries, play an essential role in bridging the digital divide. These spaces act as community hubs where individuals, regardless of socio-economic background or physical ability, can access vital information and services.

Post offices and other public institutions are increasingly adopting digital solutions to improve accessibility. Public libraries provide internet access points that empower individuals without home connectivity, allowing them to engage with e-government services, yet as we have pointed out earlier, library funding in many countries is under pressure. Accessibility goes beyond personal devices and extends to public spaces, where technology can serve as an equaliser.

Public Sentiment and Resistance

Citizen attitudes towards AI vary significantly by age, socio-economic background, and level of education, and are shaped by experiences with automation, privacy concerns, and cultural values. In regions where automation has led to job displacement, scepticism towards AI remains high. Users who are less comfortable with technology are often frustrated by software that is neither intuitive nor user-friendly. Governments must address these concerns through accessible support services, clear communication, and an open, efficient appeals process.

Moving Forward: From Talk to Transformation

Organisations understand that AI is powerful, but few have translated this awareness into significant action. This gap stems from outdated structures, unclear incentives, and a lack of institutional learning. To bridge it, the public sector must reframe AI not as a technical add-on but as a catalyst for reimagining how work is done.

Leadership matters, but vision alone is not enough. While politicians increasingly acknowledge the urgency of AI, many stop at broad proclamations. Workers need more than encouragement; they need a vivid, shared vision of an AI-enabled future. Without clarity on how AI will reshape roles, rewards, and responsibilities, adoption remains uneven and hesitant. Real-world examples that demonstrate tangible benefits to users have proven highly effective in building trust and engagement.

Employee experimentation drives results, but fear suppresses it. Many workers already use AI tools independently, reporting large productivity gains. Yet most do so in secret, constrained by unclear policies and cultural stigma. Public AI use will remain limited unless leaders explicitly reward experimentation and decouple productivity gains from job cuts.

Basic training is not enough; practice builds confidence. Initial training efforts often focus on prompting techniques, which quickly become outdated; in fact, the latest AI models are increasingly capable of handling less directive prompts. Most useful is creating a space where employees can safely test AI tools, share workflows, and explore use cases relevant to their domain expertise.

A centralised effort is still essential to scale what works. Decentralised innovation fuels early momentum, but without a dedicated team focused on fast prototyping and deployment, discoveries remain isolated. This team must be agile, cross-functional, and oriented towards rapid iteration. Their job is to turn promising ideas into reliable systems for the organisation.

Benchmarks should be built internally, not borrowed. Off-the-shelf tests don't measure what matters. Organisations must create their own evaluations based on their workflows, goals, and constraints. Subjective impressions are often more actionable than traditional metrics, especially when evaluating complex, creative, or nuanced AI output.

Change Moves Faster Than Certainty

AI technologies are evolving more rapidly than most public bodies can respond. Each new model expands the possibilities for automation, augmentation, and service acceleration. By the time an AI strategy is finalised, the landscape may already have shifted. The advantage lies with organisations that build the capacity to learn and adapt in real time, rather than those that delay action in pursuit of perfect clarity.

Transformation requires rethinking the tasks to be completed within the context of the services offered. AI shifts bottlenecks from execution to decision-making. When writing, coding, and research are instant, the real challenge becomes identifying what's worth building, exploring, or sharing. This demands a new type of strategic thinking and new kinds of organisational roles.

The key to progress lies in learning faster. Entities that treat AI adoption as an adaptive process, not a procurement task, will move first. Those that build feedback loops between leaders, innovation teams, and frontline workers will uncover breakthroughs faster. Those that wait for playbooks will be left behind.[1]

A Blueprint for Responsible AI Integration

Governments at different stages of technological readiness require tailored strategies to integrate AI responsibly. The following blueprint, as shown in Figure 15.1, provides a structured approach for navigating this complex landscape.

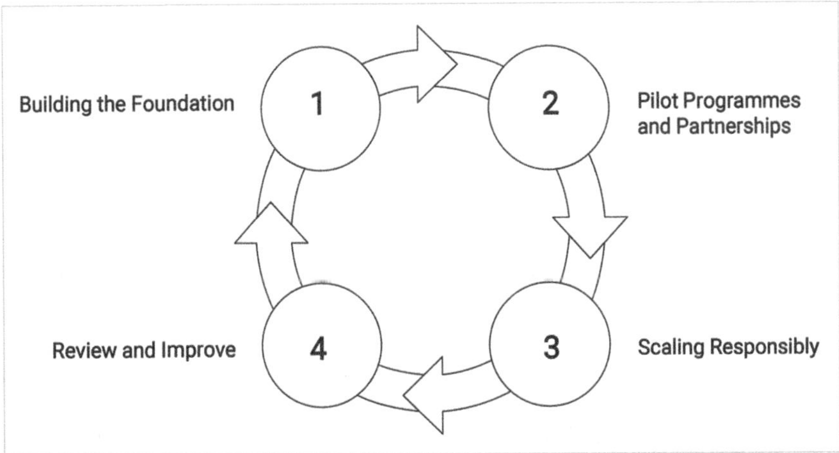

Figure 15.1 The four stages of responsible AI integration

Source: Authors' elaboration

Stage 1: Building the foundation

For governments at the beginning of their AI journey:

- Invest in infrastructure: Develop robust digital infrastructure, including broadband access and secure data systems.
- Enhance data governance: Establish standards for data collection, quality, and sharing to ensure reliable and unbiased datasets.
- Promote digital literacy: Launch public awareness campaigns and workforce training programmes to build familiarity with AI concepts.

Stage 2: Pilot programmes and partnerships

For governments with foundational capabilities:

- Focus on targeted solutions: Implement pilot projects in areas with clear, measurable outcomes, such as widely used government services and healthcare service optimisation.
- Collaborate across sectors: Partner with academia, private industry, and civil society to co-create AI solutions.
- Evaluate and refine: Use pilot outcomes to improve system design and address operational challenges.

Stage 3: Scaling responsibly

For governments with AI capabilities:

- Institutionalise oversight: Create independent AI boards to monitor ongoing projects and address public concerns.
- Embed equity: Ensure that AI systems serve a wide range of users, bridging gaps in education, healthcare, and social services.
- Foster continuous innovation: Develop adaptive policies that evolve alongside technological advancements, ensuring governance remains relevant and effective.

Stage 4: Review and improve

For governments with established AI systems seeking long-term impact and sustainability:

- Conduct regular audits: Perform comprehensive assessments of AI systems to ensure they remain ethical, secure, and effective over time.
- Incorporate public feedback: Establish transparent mechanisms for citizens and stakeholders to provide input on AI performance and societal impact.
- Update frameworks and standards: Continuously revise data governance, regulatory frameworks, and operational standards in response to new insights, emerging risks, and technological progress.

- Measure long-term outcomes: Track societal, economic, and environmental impacts of AI implementations to ensure alignment with national goals and public interest.
- Promote knowledge sharing: Document lessons learned and best practices to guide future initiatives and support other governments on their AI journey.

Envisioning the Future of AI in Public Service

The successful integration of AI into public service has the potential to redefine the provision of public services, making them more efficient, responsive, and fair. Imagine a world where:

- Real-time AI feedback loops provide policymakers with continuous insights, enabling adaptive governance that meets changing societal needs.
- Citizens can seamlessly interact with government services that are accessible through intuitive platforms that simplify processes and enhance engagement.
- The broadest number of citizens can benefit from the new technological advancements.

Leading with Vision and Values

The adoption of AI in public service is not just a technological challenge; it is also an economic and strategic imperative. Governments must lead with vision and values, ensuring that AI becomes a catalyst for dramatically improving service provision and empowering both citizens and public servants. This requires:

- Addressing ageing infrastructure to ensure systems are AI ready.
- Investing in human capital, supporting displaced workers through upskilling initiatives and career transition programmes.
- Fostering global collaboration, by sharing knowledge and resources across borders to tackle common challenges and harness shared opportunities.
- Embedding fairness at every stage, from design to deployment, with improved client service as the core principle guiding AI integration.

Conclusion: A Smarter, More Humane Future

The journey towards widespread provision of AI-enabled government services is complex, but its rewards are profound. By embracing innovation and confronting challenges with foresight and determination, governments can create systems that improve efficiency, enhance service delivery, build public trust, and uphold the dignity of all citizens. The future of public service is within reach, a future where technology supports humanity and strengthens the core values of democratic governance.

As we stand on the cusp of this transformative era, the opportunities are dazzling. We have the chance to deliver dramatically improved public services, increase citizen satisfaction, and reduce the burden on taxpayers. The challenges are real, the potential benefits are enormous, and what matters now is the courage to act, the wisdom to guide implementation responsibly, and the commitment to ensure that AI serves the public good.

Note

1 E. Mollick (2025), Making AI work: Leadership, lab, and crowd, www.oneusefulthing.org/p/making-ai-work-leadership-lab-and (accessed on 28 May 2025).

Appendices

Additional Case Studies and Resources for Policymakers

Generative artificial intelligence (AI) is transforming how the public sector manages critical operations, from incident response and supply chain management to public records accessibility. Government agencies often face challenges in processing vast amounts of data, making timely decisions, and ensuring transparency for citizens. AI-powered tools can streamline incident management by analysing real-time data from multiple sources, predicting potential crises, and optimising emergency responses. In supply chain and resource management, AI enhances efficiency by forecasting demand, optimising distribution routes, and preparing for disruptions. Furthermore, AI plays a crucial role in improving public records by simplifying complex documents, enhancing search capabilities, and promoting transparency through real-time updates. While the benefits of generative AI are substantial, responsible implementation requires careful attention to accuracy, fairness, and privacy.

Streamlining Incident Management

Public-sector organisations, such as emergency services, municipal safety departments, and public health agencies, often face real-time challenges that demand rapid analysis and response. By integrating generative AI into incident management systems, agencies can automatically process diverse data sources (e.g. emergency call transcripts, sensor feeds, social media alerts) to create a real-time, comprehensive picture of unfolding events. This enhanced situational awareness can help identify emerging crises even before traditional reporting mechanisms detect them.

Generative AI can learn from historical incident data to predict where and when incidents are most likely to occur. For example, by analysing weather patterns, traffic conditions, and past emergency events, AI models can forecast potential hotspots for accidents or public disturbances. This predictive capability enables agencies to pre-position resources, such as ambulances, police patrols, or fire trucks, thereby reducing response times and optimising the allocation of limited resources.

During and after an incident, much time is spent on post-event analysis and reporting. AI systems can automatically generate detailed reports by synthesising data, highlighting key trends, and even suggesting corrective actions. This automation not only speeds up the response process but also supports decision-makers with evidence-based recommendations, improving overall operational efficiency.

Many public-sector organisations are already part of broader 'smart city' initiatives. AI-enhanced incident management systems can integrate with existing Internet of Things networks (e.g. traffic cameras, environmental sensors) to provide a seamless flow of information. The result is a coordinated, dynamic response system where data is continuously analysed, enabling real-time adjustments to emergency protocols and resource distribution.

While the benefits are significant, implementing generative AI in incident management requires experienced human monitoring as AI systems are not flawless. The public sector must establish clear guidelines and robust safeguards to ensure that sensitive information is handled appropriately while maximising the efficiency gains offered by AI.

Optimising Supply Chain and Resource Management

The public sector, whether managing the distribution of medical supplies to public health agencies or educational materials in school districts, often contends with unpredictable demand. Generative AI models can analyse historical data, seasonal trends, and external factors (like public events or emergencies) to produce more accurate demand forecasts. This improved foresight allows agencies to plan inventory more effectively, avoiding both shortages and excessive overstock.

AI-driven analytics can revolutionise how public-sector supply chains are managed by optimising routes, reducing lead times, and managing stock levels dynamically. For instance, during a public health crisis, AI can help identify the most efficient pathways to distribute vaccines or emergency supplies, considering variables such as road conditions, real-time traffic data, and even geopolitical factors. This leads to faster, more reliable deliveries and cost savings.

Generative AI can be used to simulate various supply chain scenarios, helping public organisations plan for disruptions such as natural disasters, pandemics, or unexpected surges in demand. By modelling 'what-if' scenarios, decision-makers can test different response strategies and prepare contingency plans. This proactive approach minimises the risk of supply chain failures and ensures continuity in service delivery.

Public-sector operations are not limited to a single domain. An integrated approach to resource management, where inventory, personnel, and financial resources are managed concurrently, can greatly enhance efficiency. Generative AI tools can consolidate data across departments, providing a unified dashboard that tracks everything from equipment maintenance schedules to budget allocations. This integrated view helps managers make informed, strategic decisions that balance immediate needs with long-term planning.

Finally, optimising supply chains isn't just about speed; it's also about sustainability and fiscal responsibility. AI can identify opportunities for reducing waste, whether through better inventory turnover or more energy-efficient transportation routes, and recommend changes that align with environmental and budgetary goals. For public-sector bodies under constant scrutiny for spending and sustainability, these insights can prove invaluable.

Enhancing Public Records with Generative AI

Public records are a cornerstone of transparency and accountability in government, yet they are often complex, voluminous, and challenging for the average citizen to navigate. Generative AI offers transformative potential in making these records more accessible, comprehensible, and actionable. Here's an expanded look at how the public sector can leverage generative AI to enhance public records.

Simplifying complex documents can be achieved through automated summarisation and plain-language translation. Generative AI has the capability to process lengthy legislative documents, regulatory filings, and budget reports, condensing them into concise, plain-language summaries. This enables citizens, journalists, and watchdog organisations to quickly understand the key points without navigating dense technical jargon. In addition to summarisation, AI tools can also translate bureaucratic or legal language into clearer, more accessible terms, and it can do this in any language. By rephrasing content for better clarity, AI helps bridge the gap between technical documents and public understanding.

Improving data and accessibility can be achieved through AI-driven categorisation, indexing, and enhanced search functionality. AI can automatically categorise documents based on topic, date, or relevance, making it easier to locate specific records. This streamlined structure enables more focused searches and helps ensure that important documents aren't lost in an overwhelming archive. Additionally, natural language processing enhances search capabilities on public-sector websites and repositories. Users can ask questions in everyday language and receive direct, relevant excerpts from public records, making information more accessible and user-friendly.

Dynamic and interactive records can enhance public understanding by adding context and visual engagement to traditionally static documents. Generative AI can enrich public records with contextual annotations, linking legislative changes to historical precedents, related policy documents, or previous budget cycles. These annotations provide a deeper narrative, helping users grasp the broader implications of the data. Additionally, AI can transform static documents into interactive dashboards, allowing citizens to explore information visually. Features like trend analysis, side-by-side comparisons, and dynamic timelines can illustrate how policies evolve over time, making complex data more accessible and engaging. However, it is important to restate that AI is not infallible. It can and does make mistakes, and may at times hallucinate, producing information that is false or misleading. While there is no doubt that the models are improving, we remain a long way from being able to place full confidence in AI-generated outputs.

Promoting transparency and accountability becomes more effective with AI-driven real-time updates and enhanced oversight. In fast-changing policy environments, generative AI can continuously monitor updates and automatically refresh public records, ensuring that citizens always have access to the most current information. By offering easily digestible insights and comprehensive summaries, AI empowers oversight bodies, auditors, and the public to scrutinise governmental decisions and expenditures more effectively. This improved access to clear and up-to-date information strengthens accountability and fosters greater public trust in government operations.

While generative AI can greatly enhance accessibility, it is essential to establish robust verification processes to ensure that AI-generated summaries accurately reflect the original documents. Cross-checking these summaries helps preserve critical details and prevent misinformation. Ethical and privacy concerns must also be addressed, as public records often contain sensitive information. Deploying AI tools with strict data privacy measures and transparent methodologies helps maintain public trust. Additionally, user education plays a key role in maximising the benefits of AI-enhanced records. Providing guidance on interpreting AI-generated summaries through training sessions, FAQs, and interactive help features ensures that users can effectively navigate and utilise these tools.

By integrating generative AI into the management of public records, government agencies can demystify complex information, enhance transparency, and foster a more informed citizenry. These advancements not only improve access to vital data but also reinforce the accountability of public institutions, ultimately leading to more engaged and empowered communities.

AI Checklists

AI Implementation Checklist

This checklist is a guide for organisations to assess and mitigate the technical, operational, and reputational risks inherent in AI systems.

Table A.1 AI implementation checklist

Main Element	*Description*
Establish governance and oversight	Define clear roles and responsibilities for managing AI risks across the organisation. Create and formalise policies and procedures for governing AI systems. Ensure AI management is consistent with organisational principles, policies, and legal requirements.
Map and identify AI systems and risks	Create an inventory of all AI systems in use, outlining their purpose, data sources, and stakeholders. For each AI system, identify: • the technical risks such as model usage, cybersecurity, and data integrity issues • operational risks, including system malfunctions, integration failures, and disruptions to business processes • reputational risks like privacy violations, algorithmic bias, lack of transparency, and ethical concerns Assess compliance with relevant data protection and AI-specific regulations (for example GDPR, and EU AI Act).

(*Continued*)

Table A.1 (Continued)

Main Element	*Description*
Measure and assess risks	Create a risk matrix to assess the severity and probability of each identified risk through both qualitative and quantitative approaches. Utilise: • tools and metrics to quantify risks, including model risk management platforms to assess reliability • data quality tools to ensure robustness and accuracy, and fairness • bias detection metrics to address ethical considerations Document potential impacts, including financial losses, operational downtime, and reputational harm.
Mitigate and manage risks	Create risk mitigation strategies that are aligned with the organisation's risk appetite and strategic priorities. Implement technical safeguards, such as: • data encryption and access controls to protect sensitive information • routine audits and penetration testing to uncover vulnerabilities • bias detection and mitigation algorithms to promote fairness • fail-safe mechanisms with system redundancy for critical AI operations Establish operational safeguards, such as: • incident response plans to address AI failures or security breaches • ongoing monitoring and recalibration of AI models to manage model drift and emerging threats • regular staff training on AI risks and ethical responsibilities
Ensure transparency, accountability, and compliance	Maintain comprehensive documentation of AI system design, decision-making logic, and all risk management activities. Ensure AI decisions are explainable and auditable, particularly in high-stakes applications. Engage in transparent communication with stakeholders regarding the capabilities, limitations, and risk mitigation strategies of AI systems. Continuously monitor regulatory developments and ensure sustained compliance with evolving AI standards and legal requirements.

(*Continued*)

Table A.1 (Continued)

Main Element	*Description*
Review and continuous improvement	Regularly review and update the AI risk management framework to account for emerging risks, evolving technologies, and changes in regulatory requirements. Perform post-incident analyses to extract lessons from AI failures and enhance future risk management strategies. Collect stakeholder feedback to improve governance structures and strengthen risk mitigation practices.

Source: Authors' elaboration

By using this checklist, organisations can methodically assess and manage the technical, operational, and reputational risks of AI systems, ensuring their AI implementation is secure, ethical, and aligned with both business goals and societal expectations.

EU AI Act Compliance Checklist

This checklist is a guide for organisations to assess the key provisions of the EU AI Act. It serves as a preliminary tool to assess an organisation's AI systems for regulatory alignment.

Table A.2 EU AI Act compliance checklist

Main Element	*Description*
AI system classification and risk assessment	• Specify the AI system type and its intended purpose. • Classify the system's risk level (Unacceptable, High, Limited, Minimal). • Document and regularly update the reasoning behind the risk classification. • Perform a risk assessment considering impacts on rights, safety, and potential discrimination.
Data governance and transparency	• Record data sources, collection techniques, and data types. • Assess data quality, relevance, and potential biases. • Incorporate privacy into design principles in compliance with GDPR requirements. • Document permissions, data-sharing agreements, and ethics approvals. • Establish data traceability and audit capabilities.

(*Continued*)

Table A.2 (Continued)

Main Element	*Description*
Model documentation and explainability	• Keep comprehensive documentation of the model, including its source, version, and training data. • Clearly define the model's intended use, limitations, and decision-making logic. • Offer simplified outputs and user-friendly explanation interfaces.
Human oversight and accountability	• Designate an AI compliance officer and AI data protection officer. • Clearly outline roles and responsibilities for oversight. • Incorporate human-in-the-loop processes for high-risk decision-making. • Set up escalation procedures for appeals and reviews.
Compliance with data protection (GDPR)	• Ensure data processing complies with GDPR principles such as data minimisation and purpose limitation. • Perform Data Protection Impact Assessments (DPIAs) for high-risk systems. • Keep processing records current and accurate.
Cybersecurity and robustness	• Conduct risk analyses to identify security and privacy threats. • Apply protective measures such as anonymisation. • Carry out penetration testing and security evaluations. • Continuously monitor system performance, detect anomalies, and respond to incidents.
Post-market monitoring and continuous improvement	• Set up continuous compliance monitoring and reporting processes. • Regularly review and update assessments and documentation. • Register high-risk AI systems with EU authorities when necessary. • Prepare for internal, external, and public audits.
Ethics and social responsibility	• Perform ethics reviews and impact assessments. • Consider social, economic, and legal implications. • Provide mechanisms for redress and channels for user feedback.

Source: Authors' elaboration

This checklist should be tailored to the specific AI system and organisational context; for high-risk AI systems, ensure all mandatory requirements under the EU AI Act are strictly followed and documented.

EU AI Act Audit Checklist

This checklist is a guide for organisations to audit an AI system.

Table A.3 EU AI Act audit checklist

Area	*Key Checks*	*Status (Y/N/N/A)*	*Evidence/Comments*
Risk classification	Risk category identified and documented		
Data governance	Data sources, quality, and bias risks documented		
Model documentation	Model type and explainability documentation available		
Human oversight	Human-in-the-loop and escalation procedures in place		
GDPR compliance	DPIA completed, records of processing maintained		
Security and robustness	Cybersecurity measures and incident response plans implemented		
Post-market monitoring	Ongoing monitoring and periodic audit processes established		
Ethics and social responsibility	Ethics review and redress mechanisms documented		

Source: Authors' elaboration

EU AI Act Transparency Checklist

The EU AI Act establishes a risk-based framework for transparency, with obligations varying by risk level and by whether the system is a general-purpose AI (GPAI) model. The following checklist might support compliance with the EU AI Act transparency requirements.

Table A.4 EU AI Act transparency checklist

Category	*Obligation*
General transparency obligations (all AI systems)	• Notify users when they are engaging with AI, unless it is evident or legally exempt. • Present this information clearly, accessibly, and at the first point of interaction. • Clearly label AI-generated or altered content, such as deepfakes or synthetic media. • Disclose AI involvement in public-facing communications. • Comply with EU/national transparency laws (e.g. GDPR).
Minimal-risk AI systems	No specific obligations under the EU AI Act.
Limited-risk AI systems	• Clearly inform users when interactions or content are AI-generated. • Mark AI-created or altered images, audio, and video accordingly. • Provide summaries of any copyrighted data used in training, when applicable. • Develop models with safeguards to prevent the generation of illegal content.

High-risk AI systems	• Disclose the provider and authorised representative, if applicable.
	• Clearly state the system's intended purpose, performance metrics (accuracy, robustness), cybersecurity measures, and potential risks.
	• Describe how outputs are generated, including any variations across demographic groups.
	• Supply comprehensive technical documentation, including:
	  ◦ details on training, testing, and validation data aligned with the system's intended use
	  ◦ human oversight mechanisms
	  ◦ operational requirements such as computational resources, update schedules, and maintenance needs
	  ◦ logging and auditing capabilities
	• Register the system in the EU High-Risk AI Database with publicly accessible information.
	• Ensure documentation is regularly updated and available to relevant authorities.

General-purpose AI (GPAI) models	• Keep documentation up to date, covering:
	  ◦ model architecture and intended applications
	  ◦ sources and characteristics of training data
	  ◦ evaluation methods and performance benchmarks
	• Supply documentation to the AI Office or national authorities upon request.
	• Balance compliance requirements with the protection of trade secrets.

(*Continued*)

Table A.4 (Continued)

Category	*Obligation*
Additional notes	• Ensure transparency information is easily accessible and understandable, meeting accessibility standards. • Revise contracts to support the clear flow of transparency-related information, similar to GDPR requirements. • Adhere to EU-level codes of practice or standardised rules established by the European Commission, if applicable.

Source: Authors' elaboration

AI Usage in HR Checklist

This checklist is intended to help HR leaders and teams to responsibly and effectively integrate AI into HR functions, with a strong focus on people-centric practices, ethical standards, and alignment with organisational goals.

Table A.5 AI usage in HR checklist

Step	*Action Items*
Define objectives and scope	• Define the purpose of AI in HR (e.g. recruitment, employee engagement). • Pinpoint specific HR processes or challenges that AI aims to solve. • Establish clear, measurable goals and key performance indicators (KPIs).
Assess organisational readiness	• Assess existing HR processes and data infrastructure. • Secure leadership support and engage key stakeholders. • Identify available resources and skill sets.
Develop AI governance and ethical guidelines	• Develop or revise AI ethics policies, focusing on fairness, transparency, and accountability. • Designate roles for oversight, including privacy and ethics specialists. • Record decision-making procedures and maintain comprehensive audit trails.
Select appropriate AI tools and vendorsl	• Select AI solutions tailored to HR use cases. • Evaluate tools based on privacy, security, explainability, and localisation. • Require vendors to provide transparency regarding algorithms, data usage, and bias mitigation efforts.

(*Continued*)

Table A.5 (Continued)

Step	*Action Items*
Pilot and prioritise use cases	• Begin with small-scale, high-impact projects. • Engage end users early to gather feedback. • Utilise pilot programmes as proof of concept for wider implementation.
Integrate AI into HR workflows	• Ensure smooth integration with current HR systems. • Leverage AI to support and enhance HR staff, not replace them. • Offer clear communication and training on effective AI usage.
Foster AI literacy and change management	• Provide AI literacy and upskilling opportunities for HR teams and employees. • Clearly explain the benefits, limitations, and potential impacts of AI. • Proactively address job displacement concerns and encourage collaborative use of AI.
Monitor, evaluate, and optimise	• Monitor key indicators such as cost savings, productivity, user satisfaction, and fairness. • Conduct regular audits to assess bias, accuracy, and regulatory compliance. • Gather ongoing feedback and implement continuous improvements.
Ensure data privacy and security	• Enforce robust data protection measures and maintain regulatory compliance. • Restrict access to sensitive information and ensure secure data handling. • Regularly review and update security protocols.
Maintain a people-first approach	• Leverage AI to improve the employee experience. • Ensure transparency and retain human oversight in decision-making. • Continuously reassess ethical considerations as needs and technologies evolve.

Source: Authors' elaboration

AI Agent Development Checklist

This checklist covers the essential steps and considerations for setting up an agentic AI system, from initial planning to deployment and monitoring. It is designed to be framework-agnostic, suitable for both beginners and experienced practitioners.

Table A.6 AI agent development checklist

Step	*Task*
Define purpose and scope	• Clearly define the agent's intended goal and use case. • Outline the scope and limitations of the agent's autonomy.
Select tools and frameworks	• Select a suitable agentic AI framework or toolkit. • Install all necessary packages and dependencies.
Data preparation	• Identify and gather relevant data sources. • Cleanse, preprocess, and format the data for use.
Design agent architecture	• Specify the perception module responsible for input processing. • Define the decision-making engine (e.g. rule-based, reinforcement learning). • Establish the learning mechanism (supervised, unsupervised, or reinforcement learning). • Outline the action module for execution (APIs, actuators, etc.). • Design conversation flows, decision trees, and tool integrations.
Model training and integration	• Train or fine-tune AI models such as LLMs and classifiers. • Incorporate memory, retrieval systems, or external tools. • Facilitate interactions with APIs, databases, and actuators.
Testing and evaluation	• Conduct testing across various scenarios. • Validate outputs, decision-making logic, and error management. • Implement checkpoints for controlled step-by-step task execution.
Deployment	• Deploy the agent to the intended environment (e.g. web, mobile). • Establish infrastructure to ensure scalability, reliability, and security.
Monitoring and maintenance	• Track performance, resource utilisation, and user interactions. • Gather logs and user feedback to drive improvements. • Regularly update models, data, and system integrations.
Compliance and governance	• Maintain privacy, data sovereignty, and adherence to legal regulations. • Document the agent's capabilities, limitations, and evaluation criteria.
Support and iteration	• Offer support to users and stakeholders. • Continuously refine design and functionality in response to feedback.

Source: Authors' elaboration

Data for AI Readiness Checklist

This checklist helps ensure that an organisation's data is accurate, trustworthy, and compliant, thus laying a solid foundation for successful AI initiatives.

Table A.7 Data for AI readiness checklist

Category	*Checklist Item*
Data governance and compliance	• Data governance framework established and enforced. • Data privacy and security policies compliant with regulatory requirements (e.g. GDPR, EU AI Act). • Ethical AI guidelines developed, including data usage and bias mitigation.
Data quality assurance	• Data accuracy and consistency are maintained, eliminating errors, typos, and irrelevant records. • Uniform formatting is applied across all data types. • Data completeness is ensured, with minimal or no missing values and all essential fields included. • Outliers are detected and handled appropriately through removal, transformation, or flagging. • Data is kept current and routinely validated to ensure its relevance and accuracy.
Data structure and accessibility	• Data is organised efficiently, preferably in a tabular format. • Column headers are clear and descriptive. • Data types are consistent within columns and across different datasets. • A data catalogue and metadata management system are in place. • Data is readily accessible to AI systems and cross-functional teams, avoiding silos.
Data volume and representativeness	• Adequate data volume is available to capture patterns and variability. • Data accurately represents the intended use case. • All pertinent scenarios and populations are encompassed.
Data lifecycle management	• Ongoing data evaluation, validation, and monitoring are implemented. • Data pipeline workflows are established. • Data stewardship policies are enforced throughout the entire data lifecycle.
Data management infrastructure	• Infrastructure is designed to meet AI workload demands, including storage, processing power, and bandwidth. • Systems are scalable and seamlessly integrate with AI platforms and tools. • Cloud-based solutions are evaluated to enhance scalability and cost efficiency.
Documentation and transparency	• Comprehensive documentation exists for data sources, transformations, and lineage. • Data processes and quality controls are transparent and can be audited.

(*Continued*)

Table A.7 (Continued)

Category	*Checklist Item*
Organisational alignment and training	• AI project staff receive data literacy training. • A cross-functional task force is established to promote collaborative data management. • Executive sponsorship and leadership commitment have been secured.

Source: Authors' elaboration

Frameworks for Ethical AI Implementation

The G7 Hiroshima Process: A Comprehensive Policy Framework

The Hiroshima AI Process was launched by G7 leaders to develop a coordinated international response to the rapid advancements in AI. The G7 digital and tech ministers met on 1 December 2023, in collaboration with the OECD and the Global Partnership on AI (GPAI), to discuss AI governance.[1] Their discussions focused on addressing AI risks while promoting trustworthy AI, developing a structured framework for AI policies and governance, and fostering AI innovation while ensuring ethical considerations.

The Hiroshima AI Process represents the first global framework that includes guiding principles, and a code of conduct specifically designed to regulate advanced AI systems.

The key objectives of the framework are to promote safe, secure, and trustworthy AI, establish international cooperation on AI governance, ensure that AI development aligns with democratic values and human rights, and develop a risk-based approach for AI regulation.

The Hiroshima AI Process Comprehensive Policy Framework serves as a foundation for AI governance and includes four main elements:

Table A.8 The four main elements of the Hiroshima AI Process Comprehensive Policy Framework

Key Component	*Description*
OECD's report *Towards a G7 Common Understanding on Generative AI*	The OECD report provides a structured analysis of AI risks and benefits, serving as a reference document for G7 nations. It identifies key challenges in generative AI, such as bias, misinformation, and deepfakes; recommends best practices for AI risk management; and serves as a knowledge base for future AI governance decisions.
International Guiding Principles for AI Actors	The International Guiding Principles apply to all AI actors, including governments, private companies, researchers, and members of civil society. They provide ethical standards and best practices for AI development and use.
International Code of Conduct for AI Organisations	The Code of Conduct is a voluntary set of commitments for organisations developing advanced AI systems. It serves as a practical guide for AI developers to ensure transparency, accountability, and security.
Project-based AI cooperation	G7 nations collaborate with international partners to implement AI safety measures, including establishing transparency mechanisms for AI-generated content, countering AI-driven disinformation through labelling and authentication tools, and promoting AI adoption in areas such as climate action, healthcare, and education.

Source: Authors' elaboration from the Japanese Ministry of Economy, Trade and Industry (2023), Hiroshima AI Process G7 digital & tech ministers' statement, www.meti.go.jp/english/press/2023/1201_001.html (accessed on 28 December 2024)

Together, these elements form a holistic approach to global AI governance.

The *Work Plan to Advance Hiroshima AI Process* under Italy's 2024 G7 Presidency has driven the evolution of the Hiroshima AI Process through three main strategies:

Table A.9 Hiroshima AI Process – three main strategies

Main strategy	*Description*
Expanding international outreach	• Engage non-G7 countries and encourage them to adopt the International Guiding Principles and Code of Conduct. • Present AI governance principles at international forums (e.g. United Nations, OECD, GPAI, UNESCO).
Strengthening AI accountability	• Encourage AI companies and governments to publicly commit to AI governance standards. • Develop monitoring tools to ensure adherence to ethical AI guidelines. • Work with OECD and AI experts to track AI developments.
Enhancing AI collaboration	• Collaborate with OECD, GPAI, and UNESCO on AI disinformation, transparency, and accountability. • Launch a Hiroshima AI Process website to provide: ◦ updates on AI policy developments ◦ a public list of entities that have committed to responsible AI

Source: Authors' elaboration from the Japanese Ministry of Economy, Trade and Industry (2023), Hiroshima AI Process G7 digital & tech ministers' statement, www.meti.go.jp/english/press/2023/1201_001.html (accessed on 28 December 2024)

The *International Guiding Principles for AI Actors* serve as ethical and practical guidelines for AI actors, ensuring AI safety and accountability. The core principles are the following:

Table A.10 Core principles of the *International Guiding Principles for AI Actors*

Core Principles	*Description*
Risk mitigation	Implement AI safety measures from design to deployment.
Post-deployment monitoring	Identify and address misuse and security risks.
Transparency	Clearly communicate AI capabilities, limitations, and risks.
Incident reporting	Establish mechanisms for sharing AI risks among stakeholders.
AI governance and risk management	Develop AI policies aligned with human rights and privacy standards.

(*Continued*)

Table A.10 (Continued)

Core Principles	*Description*
Security and cyber protection	Implement robust cybersecurity and data protection protocols.
Content authentication	Use watermarking and other verification methods to detect AI-generated content.
Investment in AI safety research	Prioritise research in AI ethics and safety.
AI for social good	Promote AI applications in climate, healthcare, and education.
Technical standards	Support international AI standards to ensure global consistency.
Data protection	Protect personal data and respect intellectual property rights.
AI literacy and awareness	Educate users on AI risks and promote responsible AI adoption.

Source: Authors' elaboration from the Japanese Ministry of Economy, Trade and Industry (2023), Hiroshima AI Process G7 digital & tech ministers' statement, www.meti.go.jp/english/press/2023/1201_001.html (accessed on 28 December 2024)

The *International Code of Conduct for AI Organisations* is a non-binding framework that offers practical recommendations for organisations developing advanced AI systems. Its main objectives are to encourage AI companies to adhere to ethical guidelines, promote accountability and transparency in AI development, and ensure AI aligns with human rights, democracy, and sustainability goals. The implementation plan includes inviting AI organisations to endorse the Code of Conduct and continuously updating the framework to address emerging AI challenges.

G7 countries, in collaboration with the OECD, GPAI, and UNESCO, have launched a Project-Based AI Collaboration, a series of global initiatives aimed at addressing AI misuse and disinformation. A central project, the Global Challenge on Trust in Generative AI, focuses on developing reliable methods for AI content authentication and tackling issues such as misinformation and AI-generated deepfakes. Another key initiative, AI Labelling & Authentication, seeks to implement watermarking techniques to clearly distinguish AI-generated content and ensure transparency in AI-produced text, images, and videos. Furthermore, international AI partnerships like the US–EU AI Cooperation promote joint research on AI safety and governance, while the US–UK-Canada AI for Development Initiative drives AI solutions for economic and social development.

In conclusion, the Hiroshima AI Process stands as a significant international initiative dedicated to ensuring the safety, transparency, and responsible innovation of AI. By establishing a global governance framework, encouraging ethical practices among AI organisations, fostering collaboration between governments, companies, and researchers, and aligning AI development with democratic values, human rights, and public trust, it paves the way for a more ethical and transparent AI future.

The Hiroshima Process International Code of Conduct for Organisations Developing Advanced AI Systems

The *Hiroshima Process International Code of Conduct* aims to provide voluntary guidance for those developing advanced AI systems,[2] including foundation models and generative AI. It promotes safe, secure, and trustworthy AI while addressing emerging risks. This document builds on the OECD AI Principles and will evolve through multi-stakeholder consultations.

Organisations from academia, civil society, and the private and public sectors are encouraged to adopt these guidelines. Implementation varies by jurisdiction, and the document serves as a complement to future regulatory approaches.

They should take proactive steps to identify, evaluate, and mitigate risks across the AI lifecycle. Entities creating advanced AI systems should adopt a proactive, risk-focused strategy across the entire AI lifecycle, from design through deployment and continued operation. Comprehensive testing, including internal evaluations and independent external assessments like red teaming, a structured practice used to test the effectiveness and security of systems, should be employed to identify vulnerabilities. Ensuring traceability by maintaining detailed records of datasets, processes, and decisions is essential for accountability. Testing should take place in secure environments at multiple checkpoints, particularly before deployment, to address risks in areas such as cybersecurity, public safety, and societal impact. Risks that require special attention include AI's potential role in facilitating the development of chemical, biological, radiological, and nuclear weapons, as well as its capacity for enabling offensive cyber capabilities that may be exploited for hacking or cyber warfare. Furthermore, it is crucial to mitigate risks associated with AI-controlled physical systems that may impact critical infrastructure, as well as risks related to self-replicating AI models that could proliferate unchecked. Societal concerns such as harmful biases, privacy violations, and discrimination must also be considered, along with threats to democratic values, including the facilitation of misinformation and suppression of fundamental rights.

Collaboration across industries and with governments is essential to tackle systemic risks and invest in research focused on improving the safety, robustness, and trustworthiness of AI systems. AI safety and security measures must extend beyond initial deployment, with continuous monitoring and evaluation of AI systems to identify emerging threats, vulnerabilities, and patterns of misuse. It is important to implement post-deployment risk assessment processes that facilitate the identification of real-world impacts and offer solutions for required adjustments. Vulnerability reporting systems, including bug bounty programmes and public disclosure portals, can enable external stakeholders to contribute to identifying flaws and misuse cases.

Maintaining a comprehensive record of incidents and collaborating with third-party evaluators will improve the ability to refine security measures. Collaboration with external stakeholders, including government agencies and independent researchers, will further aid in the development of effective mitigation strategies for addressing unforeseen AI-related risks.

To promote accountability and trust in AI systems, organisations must commit to transparency by publicly reporting the capabilities, risks, and appropriate uses of their AI models. Transparency reports should contain clear and accessible explanations of AI system capabilities, limitations, and significant risks, including safety and security concerns, societal risks, and privacy implications. These reports should also outline the results of evaluations conducted to assess threats, such as bias, misinformation, and discrimination. Additionally, they should provide clear guidance on the appropriate use of their AI models, ensuring that users understand both the strengths and limitations of the technology. Effective documentation processes should support transparency efforts, enabling users and stakeholders to make informed decisions about AI interactions.

Collaboration between AI developers, governments, and civil society is critical in mitigating risks associated with advanced AI systems. It is essential to establish mechanisms for responsible information sharing, enabling the exchange of security insights, risk assessments, and incident reports while safeguarding intellectual property rights. By contributing to the development of industry-wide safety standards, stakeholders can ensure that best practices are adopted universally. Standardised reporting mechanisms should be established to facilitate the secure exchange of information about vulnerabilities, misuse cases, and emerging risks, thereby strengthening collective efforts to enhance AI security and trustworthiness.

A robust governance framework is essential for ensuring responsible AI development and deployment. Organisations should establish formal AI governance structures that define risk management policies, accountability mechanisms, and oversight processes. These policies should be regularly updated based on evolving risks and technological advancements. Privacy and data protection measures should be explicitly incorporated into AI governance strategies, detailing how user data, model outputs, and AI-generated interactions are handled. Organisations should also ensure that AI governance frameworks align with international ethical standards, providing clear accountability pathways for addressing AI-related risks and ensuring compliance with legal and regulatory obligations.

Protecting AI systems from cyber threats and insider risks is a crucial component of responsible AI development. Organisations must implement strong cybersecurity measures to prevent unauthorised access, data breaches, and theft of proprietary AI models. Security controls should include restricted access to AI model weights, datasets, and algorithms, alongside regular security audits to detect vulnerabilities. Secure storage environments must be established to prevent the unauthorised release or misuse of AI models. In addition to external threats, insider risks must be addressed through strict access management, employee training, and continuous monitoring of AI-related activities. They should adopt robust cybersecurity policies and ensure compliance with evolving security standards to safeguard AI systems against emerging threats.

To combat misinformation and disinformation, it is essential to implement effective mechanisms for authenticating AI-generated content. Watermarking and other provenance techniques should be employed to help distinguish AI-generated media from human-created content. Organisations should also develop tools that allow users to verify the authenticity of AI-generated outputs, ensuring that digital consumers are aware when they are interacting with machine-generated material. Additional efforts, such as content labelling and disclaimers, can further aid in preventing AI misuse for deceptive purposes. Investing in research and innovation to advance content authentication technologies will play a key role in maintaining public trust in AI-generated information.

AI developers must prioritise research and investment in mitigating societal, safety, and security risks associated with advanced AI systems. This includes supporting research initiatives focused on explainability, fairness, bias reduction, and misinformation prevention. AI development should uphold democratic values, human rights, and data protection principles while safeguarding against potential harms. Investment should also be directed towards developing mitigation tools that address risks related to AI-generated disinformation, algorithmic bias, and security vulnerabilities. Additionally, it is important to evaluate the environmental impact of AI systems, particularly their energy consumption and carbon footprint, and work towards developing sustainable AI technologies.

Beyond risk mitigation, AI should be leveraged as a tool for addressing some of the world's most pressing challenges, including climate change, global health crises, and education accessibility. AI-powered innovations can support sustainability efforts, optimise healthcare delivery, and expand educational resources to underserved communities. Organisations should align their AI development initiatives with the United Nations Sustainable Development Goals, ensuring that technological advancements contribute to positive societal outcomes. Furthermore, AI literacy and education programmes should be promoted to equip the public with the necessary knowledge to engage with AI responsibly. By working with civil society and community groups, AI developers can identify priority challenges and develop solutions that maximise AI's potential for societal good.

A unified approach to AI safety and governance requires international collaboration in the development of global technical standards. Entities should contribute to establishing widely accepted AI standards by working with international regulatory bodies and industry stakeholders. Standardised frameworks should address key areas such as AI system evaluation methodologies, content authentication protocols, cybersecurity best practices, and public transparency guidelines. Organisations should also promote the development of interoperable AI systems that allow for seamless cross-border collaboration while maintaining consistent safety and security measures.

Organisations must implement rigorous data protection policies to ensure the responsible handling of personal data and intellectual property in AI systems. Data quality should be carefully managed to prevent harmful biases in training datasets, while privacy-preserving techniques such as differential privacy and data anonymisation should be adopted. Intellectual property rights must be respected, ensuring that AI systems do not inadvertently infringe upon copyrighted content or expose confidential information. They should also establish compliance frameworks that align with global data protection laws, such as the General Data Protection Regulation (GDPR).

In conclusion, the *Hiroshima Process International Code of Conduct* provides a comprehensive framework for ensuring the ethical, safe, and responsible development of advanced AI systems. By integrating strong governance structures, security measures, and transparency efforts, AI developers can mitigate risks while harnessing AI's potential for positive societal impact. As AI technologies continue to evolve, it is crucial to remain committed to refining risk management approaches and engaging in international collaborations to uphold the highest standards of AI safety and accountability.

The *United Nations System White Paper on AI Governance*

The *United Nations System White Paper on AI Governance*,[3] developed by the UN Inter-Agency Working Group on Artificial Intelligence, provides a detailed examination of governance structures, regulatory frameworks, and institutional mechanisms that can be leveraged to ensure responsible AI development. The exponential rise of AI, particularly generative AI and large language models, has raised global concerns regarding ethical risks, digital inequalities, and regulatory gaps. The governance of AI is now an urgent priority, given its potential to influence all aspects of society, including economic systems, political structures, and social interactions. The UN has recognised the need for a coordinated response to address AI-related risks while ensuring that its benefits are shared fairly among all nations.

The white paper serves as a foundational document for AI governance discussions within the UN system and contributes to the work of the High-Level Advisory Body on Artificial Intelligence. It highlights the necessity of an inclusive, multi-stakeholder approach to AI regulation, emphasising that AI governance must be guided by just principles, international human rights law, and Sustainable Development Goals. By analysing existing governance models and international regulatory frameworks, the white paper aims to provide actionable recommendations for shaping global AI governance in a manner that prioritises human rights, safety, transparency, and fairness.

The governance of AI within the UN system is grounded in a variety of normative and policy instruments that establish principles for ethical AI development and deployment. One of the key pillars of AI governance is international human rights law, which provides a legal foundation to regulate AI systems in ways that uphold principles of fairness, accountability, and non-discrimination. Key human rights documents, including the Universal Declaration of Human Rights (UDHR), the International Covenant on Civil and Political Rights (ICCPR), and the Convention on the Rights of the Child (CRC), serve as global standards that guide AI regulation. These legal frameworks emphasise that AI technologies should not infringe on fundamental rights such as privacy, freedom of expression, or the right to a fair trial.

In addition to human rights law, the UN has developed technical and regulatory standards to address the challenges posed by AI. The International Telecommunication Union (ITU) has played a leading role in establishing international standards for AI interoperability, data governance, and cybersecurity. UNESCO, through its *Recommendation on the Ethics of Artificial Intelligence*, has provided a globally recognised framework for AI governance, advocating for transparency, accountability, and sustainability in AI development. Other UN entities, such as the United Nations Children's Fund (UNICEF), the World Health Organization (WHO), and the United Nations Interregional Crime and Justice Research Institute (UNICRI), have also contributed to AI governance through sector-specific policies. UNICEF has focused on AI's impact on children's rights, while WHO has explored AI's role in healthcare, including diagnostics and disease surveillance. UNICRI, in collaboration with INTERPOL, has examined the use of AI in law enforcement, ensuring that AI-driven security systems respect human rights principles.

The UN's governance efforts are further strengthened by lessons drawn from other international regulatory models. Agreements such as the Montreal Protocol on Substances that Deplete the Ozone Layer and the WHO Framework Convention on Tobacco Control illustrate how global governance structures can establish compliance mechanisms, safety standards, and international cooperation. These models demonstrate that AI governance must integrate scientific consensus, multi-stakeholder engagement, and robust regulatory oversight to address both the opportunities and challenges posed by AI technologies.

The findings of the white paper emphasise that AI governance should be rooted in existing international legal frameworks while incorporating new regulatory mechanisms that address AI's unique risks. The integration of cross-sectoral policies, technical standards, and multi-stakeholder engagement will be critical in shaping a governance framework that promotes moral AI development, regulatory accountability, and fair technological distribution.

The UN plays a critical role in fostering scientific research, regulatory coordination, and capacity-building initiatives to support AI governance. One of the key institutional functions identified in the white paper is the need for rigorous scientific assessments and research to inform policy decisions. Independent, multidisciplinary evaluations of AI technologies are essential for identifying risks and establishing best practices for AI governance. The UN has already developed expert panels, task forces, and observatories to monitor AI's societal impact and recommend appropriate regulatory responses.

Norm-setting and standardisation are fundamental to AI governance, ensuring that AI technologies adhere to principled guidelines and safety standards. The UN must develop governance mechanisms similar to those used in aviation, nuclear safety, and public health to regulate AI's deployment. Existing global regulatory bodies, such as the International Civil Aviation Organisation (ICAO) and the International Atomic Energy Agency (IAEA), provide valuable insights into how AI safety standards can be established. AI governance should incorporate similar compliance mechanisms, including certification programmes, risk assessments, and enforcement procedures, to ensure that AI systems operate within legal boundaries.

Another essential function of AI governance is regulatory coordination and monitoring. The UN has extensive experience in coordinating international regulatory frameworks, particularly in cybersecurity, environmental protection, and public health. The white paper highlights lessons from ICAO's aviation safety regulations, WHO's pandemic response mechanisms, and IAEA's nuclear safeguards, which demonstrate the importance of creating international oversight bodies to monitor AI's development. AI governance efforts should integrate similar monitoring mechanisms, ensuring that AI applications remain transparent, accountable, and aligned with international standards.

Many developing nations lack the necessary infrastructure, expertise, and regulatory capacity to engage in AI governance effectively. The UN has a unique opportunity to bridge this gap by promoting fair access to AI technologies, supporting AI literacy programmes, and strengthening global AI policy frameworks. Ensuring that AI development benefits all nations, regardless of their technological capabilities, is essential for reducing the AI divide and promoting global access to technology.

AI governance must also be cross-sectoral, incorporating principles from related policy domains such as data governance, cybersecurity, and sustainable development. By enhancing inter-agency collaboration and fostering partnerships with governments, industry leaders, and civil society, the UN can ensure that AI governance remains comprehensive and adaptable to emerging technological challenges.

AI governance must be structured to be inclusive, adaptive, and forward-thinking. The UN's experience in developing international regulatory frameworks provides valuable insights into how AI governance mechanisms can be structured. A key lesson from existing governance models is the importance of multi-stakeholder engagement, ensuring that AI governance frameworks incorporate perspectives from governments, private-sector actors, academic institutions, and civil society. The UN's ability to facilitate international consensus building allows it to play a crucial role in shaping AI governance.

Agility and foresight are also essential in AI governance, given the rapid pace of AI advancements. AI systems evolve much faster than traditional regulatory frameworks, necessitating the development of flexible, anticipatory governance mechanisms. The UN's work in climate change, cybersecurity, and public health provides useful models for structuring adaptive AI governance frameworks that can respond to emerging risks while promoting responsible AI innovation.

A human rights-centred approach to AI governance is essential to ensure that AI technologies promote fairness, prevent discrimination, and protect democratic institutions. AI governance frameworks should prioritise ethical AI development, ensuring that AI systems do not reinforce biases, exacerbate inequalities, or violate human rights.

The white paper discusses the impact of AI on the public sector across various dimensions, including governance, law enforcement, healthcare, urban planning, and administrative processes. The document underscores both the opportunities AI presents for improving government efficiency and the challenges it poses, particularly in terms of regulation, equity, and ethical considerations. The white paper highlights that some UN member states have begun incorporating AI methodologies developed by UN bodies such as the UN Conference on Trade and Development (UNCTAD) and the UN Development Programme (UNDP) to support governance reforms and sustainable development initiatives. However, AI also presents regulatory challenges. As AI systems become more integral to governance, ensuring accountability and transparency in automated decision-making is crucial. The document warns against the unchecked proliferation of AI governance principles without effective enforcement mechanisms, emphasising that ethical AI governance requires not only voluntary commitments but also robust accountability structures.

The document notes that AI is increasingly being deployed in law enforcement for surveillance, crime prevention, and forensic investigations. AI-powered facial recognition and predictive policing tools are being trialled in various countries, with support from UN agencies such as UNICRI in collaboration with INTERPOL. However, the use of AI in law enforcement raises significant ethical and human rights concerns. There is a risk of algorithmic bias leading to discriminatory policing practices, as well as concerns about mass surveillance infringing on privacy rights. The white paper calls for stronger regulatory oversight to ensure that AI deployment in public safety respects fundamental rights and international legal standards.

AI is playing an increasingly prominent role in urban planning and the management of smart cities. UN-Habitat, in collaboration with other UN agencies, has developed reports and frameworks to guide AI implementation in urban governance. AI-driven systems are being used for optimising traffic management, improving public transportation networks, and enhancing environmental monitoring. The document highlights that AI applications in urban planning should be designed with inclusivity in mind, ensuring that marginalised communities are not excluded from the benefits of smart city innovations.

The application of AI in healthcare is another key area of public-sector transformation. AI-powered diagnostics, predictive modelling, and robotic-assisted surgeries are revolutionising medical practice. During the COVID-19 pandemic, AI played a crucial role in tracking the spread of the virus, optimising vaccine distribution, and improving crisis response efforts. The World Health Organization (WHO) has been actively working on AI governance frameworks to ensure that AI in healthcare adheres to ethical guidelines and patient safety standards. However, the white paper also highlights risks related to data privacy, cybersecurity, and the ethical use of AI-driven medical decisions.

The white paper acknowledges that AI-driven automation poses both opportunities and risks for the labour market. While AI can improve efficiency and reduce the workload of public employees, it may also lead to job displacement, particularly for administrative roles that involve repetitive tasks. The International Labour Organization (ILO) has been studying the implications of AI for employment and is working on developing labour standards that ensure fair transitions for workers affected by AI-driven automation. Additionally, there is concern that over-reliance on AI systems could lead to a decline in human expertise as people become increasingly dependent on automated decision-making tools.

The white paper warns of the growing AI divide, where advanced economies are better positioned to leverage AI innovations, while developing countries face significant challenges in AI adoption. Many governments lack the technical expertise, infrastructure, and financial resources to develop AI capabilities, putting them at a disadvantage in the global AI landscape. The UN calls for increased investment in capacity-building programmes to ensure that all member states can benefit from AI advancements. The document stresses that AI governance should be inclusive, and that special attention should be given to the needs of developing nations.

The white paper underscores that AI has the potential to enhance public-sector operations, improve governance, and contribute to sustainable development. However, it also emphasises that AI adoption in the public sector must be accompanied by robust governance frameworks, ethical guidelines, and equitable access to AI resources. The UN plays a critical role in facilitating AI governance discussions, ensuring that AI policies align with international law and human rights standards while fostering global cooperation to bridge the AI divide.

In conclusion, the *United Nations System White Paper on AI Governance* presents a structured approach to AI governance that balances regulatory oversight with ethical considerations. The white paper highlights the importance of anchoring AI governance in international human rights law, integrating scientific research into policymaking, and fostering multi-stakeholder collaboration. As AI technologies continue to evolve, the UN must take a leadership role in establishing a globally coordinated governance framework that ensures AI's benefits are distributed equitably while mitigating its risks. Through ethical governance, international cooperation, and policy innovation, the UN can shape an AI future that is safe, transparent, and beneficial to all of humanity.

The United Nations *Governing AI for Humanity* Framework

The United Nations has made significant progress in establishing a global framework for AI governance. In September 2024, it introduced a proposed framework titled *Governing AI for Humanity*.[4]

The rapid advancement of AI presents significant opportunities and challenges for humanity. The United Nations' High-Level Advisory Body on AI has recognised the urgent need for a global governance framework to ensure AI benefits all and does not exacerbate inequalities.

AI's transformative power affects multiple sectors, from healthcare and energy to education and security. While AI has the potential to advance the Sustainable Development Goals (SDGs), its risks include bias, misinformation, surveillance, and ethical dilemmas. Unregulated AI development could concentrate benefits in a few hands, widening the digital divide and limiting global progress.

A robust international governance mechanism is necessary due to AI's transboundary nature. The lack of a comprehensive governance structure means that accountability mechanisms remain weak, leading to risks such as unfair AI applications, the spread of misinformation, and security threats.

The urgency for AI governance is heightened by its rapid evolution and increasing integration into critical areas of human life. The global AI landscape is currently shaped by fragmented regulations and voluntary compliance measures that vary significantly across countries and regions. This fragmented approach has led to inconsistencies in AI safety standards, ethical considerations, and the equitable distribution of AI benefits.

Moreover, AI's global reach means that decisions made by a few countries or corporations can have widespread ramifications, affecting economies, societies, and even global security. AI-driven automation and decision-making systems influence everything from financial markets to employment, healthcare access, and cybersecurity. In the absence of coordinated governance, issues such as algorithmic bias, data privacy violations, and potential misuse of AI in warfare and surveillance can proliferate unchecked.

Given these challenges, AI governance must be designed to ensure that its development and deployment align with universally recognised international laws and human rights. The governance framework must be inclusive, bringing in voices from all regions, including developing nations that currently lack representation in AI policymaking. It should also facilitate collaboration among governments, the private sector, academia, and civil society to create a regulatory environment that fosters responsible AI innovation while mitigating its risks.

A strong global governance framework should prioritise transparency, accountability, and fairness. Mechanisms for international cooperation, such as standardised safety protocols, AI impact assessments, and independent oversight bodies, will be essential. The UN's role in this process is crucial, as it provides a platform for multilateral dialogue and coordination, ensuring that AI governance serves humanity as a whole rather than benefiting only a select few.

The platform for multilateral dialogue and coordination will serve as a dedicated forum within the United Nations to facilitate continuous discussions on AI governance. This platform will have the following structure:

Table A.11 The structure of the UN platform for multilateral dialogue and coordination on AI governance

Structure	*Description*
Global AI Governance Council	A high-level body comprising representatives from UN member states, AI industry leaders, academia, and civil society. This council will set strategic priorities for AI governance and oversee international cooperation efforts.
Technical and Ethical Advisory Committees	Expert groups tasked with assessing AI risks, ethical considerations, and emerging trends. These committees will provide science-based recommendations to policymakers.
Multi-Stakeholder Working Groups	These groups will focus on specific issues such as AI safety, ethical AI deployment, data governance, and responsible AI innovation. Each working group will include representatives from governments, businesses, research institutions, and advocacy groups.
Annual Global AI Summit	A yearly event hosted by the UN, bringing together key stakeholders to evaluate progress in AI governance, share best practices, and update policy frameworks as needed.

Source: Authors' elaboration from the United Nations (2024), *Governing AI for Humanity*, www.un.org/sites/un2.un.org/files/governing_ai_for_humanity_final_report_en.pdf (accessed on 27 December 2024)

The platform will have the following implementation strategy:

Table A.12 The implementation strategy of the UN platform for multilateral dialogue and coordination on AI governance

Main Strategy	*Description*
Policy harmonisation	The platform will work towards creating globally recognised AI regulations and ethical standards, minimising discrepancies between national and regional governance approaches.
Capacity building and knowledge sharing	Developing nations will receive technical support, resources, and training to ensure equal participation in AI governance. Open-access research, case studies, and policy recommendations will be shared globally.
Real-time AI risk monitoring	Establishing an AI Observatory that continuously assesses emerging AI risks, ensuring rapid response mechanisms are in place for potential crises.

(*Continued*)

Table A.12 (Continued)

Main Strategy	*Description*
Public–private partnerships	Encouraging collaboration between governments, industry leaders, and civil society to drive AI research and development while maintaining ethical safeguards.
Legal and ethical frameworks	The platform will promote AI accountability by advising on international agreements, treaties, and guidelines that align with human rights and global security interests.

Source: Authors' elaboration from the United Nations (2024), *Governing AI for Humanity*, www.un.org/sites/un2.un.org/files/governing_ai_for_humanity_final_report_en.pdf (accessed on 27 December 2024)

The report identifies three primary gaps in global AI governance.

The first gap is representation. Many developing nations lack a voice in AI policymaking, leading to policies that favour a few powerful countries and corporations. This exclusion perpetuates existing inequalities, as developing nations often lack the necessary infrastructure, expertise, and financial resources to contribute meaningfully to AI governance discussions. Without global representation, AI policies and regulations are shaped by a limited set of interests, leaving vast portions of the world unable to influence how AI impacts their economies and societies.

The second gap is coordination. Various AI governance initiatives exist, but they often work in silos, creating regulatory fragmentation. Governments, corporations, and international organisations are developing AI guidelines independently, leading to overlapping, conflicting, or incomplete regulations. This lack of coordination results in inefficiencies, where some regions face excessive restrictions while others operate in regulatory vacuums. A harmonised approach is necessary to ensure that AI governance efforts align across jurisdictions, fostering global interoperability and compliance.

The third gap is implementation. Even when policies are proposed, they often lack enforcement mechanisms or clear pathways for practical implementation. Many AI-related agreements and guidelines remain aspirational due to insufficient resources, monitoring capabilities, and legal mandates. Without clear accountability frameworks, commitments to AI safety, ethics, and human rights remain largely voluntary. Stronger enforcement mechanisms, capacity-building initiatives, and resource allocation strategies are needed to translate governance principles into actionable and effective regulations.

The *Governing AI for Humanity* report proposes a multi-pronged approach to global AI governance, emphasising common understanding, common ground, and shared benefits.

It calls for the creation of an International Scientific Panel on AI to regularly assess AI capabilities, risks, and opportunities. This panel would be responsible for horizon-scanning and knowledge sharing to bridge the gap between AI developers, policymakers, and the public. By fostering a deeper understanding of AI's evolving landscape, the panel would play a pivotal role in setting international benchmarks for ethical AI development and deployment.

The report suggests policy dialogues to facilitate discussions among countries, corporations, and civil society. A Global AI Standards Exchange would harmonise AI safety and ethical standards across borders, ensuring that AI is developed responsibly. This exchange would help establish universal guidelines that address ethical concerns, safety measures, and governance protocols, reducing regulatory inconsistencies and ensuring alignment in international AI governance efforts.

To ensure equitable AI access, the report recommends:

- AI Capacity Development Network focused on training policymakers, public-sector officials, and entrepreneurs, particularly in underrepresented regions. This initiative aims to bridge the AI skills gap and promote digital inclusivity by providing education and resources to nations that currently lack technical expertise.
- Global Fund for AI: A funding mechanism to support AI research and applications in low-resource settings. This fund would enable developing nations to access AI tools and technologies that can drive sustainable development and economic growth.
- Global AI Data Framework: A set of policies to facilitate the ethical collection, sharing, and use of data to improve AI systems. This framework would establish principles for data governance, ensuring data privacy, security, and equitable access while fostering innovation.

The Global AI Standards Exchange is envisioned as a mechanism to facilitate the alignment and interoperability of AI regulations, standards, and best practices across different jurisdictions. Its core objectives are:

Table A.13 The core objectives of the Global AI Standards Exchange

Objective	*Description*
Establishing a common framework	Developing universally accepted AI safety and ethical guidelines that can be adopted across industries and national regulatory bodies.
Promoting regulatory consistency	Encouraging alignment between national AI laws to prevent regulatory fragmentation and ensure smoother global AI governance.
Facilitating knowledge sharing	Creating a repository of best practices, compliance requirements, and impact assessments to support policymakers, businesses, and researchers in navigating AI governance.

(*Continued*)

Table A.13 (Continued)

Objective	*Description*
Encouraging industry collaboration	Bringing together technology firms, regulatory agencies, and academia to collaboratively define and refine AI standards in areas such as transparency, accountability, and bias mitigation.
Building compliance mechanisms	Assisting nations and organisations in implementing AI governance measures by providing standardised audit tools, certification programmes, and compliance benchmarks.

Source: Authors' elaboration from the United Nations (2024), *Governing AI for Humanity*, www.un.org/sites/un2.un.org/files/governing_ai_for_humanity_final_report_en.pdf (accessed on 27 December 2024)

The exchange will operate as a decentralised yet coordinated effort, with regular policy dialogues, working groups, and cross-border partnerships to ensure standards evolve alongside technological advancements.

The report explores different institutional models for AI governance, considering whether a dedicated International AI Agency should be established. While the advisory body does not immediately recommend creating a new AI-specific agency, it underscores the need for an AI Office within the UN Secretariat to coordinate AI-related initiatives across UN entities and its partners. This office would serve as a central coordinating body, ensuring that AI governance remains adaptive, inclusive, and aligned with global development goals.

The report explains that AI adoption in the public sector has the potential to improve governance, enhance service delivery, and increase efficiency in policy implementation. However, it also presents unique challenges that require careful oversight and strategic planning. The key aspects influencing AI in the public sector include:

Table A.14 The key aspects influencing AI in the public sector

Main Element	*Description*
Policy and regulation	Governments must establish clear legal and ethical guidelines to ensure responsible AI deployment in public administration and services.
Transparency and accountability	AI systems used in public decision-making must be explainable and subject to oversight to maintain public trust.
Data governance	The collection, management, and protection of data are critical in AI-driven public services, requiring robust privacy and security measures.

(*Continued*)

Table A.14 (Continued)

Main Element	*Description*
Bias and fairness	AI systems must be designed to mitigate biases and ensure equitable access to public services for all citizens.
Infrastructure and resources	Adequate computing power, skilled workforce, and financial investments are necessary for effective AI implementation.
Public–private partnerships	Collaborations between governments, tech firms, and academic institutions can enhance AI-driven innovations while maintaining regulatory compliance.
Citizen engagement	Public participation in AI policymaking ensures that AI applications align with societal needs and values.
AI ethics and human rights	AI deployment must align with human rights principles to prevent discrimination and ensure ethical decision-making in public services.

Source: Authors' elaboration from the United Nations (2024), *Governing AI for Humanity,* www.un.org/sites/un2.un.org/files/governing_ai_for_humanity_final_report_en.pdf (accessed on 27 December 2024)

Governments must navigate these challenges through inclusive policymaking, capacity building, and international cooperation to ensure AI serves as a tool for public good rather than exacerbating inequalities.

The report's overall recommendations for immediate action emphasise the need to strengthen scientific research on AI risks and benefits by supporting independent, international studies that can guide policymaking and inform governance frameworks. It also highlights the importance of developing AI standards by encouraging the implementation of safety protocols and transparency mechanisms to ensure responsible AI use. Additionally, the report calls for more inclusive participation in AI governance discussions, ensuring that stakeholders from the Global South, marginalised communities, and emerging economies have a voice. Finally, it stresses the necessity of aligning AI with the UN Charter and human rights principles to safeguard individual freedoms and promote social equity.

The UN stresses that AI's future depends on proactive governance that balances innovation with safeguards for users. A fragmented approach relying on voluntary compliance and national regulations will be insufficient. The report urges global cooperation to develop a unified, transparent, and accountable AI governance structure that serves humanity equitably.

The way forward requires sustained dialogue, investment in AI governance capacity, and a commitment to democratic AI principles. The UN envisions a governance model that is agile, inclusive, and responsive to AI's evolving risks and opportunities. Achieving this vision necessitates a coordinated effort among governments, private-sector actors, civil society, and international organisations to ensure AI remains a force for good.

Notes

1 Japanese Ministry of Economy, Trade and Industry (2023), Hiroshima AI Process G7 digital & tech ministers' statement, www.meti.go.jp/english/press/2023/1201_001.html (accessed on 28 December 2024).

2 European Commission (2023), *Hiroshima Process International Code of Conduct for Advanced AI Systems*, https://digital-strategy.ec.europa.eu/en/library/hiroshima-process-international-code-conduct-advanced-ai-systems (accessed on 28 December 2024).

3 UNESCO (2024), *United Nations System White Paper on Artificial Intelligence Governance: An Analysis of Current Institutional Models and Related Functions and Existing International Normative Frameworks within the United Nations System That Are Applicable to Artificial Intelligence Governance*, https://unsceb.org/sites/default/files/2024-11/UNSystemWhitePaperAIGovernance.pdf (accessed on 27 December 2024).

4 United Nations (2024), *Governing AI for Humanity*, www.un.org/sites/un2.un.org/files/governing_ai_for_humanity_final_report_en.pdf (accessed on 27 December 2024).

Index

Note: if a word is presented in italics in the book, the corresponding entry in this index is in italics.

For Product Safety Concerns and Information please contact our EU representative GPSR@taylorandfrancis.com Taylor & Francis Verlag GmbH, Kaufingerstraße 24, 80331 München, Germany